The Mystery of Spiritual Sensitivity

The Mystery of Spiritual Sensitivity

YOUR PRACTICAL GUIDE TO RESPONDING
TO BURDENS YOU FEEL FROM GOD'S HEART

CAROL A. BROWN

DESTINY IMAGE® PUBLISHERS, INC.
P.O. Box 310, Shippensburg, PA 17257-0310

"Speaking to the Purposes of God for this Generation and for the Generations to Come."

This book and all other Destiny Image, Revival Press, Mercy Place, Fresh Bread, Destiny Image Fiction, and Treasure House books are available at Christian bookstores and distributors worldwide.

For a U.S. bookstore nearest you, call 1-800-722-6774.
For more information on foreign distributors, call 717-532-3040.
Reach us on the Internet at: www.destinyimage.com.

ISBN 10: 0-7684-2592-1
ISBN 13: 978-0-7684-2592-5

For Worldwide Distribution, Printed in the U.S.A.

1 2 3 4 5 6 7 8 9 10 11 / 11 10 09 08

Dedication

Dedicated to the uncounted number of God's "Special Forces." God made no mistake when He made you.

Acknowledgments

Special thanks to the following—I would not have completed this work without you.

Deb Finck, for editing, sequencing, encouraging, believing in me, and for helping me dig the "MS" out of the manuscript! You kept me going.

Jim Wilder, for your expertise and encouragement. You give me perspective

John Sandford, for seeing in me what I did not. You gave me inspiration and loving feedback.

Paul and Gretel Haglin, for comfort and understanding when I most needed it.

Joan Feikema, Ludie and Inga Huppman, for your support, encouraging, supporting, and helping me make the final steps to publication.

Mark Sandford! I owe you a debt of gratitude. Thank you for your generous and gracious spirit—you bring the Father's flavor into what you do. I am eternally grateful for your uncanny, God-given ability to separate the forest from the trees and to see far enough ahead on the path to spot the theological stones that might cause a reader to stumble. Your gracious contribution to this work cannot be measured this side of Heaven.

David, my husband, you persevered in helping me overcome the computer gremlins. You believed in this work and my ability to do it. Sometimes your ADD has driven me up the proverbial wall, yet you have also saved my life. Your own sensitivity has helped me recognize when I was literally not myself and needed Jesus' help to release burdens. Your passion for setting captives free through Jesus is the source of many of the stories in this book. When I gave up on myself, you kept faith in me.

And finally, thank you to all the people who kept asking, "Is the book out yet?"

Endorsements

Carol has put her finger on a huge problem in a way that brings healing and understanding about one of God's great gifts. Emotional, spiritual, and neurological sensitivity is a painful gift and we must cherish and protect those who carry such deep links between us, God, and each other. Everyone who has cringed at the pain they feel in the world should read this book and learn a way back to peace.

E. James Wilder, PhD
International teacher, counselor,
cofounder of Shepherd's House
Pasadena, California

Some people write about healing from their extensive studies. Some people write based strictly on their perceptions of God's Word. Carol Brown writes from both of these viewpoints plus many years of living God's healing answers and revealing His resurrecting revelations to saints in deepest need. This is a workbook for healers written by a healer who has persevered through her own healing at the side of a trustworthy God. You will not just read Carol's book, you will devour and re-read it and appropriate it into your life and ministry.

Paul and Gretel Haglin
Engineer, pastor, radio teacher, international speaker,
founder of Resurrection Ministries,
Hawk Point, Missouri

Carol Brown's book about the mystery of spiritual sensitivity is an innovative exploration of "intercession that begins in the heart of God." She does an excellent job of showing how God created us with everything necessary to accept the challenge of bearing one another's burdens. Carol's book is full of interesting stories that helped me understand and relate to her premise of how important it is to synchronize with others. Carol's writing is expressive, motivational, and exciting. She brought to my attention how important it is to look at my weaknesses that could create more of a burden to the person to whom I want to help. This book will help many people in the church.

Cheryl Knight
C.A.R.E., Inc.

Contents

Foreword

Many have written articles and some have composed books that include passages about burden bearing. Some have inadvertently revealed how little they really understand about this most mystical and mysterious of the Lord's callings upon our lives. Carol Brown has written a comprehensive work replete with comprehension because she has lived burden bearing from its bumbling beginnings in her heart to its climax in expertise. She knows the subject inside out, as you will if you persevere not only in reading but in practicing burden-bearing prayer and ministry.

"My people are destroyed for lack of knowledge..." (Hosea 4:6). As the Holy Spirit has tumbled us into new revelations and gifts, increasingly since the middle of the 20th century as Joel 2:28 is being fulfilled before our wondering eyes, we have all come to understand Hosea's text experientially, sometimes ruefully. It seems we can't enter into anything new in the Spirit without suffering the pains of trial and error—which is probably the Lord's providential wisdom. How else would we come to fully own what He wants us to know? Pearls are the symbol of wisdom because when a grain of sand irritates an oyster, it works to cover it, and beauty is formed. So it is with us.

Burden bearing, though a most basic calling for all Christians, has been almost totally neglected by Christian teachers, and very little understood by most—teachers and pupils alike. The depths of it remain new revelation to all but a miniscule portion of the Body of Christ. Now comes Carol Brown, uniquely prepared by the route of trial and error and the fires of the illness of multiple sclerosis (MS) to expose the secrets and joys of burden bearing to the Body of Christ.

As readers will learn, burden bearing is not something exotic and thus the exclusive property of a few elite. It is a calling upon us all, and an elevation into ministry to the very heart of our loving Lord Jesus Himself, a constant practice in the art of loving others as Jesus loves, a supreme labor that is love itself. As Galatians 6:2 tells us, "Bear one another's burdens, and thus fulfill the law of Christ." The law of Christ is to love as He loved, which is to lay our lives down for each other. Hopefully you will come to appreciate the fullness of what that means as you read and put into practice what you learn here.

Precisely because burden bearing is such a priceless gifting and high calling, it can to that degree be subject to error and consequent suffering. Carol makes that abundantly clear throughout the book, and teaches how to avoid pitfalls and bear burdens rightly in our Lord Jesus. You may find great relief as Carol explains the dynamics of burden bearing in marriages and other close relationships (Chapters 5 and 6).

For more than 40 years Paula and I have pioneered in the discovery and teaching of inner healing. Know then our qualifications when we say that except possibly for the field of deliverance ministry, we know of no other calling more fraught with pains and aches from lack of knowledge than the field of burden bearing. That is one reason why this book is so timely and so desperately needful for the Church in these days, as the Lord purifies His servants a la Malachi chapter 3 for ministry to His broken and tattered world. We must know the rightness and the pitfalls of burden-bearing intercession and ministry as the times crescendo to mountains of need and the Lord calls His own to stand in the gap for the multitudes, and as He trains us for the coming greatest revival in all of history.

"Faith comes from hearing, and hearing by the word of Christ" (Rom. 10:7). We all know that. But how often did Jesus say, "Let him who has ears to hear, hear"? Many if not most peoples' hearts are too laden and confused for the mind to hear the good news of the Gospel. Therefore, all too often the preaching of the "word of Christ" falls on deaf ears. There has never yet been a great revival without first great intercessory prayers. Burden-bearing intercession uniquely prepares the hearts of people to hear God's word and respond. If multitudes are to be converted, and then healed unto salvation, thousands, even millions, must come to join the ranks of God's burden-bearing intercessors.

And beyond the great revival, as the prophesied tribulations of the endtimes increase exponentially, we are going to have to have an increasing army, a vast host, who know how to stand for the Lord in burden-bearing intercession and ministry for the transformation of the Father's broken children. Today, there are yet too few.

Read with expectancy. You are being led onto the ground floor of the vast newness God is building. You are privileged to be part of it—partners with Him in the coming glory. Therefore, study to show yourself worthy...this book is full of revelation.

John Sandford
Elijah House

Preface

Mystery is a word you use to describe those things that, try as you may, you cannot find words to communicate what you experience. You use mystery to describe the things that elude reason and logic, yet there they are. They cannot be completely defined, measured, and repeated in a scientific setting. You cannot wrap your mind around it; not completely.

For example, have you ever wondered what comes over you from time to time? Ever have, oh, say, two mood swings before you reach the top of the stairs? Ever have excessive emotions or feel completely out of sync with the circumstances of your life? Often feel of little value, not chosen? Do you feel used up, burned out, and cast aside, not at all like a son or daughter of God? Do you become irritated and overwhelmed with people, lights, noise, or too much motion—like when shopping at the mall? Do you feel sad or angry when you have nothing to be sad or angry about?

I want you to know that you are not crazy; you are different. You are not wired like most people, and God has a reason for making you that way. I have walked this path and I know how hard it is. I know what it is like to feel God planned "something" for you, but you have no idea what or how to become the person He intends you to be. I know the temptation to try to make life better for other people, but at the same time must narrow your own life to make it manageable, which makes it hard to help others. I know what it is like to feel like a magnet walking through the pin factory of life, with all the pins and needles flying at me point first. Life hurts.

Life really hurts for those who feel like an emotional soccer ball—kicked about, used, and dropped with little regard. After a while you begin to wonder why God put you here, why you have so little value. No one seems to understand— and no one seems able to help. Pressure builds within, but then you meet someone who hurts more deeply than you do and your heart pulls you back to reality. And there you go again, helping and going home overwhelmed. Why? You may be one of God's "Special Forces," designed with a highly sensitive nervous system that allows you to empathize on deep levels with God and others.

Readers

Although I address readers who resonate with these and other feelings that will be described, I also want you who are not aware of having such feelings to read as well. If you live with someone I've described, this book will help you understand them—your mate, your children, or someone who you work with or for. Understanding will help pastors and church leaders prepare people for what the Lord may ask of them. The examples you will read about are actual people and experiences. Names have been changed to protect their privacy, with a few exceptions which include individuals who have given me permission to use their names.

Why I Write

I don't want you, or someone you know, to live one day longer with a sadness that seems bottomless. I don't want your inner pressure to build to the point that you are tempted to cut yourself to release it, or do something self-destructive to numb the pain you feel. You are one of God's "Special Forces." Your nervous system is different than most. You are uniquely designed as a highly sensitive person, one who can join Jesus in the work He began and continues to do—reconciling people to God, people to themselves, and restoring relationships between people.

But you need to learn how to bear burdens rightly. From unravelling my own mystery of spiritual sensitivity life experiences, I explain our unique design to help you understand yourself. Understanding what it looks and feels like, how it affects you, and discovering common reflex reactions to high sensitivity—physical, emotional, and spiritual—will allow God to use your sensitivity to develop spiritual maturity—yours and others. This is empathetic burden-bearing intercession. The high sensitivity required to sense and feel what other people experience is what makes life painful; it also makes it possible to sense, feel, and hear from God.

Being a pastor's wife, mother of two lively girls, and a college instructor can be a full plate. However, I experienced an exhaustion that my circumstances could not explain. That's when I heard Mark Sandford teach about burden bearing. I was desperate. "OK, God, if there is anything to this, let's do it." I began to pray through my life, period by period, cleaning out the residue of burdens I had accumulated throughout my life. When I finished, I felt 40 pounds lighter.

My learning curve began at that point. I began to pray first and then call people when I experienced a sudden severe headache, strange (to me) thoughts, chest pains, flashes of uncharacteristic anger or sensations, overwhelming sadness, etc. Time after time they confirmed that I was indeed sharing what they themselves were experiencing. My husband, David, affectionately called me his "canary." He could understand people dynamics by watching my reactions. I was drawn more and more into ministry with David, He was the counselor/teacher and I was the teacher/intercessor.

When I was diagnosed with multiple sclerosis in 1995, my life changed dramatically. Life would be different, but not ruined! Previously, through the gift of knowledge (1 Cor. 12:8), the Lord allowed me to feel powerfully what another person experienced—to give vocabulary and a voice to those who had no voice. It is my hope the writing of this book will give voice and vocabulary in ways I could never imagine, and can no longer do. My loving Father is not requiring my body to experience burden bearing in the same way since December 1995 because He knows my frame. Stress is not healthy for me, so He gives me another way to discharge my calling.

Five months after being diagnosed, I woke up to life well enough to do something but not well enough to do anything. I had to do something or go mad. I could not teach or speak before an audience now...my thoughts were disjointed fragments. I could not be on my feet for more than a moment. Visual images didn't stand still, and reading is still difficult. I had no endurance. The enemy of my soul tried to remove every reference that told me who I was. I think he hoped I would be so depressed I'd forget to pray. All I could do was sit.

I taught myself to knit and began to write, sometimes for only five minutes, then ten, then maybe half an hour. The fog in my brain would clear and a thought would stand out so I wrote it down, phrase at a time, story at a time. But always the thoughts and stories were about burden bearing and the mystery of spiritual sensitivity. I can't remember for how many years that went on, but at some point I realized I had a pile of incoherent, disjointed pieces that could become a book—this book.

The Lord is redeeming the time the enemy thought he could steal! Scripture says, "all things work together for the good of those who love the Lord!

Understanding

You will learn what the characteristics of a natural burden bearer are, the elements foundational to this form of intercession, and what is involved in the process of solving the mystery of spiritual sensitivity. Burden-bearing dynamics work in all relationships, but we look at the two most fundamental in everyone's life—husband and wife, parent and child. Blessings come to you when you bear burdens, but there are also inherent vulnerabilities that complicate life for the highly sensitive. Lack of nurturing or misunderstanding of your sensitive nature can cause wounded spirits and emotions, and can negatively impact your life, so these issues have been addressed. You also need to know how to pray for healing. You will learn that burden bearing, for you, may be a very important feature of your development into your destiny—a son, a daughter of the King. And finally, I share another perspective on burden bearing—one you may not have imagined!

Having been a burden bearer these many years, I can assure you that any struggle you may have is redeemable. Hurt you have endured can be healed. Spiritual sensitivity can become a blessing. The blessing of knowing yourself as one who inherits His Kingdom and being close to the heart of God is worth understanding and accepting your unique design.

CHAPTER 1

Perspective

J esus' dear friend Lazarus fell ill. In John 11:1-44 we read that his sisters sent word to Jesus, but rather than quickly going to heal his friend, Jesus stayed where He was for two more days. Lazarus died. When Jesus finally arrived, He walked into a cloud of grief. "When Jesus saw her [Mary] weeping, and the Jews who had come along with her also weeping, He was deeply moved in *spirit and troubled*" (John 11:33).

In John 11:35, "Jesus wept." In verse 38 Jesus, was "once more deeply moved." Jesus had no reason to grieve His own tears, He knew Lazarus would rise from the dead. Indeed, earlier (John 11:14) He said, "*I am glad,* for your sake, that *I was not there,* so that you may believe." Jesus' display of emotion is most likely a result of burden bearing. He came alongside His friends and drew some of their burden into His spirit and soul, thus lightening their emotional load. He felt what the sisters and friends were feeling—He was fully in sync with them. He felt their grief and sadness, and was moved to tears. Always in touch with the Father's heart, He was able to speak God's response of life to Lazarus.

So what, exactly is burden bearing? Let's back up for perspective.

"But I say to you..."

Pure and undefiled religion in the sight of our God and Father is this: to visit [look after] orphans and widows in their distress... (James 1:27 NASB).

Giving alms to the poor, providing for orphans, widows, the blind, and lame have been accepted as appropriate ways to bear one another's burdens (Gal. 6:2)—ways to come alongside, to lighten the loads of others. The Lord began to teach a deeper level of understanding of the Scriptures in Matthew 5:17. He said He came, not to abolish the law, but to fulfill it. He said that your righteousness must surpass that of the scribes and Pharisees. Throughout chapters 5 and 6 of the Book of Matthew, He offered examples that went beyond the currently accepted righteousness: "you have heard it said that...but I tell you...," challenging every Christian to go beyond what is normally accepted.

In this same spirit of expanding upon that which is already right and good, I would say that all material and tangible means of lightening a person's load pleases God. But, He does not want you to stop there. Rather, He designed you and me to be highly sensitive, with a remarkable and quite human capacity to share in, carry, and thus relieve emotional and spiritual burdens as well. This is empathy, the foundation for the kind of burden bearing explored in this book.

This type of "burden bearing" is a form of intercession that begins in the heart of God. The burden forms in the heart of God as He sees a need in someone's life. Rather than barge in and fix it, He respects a person's free will and asks you, His servant, to be part of His solution. He wants you to be the **person** *through whom* He draws the pain of a hurting person to Himself. He asks you to be His hands on earth to relieve physical suffering, and to stand for Him as an emissary of comfort and freedom from emotional and spiritual bondage.

To this end He designed your body, not only to be an instrument of praise, but of prayer. This type of "burden bearing" involves the body, the emotions, and senses all working together. I believe this is what the apostle Paul was talking about when he said, "Now I rejoice in what was suffered for you, and I fill up in my flesh what is still lacking in regard to Christ's afflictions, for the sake of His body, which is the Church" (Col. 1:24).

Empathy is key. Without empathy you cannot sense the heart of God where burden bearing originates.

Sadly, most are not aware of their capacity for empathy, nor imagine in their wildest dreams God's purposes for it. Most live unaware of the extent to which others' troubles affect them, and vice-versa. Everyone bears burdens because that is how humanity is designed, but many do it wrongly. God designed burden bearing so as not to harm a person. When sin entered the picture, humankind has been turned around, upside down, and operating only somewhat according to design—there is something missing, causing us hurt.

There is much to be gained for the Kingdom of God when you bear burdens rightly, and much error and suffering when you bear burdens wrongly due to lack of knowledge. Our lack of knowledge caused us to live out only a portion of our "design capabilities."

God's design for humankind, and you individually, is perfect. His plan for your maturity is perfect. I believe burden bearing is an important part of His plan. You bear burdens because that is who you are, much as a gifted composer composes because he must. You are highly sensitive; you empathize and bear others burdens because you cannot do otherwise.

The Sensitive Human

God designed you with a broad capacity to relate, to connect with others (but especially Him), and to experience something of what others experience. This is a primary function of your human spirit—that eternal part of you that will return to God.

The neural hardware you are born with determines your conscious capacity for sensitivity.[1] This neural hardware is responsible for how much data you take in. It simply is—it has nothing to do with personal worth or value, and varies person to person. It is part of what makes you a unique individual.

Empathy is the ability to feel what another person experiences by matching their inner state of being and energy level. This is possible because of our neural hardware. Life experiences (family, school, work, etc.), positively or negatively, affect your ability to function empathetically. Your ability to connect empathetically can be even further diminished to the extent sin separates you from yourself, and distorts your sense of who you are in relation to God and others. Conversely, you strengthen your empathy muscles when you experience nurture, acceptance, support, seek hard after God, and develop a deep personal relationship with Him—a deep, mature prayer life.

Synchronization is another term for the brain's ability to match the state of mind and/or energy level of another person by means of communication from right brain to right brain.[2] This communication happens at such a speed that you seem to experience another person's state of mind or energy level simultaneously. High sensitivity is pivotal for the ability to synchronize with another; it is the core of empathy, and empathy is the core of burden bearing. It is a physical, mental, emotional, *and* spiritual activity.

God designed people physically and biologically for relationships. Every human being is born with the raw materials needed for empathy, and all experience it to one degree or another. When you actually "touch" what other people think and feel, you gain a "knowing" about them that is deeper than if you simply identify with, imagine, or feel sorry for how they might feel. Empathy allows you to begin to share in the emotional life of another.

Have you ever experienced a horrible feeling in the pit of your stomach, like you were going to be ill, and at the same time "know" a loved one was in some kind of trouble? Later you learned the trouble was—a car accident, a marriage crisis, or perhaps a severe illness.

A son sadly confides in his father that he "knows" the coach is going to cut him from the team. He cannot say why he knows. Soon the coach, with grief in his voice, admits he must bow to the pressure of politics and drops the young man from the team. The boy felt the coach's grief; he felt his burden and that was how he "knew" his coach was about to cut him from the team.

A wife working at home or elsewhere may experience weariness or anxiety as her day progresses that she cannot explain from her circumstances. She finds later that her spouse had a very frustrating and unproductive day at work.

My friend shares a story about the time when her mother called the school because she felt certain something horrible had happened. At the time my friend was attending junior high school and was wandering the hallway near the principle's office in tears after receiving her *very first* low grade on a math test. Her mother felt her daughter's distress.

Certain individuals or places give you "creepy" feelings. You instinctively know to avoid some people but have no concrete reason to do so. Sometimes you do not trust people who are "so sweet." What do you sense below consciousness? The Holy Spirit plays an important role in unraveling the mystery of spiritual sensitivity.

The Oxford Dictionary 10th edition says that empathy is the ability to understand and share the feelings of another. But I define it a bit differently, to be more pertinent to burden bearing. Empathy is "receptivity to the sensory and emotional experiences of another to the point that you feel what they are experiencing." This is not extrasensory perception (ESP). Scripture is quite clear that God speaks to His people as written in the Books of Joel, Acts, and specifically Job 33:13-14.

Sometimes God speaks audibly. For such cases, He built us with physical ears to hear Him. But, usually He speaks inaudibly. For those times, He built us with spiritual ears. It is not evil to have such "ears." But it is indeed evil to turn them toward any other source than the Holy Spirit. Turning spiritual ears toward a source other than the Holy Spirit is called extrasensory perception.

ESP is using God-given abilities without the boundaries and protection of the Holy Spirit. In the use of these abilities a "spirit" may unknowingly aid some; others consciously use a spirit other than God. Dependence upon a source other than God is what you are not to do! No one cares for you more than God. He knows what is in your best interest. Such dependence is an open door for forces of darkness, and such use of high sensitivity is divination.

The Oxford Dictionary defines *divination* as "the art or practice if obtaining hidden knowledge from supernatural powers" other than God. A second definition is "unusual insight; intuitive perception." I would add to that definition by saying that it is unusual insight and intuitive perception without God's authorization or protection. In other words, peering where not invited, out of curiosity, seeking status, control or personal gain—such as fortune telling, taro cards, Ouija boards, séances, etc. God does not endorse such practices. Scripture is clear that believers are *not* to be involved in such practices. (See Deuteronomy 18:10,14; First Samuel 15:23; and Second Chronicles 33:6.)

Burden bearing is different from ESP. To burden bear rightly, you die to your ability to see, sense, and feel and instead ask God to allow you see, feel, or sense only through the direction of the Holy Spirit. Your abilities are crucified, resurrected, and harnessed to God's will. It is no longer you who is doing this work, but the Holy Spirit in you. The Holy Spirit is central to burden bearing rightly. Without the Holy Spirit, burden bearing rightly does not happen.

The Holy Spirit uses your resurrected and redeemed ability to empathize and connects you with those who need His love, help, and healing touch. This is one expression of the gift of "word of knowledge" (1 Cor. 12). At the Holy Spirit's direction you feel their pain. Their pain alerts you to their needs and informs your prayer so you will accurately and compassionately invite the Lord to aid or heal that hurting person. Like a neural synapse in the brain, the Holy Spirit forms a "spiritual synapse" from a hurting person to one who can help lighten the load.

For whom do you empathize?

You have proportionately more opportunities for empathy with your loved ones than for others. You become aware of the cares, troubles, and woes of those with whom your life most frequently intersects. Exceptions are when the Lord specifically assigns the task of empathizing with or interceding and bearing burdens for a person or a group—say your church, the city in which you live, your tribe or clan, your province, state, nation.

Worth a Thousand Words

Your neural hardware makes it possible to subconsciously receive spiritual, physical, and emotional information—state-of-being information. As an infant you learn how to interpret and respond to that information. Empathy is to the spirit and emotions what words are to the mind. Words can be inadequate sometimes when you try to express emotion or your state of being! You try to express yourself with zero success, and have a sinking feeling as you watch your loved one walk away. You think, "They don't have a clue about what's going on with me." The problem intensifies when you, yourself, do not know what is churning around inside.

Imagine the value of the empathetic friend or loved one, who somehow knows you better than you do, and can put words to your feelings. When you learn to recognize, interpret, and respond appropriately to state-of-being information gathered by means of empathy with others, they receive the gift of companionship, and at a deep level—a sense of connection. Empathy is good as far as it goes, but it is not yet burden bearing, not until it is crucified, resurrected, and dedicated to the Lord's service.

Angie (not her real name) was receiving ministry from my husband. Her emotions were one massive ball. At any given time she didn't know how to express what she was feeling. David invited me into some of their sessions, and the Lord connected me to her. My function was to empathize with Angie and give her vocabulary. She experienced feelings, but had never learned the label associated with the feeling. The Lord connected us so completely that I would call her outside of the sessions when I suddenly had a headache that I knew was hurting Angie. "Do we have a headache?" I'd ask her on the phone. "Uhhh..." "Right side of your head? Right above your eye?" Angie would respond, "Yes, yes, you are right!" And so it went with other feelings and symptoms.

This is burden bearing, but if we had stopped at this point, it would have been "unredeemed" burden bearing. I would have been bearing the burden in my body by my own strength for another. However, Angie and I went on to ask the Lord for prayer direction. Often physical pain calls us to attention, but the problem the Lord wants to address lies elsewhere. Listening to the Lord's directions and praying accordingly, the Holy Spirit gathered all the burden from all the places it lodged in my body (and Angie's life) and lifted it out of me, drawing that burden through me and onto the cross of Jesus.

How Light the Yoke?

Jesus said *His yoke was easy and His burden light* (Matt. 11:30), but how easy, how light? Actually experiencing the feelings, thoughts, or attitudes of another can confuse the heck out of you! The biggest problem is to learn to recognize when these things are not your own, to know when it is not your pain, your heartache, or headache, as much as it hurts—to recognize when the burden is Holy Spirit initiated.

The wife who felt a seemingly baseless anxiety throughout her day was surely confused. Not until her husband came home from work did she recognize she had been experiencing all day long his emotional burden, stress, and pressure. She lightened his emotional/psychological load so he could continue to function in his workplace. However, if understanding is all the further she processes the burden, she is burden bearing in her own strength, without the aid of the Holy Spirit. This not God's original design for burden bearing. But, it is exactly what happens to far too many people.

This woman needs to build in the reflex of turning to the Lord and asking why she feels as she does, and interceding as the Lord directs. As she seeks the Lord's direction and prays accordingly, the Holy Spirit draws her husband's burdens through her, neutralizing them on His Cross, keeping her from becoming exhausted. With no prayer involved, without the Holy Spirit drawing the burden through her to the Cross, the residue becomes a weight upon her spirit, emotions, and body. Burden bearing rightly, which works into us the nature and character of Christ, is discussed at length in Chapter 3.

Empathy confuses the mind because most of us are not skilled in identifying and acknowledging our emotions. Unfortunately, as children many of us learned that feelings are not safe or acceptable to have, and we erected barriers to them—these barriers carried over into adulthood. Some put uncomfortable feelings away and escape into whatever will distract them. Some keep a full or over-full social or work schedule that will eliminate the time to feel. Emotions are left unidentified when pushed out of the way. Most people condemn what they do not understand. Most people remain woefully ignorant of what is inside.

If you are fearful of emotions, you will try to barricade empathy from your life. Family and society teach you not to pay attention to emotional information—your own and other's. All too often, you do to yourself what someone did before—disbelieve, minimize, and repress. As an adult, you think you are unable to sense what another feels. Or, you may admit to being empathetic but not to being able to sense. However, empathy is part of the human package, and cannot be suppressed altogether; it will manage to operate to some degree. When you do not understand empathy, most of the time you do not know what is happening. Almost certainly, you will not at all like being so sensitive. You do your best to cope anyway.

Coping With Emotional Pain

Everyone develops coping mechanisms to protect against the onslaught of our own sensitivities as well as others' reactions. We *have* to develop defenses. *At a foundational level, people tend to avoid emotional, psychological, and spiritual pain, trouble, and turmoil.* We find ways not to be where emotional pain is; we huff and puff to make it go away and leave us alone, or try to fix the person or the problem and make the pain go away. When we fix a troubled person, and lower their distress level, we feel less distress ourselves. When done rightly, in Jesus and for His sake, lowering someone's pain is good—but when done only to escape feeling it, is not good.

Avoidance by Creating Distance

Your parents may have used emotion (anger or sadness) to shut down expressions of emotion so the force of the combined energies of the family would not overwhelm them. As an adult you may use the same technique to create distance from the source(s) of turmoil.

Another way to avoid emotional pain and troubles is to *fade quietly away*. You create distance by staying around the fringes of life. In doing so you may *appear* shy, timid, or introverted when in reality you may not be shy at all, but rather, unwilling to come close to people. You learned that interaction is burdensome, confusing, and even painful. Some continually battle with the desire to withdraw from life.

At the far end of the spectrum, some natural burden bearers develop a hermit-like existence, shutting out the world in an attempt to escape the turmoil they cannot turn off. You can become so overwhelmed you want to escape from life. You can walk a mile through the forest and not be tired, but walk 100 feet through a mall or market and be exhausted. For others, malls and markets are OK, but parties are torture. These places become problematic because your spiritual pores are open. You soak up all the trouble, tension, and anxiety around. You quickly become exhausted, and flee to whatever refuge you have. This will be the case until you learn to call on the Lord to be your filter. He can block out everything except what He knows you can bear.

God designed you to be a "people" person, able to be with hurting people and carry a portion of their load to Jesus. Many do not understand themselves or know how to function properly, so they color themselves "gone," and quietly withdraw from people and life. Everyone loses when a burden bearer resigns.

Avoidance by Stifling Others

Some "avoiders" *appear* to be insensitive because they stifle others' expressions of distress. They fill up with emotional freight until they cannot bear one drop more. My husband, David, and I knew such a woman—Jane (not her real name).

With one big generous breath, Jane would do incredibly loving things, go out of her way, and use great quantities of energy and money to care for other people. However, her next breath could be harsh, critical, resentful, and insensitive. Her moods were as stable as wind in a storm.

A couple in Jane's church volunteered as youth leaders. Their first-born died three days after he was born due to complications during the birthing. A year passed and it was Christmas time. We were rehearsing Christmas music, a beautiful lullaby about Mary and the baby. Quiet tears began to roll down the woman's cheeks. Jane saw the tears and said, "Oh, are you *still* crying about *that*? Don't you know your baby is better off in Heaven?" The mother was devastated. The grief that she had been quietly giving to the Lord was rudely jammed back down her throat. The message was that her grief was unacceptable and inappropriate.

We discovered later that Jane's first husband had died 20 years before and she had vowed never to cry. She felt she had to be strong for her children. She had not allowed herself to cry since then. The mother's quiet, appropriate grief called to Jane's grief, which threatened to spill out in her own tears. *That* was what was unacceptable to Jane. In her childhood, she learned that only weak people show tender feelings. Jane was unconsciously trying to protect herself from her own grief by stifling the grieving mother's.

Avoidance by Denial

Some choose to separate, or dissociate, themselves from their feelings and hide, often in the intellect. Books, ideas, and concepts do not talk back or lash out. Libraries, laboratories, and research are wonderful places to avoid interaction with people, and what interaction there is can be objective and non-personal. Logic, causes and effects, rules, and formulas appeal. Your mind can wrap itself around science and logic. That is much easier to manage than the irrational, illogical world of feelings and emotions.

Consequently, many highly sensitive, creative burden-bearers can be found with their legs wrapped around laboratory stools, among the musty tomes of libraries, hiding behind computers and Petri dishes, seeking welcome refuge from trouble and confusion. These are socially acceptable and often lucrative hiding places! For many the body exists to carry the head from one place to another. Some disdain those less successful in coping with or hiding from spiritual, emotional, or psychological pain. I can understand why a person would choose this refuge; I did for a long time. Nonetheless, it is an escape; fleeing from the good works the Lord designed for us to accomplish.

Avoidance by Hiding in Hobbies

Losing yourself in a hobby or avocation is another socially acceptable refuge from relationship. Those who choose this avenue concentrate on the hobby and block out cries for help, silent or otherwise. If you acknowledge someone's cry for help, you will feel obligated to do something. You create your ruts, and appreciate people who do not intrude, who do not show you a larger picture of life, or call you out. You feel justified in hiding.

Avoidance by Narrowly Focusing

Avoiding the ocean of need by focusing on one small wave narrows your focus. Sometimes the "fix it" response is an attempt to rescue people and become their savior. This way you can narrow your focus and concentrate only on one slice of life, not all of it. Focusing narrowly allows you to push the clamor for attention into the background. The subconscious rationalization for not responding to all you sense and feel is that if you spend all your time and resource on one person or cause, you have neither time nor resources to attend to anything else. You cannot do everything, but you can do this. You cannot be everything for everyone, but one bit you can do.

Saving someone from his or her situation is not always pure selflessness. It can be an attempt to lessen other people's pain not so much for their benefit but to lessen the intensity of what you feel empathetically. There is a payoff in lowering the intensity of someone else's pain. You may very well be concerned for that person, but at the same time indulge a self-serving motivation.

For example, I could feel Deedee's distress over a looming work deadline. Helping would shorten the time I had to feel her distress. If I did not want to endure those feelings, all I had to do was step up—a self-serving motivation. My choices were to help do her work—actually do some of her work—or not help and pray that the Lord strengthen her so she could endure the stress of learning the lessons she needed to learn so that deadlines did not become crises. For me, it was an opportunity to learn when and how to intercede and encourage rather than enable dysfunction. I could have been her savior and stepped in to help, thus lowering my stress level, but doing so would deprive her of an opportunity to mature.

The Sponge Effect

The burden-bearing design is such that, like a sponge, you sop up a portion of someone else's emotional load. A sponge retains dirt after water evaporates. As I said earlier, you retain residue from another person's trouble even though time and distance separates you. This is true whether it is a positive or a negative load. You probably know people who are light and bright and you always come away from times with them feeling lifted up. It is a blessing to absorb and retain some of their positive emotion.

In the same way, when you are around negative people—you come away feeling heavy, sad and confused, angry or depressed. This is true of Christian and non-Christian alike—empathy, that drawing, absorbing, retentive quality of your spirit operates whether you realize it or not. Any created being must operate according to its design—fish swim, horses gallop, birds fly, and your spirit connects through empathy whether you like it or not, whether you believe it or not, and whether you intend to empathize or not. It is something your spirit knows to do and does. Like gravity or the laws of physics, the absorbing qualities of your spirit operate whether you know, understand, or believe.

Whoa!

Whoa! This is way too much sensitivity! When you are unaware that you absorb what is in other people, you walk around like a sponge with your spirit open and unprotected. You indiscriminately attract all sorts of things, such as other people's emotion, trouble, and turmoil—and it feels like your own! When you look at your home life and work life you see no reason for the feelings you have. Your family life is relatively smooth, your schedule isn't crazy—yet you feel grief and sadness, confusion, anxiety or rage. The confusion from the disparity between what you feel and what you intellectually know your circumstance to be multiplies the feelings, which compounds emotion to the point of excruciating intensity. People look at you and shake their heads when you share such feelings. They say, "It's not all *that* bad!" "What *is* your problem?" The problem is the weight of an overwhelming, crushing load you did not even know you were carrying!

For example: I met my friend Vivian for coffee. We talked through a series of her losses. On this particular day she was numb with grief. She spoke in monosyllables, her face was emotionally flat, her eyes were dull, but she insisted she was fine. It was obvious she was not fine. For half an hour, I tried to engage her and finally flashed with an intensely impatient irritation. I was only conscious of feeling compassion for the state she was in. My reaction was entirely inappropriate and surprised both of us. I apologized and ended the visit. I went away shaking my head—what was that all about? I wanted to comfort my friend, not be angry with her. She needed comfort, and I made matters worse. I felt like a lousy friend.

Damage to Others

When you absorb a portion of someone else's crushing load and do something that is *appropriate to that load*, your behavior can still be inappropriate for you—like my angry, irritated response to Vivian. My response was inappropriate; it did not express my feelings of care and compassion for her. Even if I had been irritated because she would not share, irritation would not help her. However, if Vivian were the one being angry over her loss, that would have been appropriate. I expressed anger that she was not yet in touch with. Inappropriate responses wound and confuse others. God wants you to soak up pain and trouble and pray it to the Cross and thereby help people, bringing them closer to their source of healing.

Be aware that satan will turn these potentially healing encounters into hurt and division. When you are inappropriate, you can wound a person who is already hurting. When your responses seem insensitive, wounded people will not come your way again with any expectation of comfort, help, or healing.

"What's wrong with me?"

Even for the strongest, carrying heavy loads can result in chronic energy drain. Making empathetic connection with others consumes large amounts of physical, emotional, and psychological energy. Collecting, and carrying everything you collect, requires even more energy; thus, many burden bearers are tired beyond their circumstances. You may wonder why you are constantly weary, and succumb to the growing sense that there is something drastically wrong with you. "I can't cope. I am so lazy. I must be crazy." Condemning thoughts affect your self-esteem and color how you see your-self, in some cases to the extent that they threaten your men-tal health.

Why Is it Killing Me?

If God designed me to empathize, why is it killing me? Are you supposed to walk around soaking up "stuff," filtering the spiritual environment? Yes, and no. Any filter left unat-tended clogs, resulting in great damage to the system. You can hurt yourself by doing too much for too long. Isn't God sup-posed to protect us? Yes, but...He also gives you spiritual armor. Wouldn't you assume He expects you to become adept in its use? He gave you intelligence and common sense for the same purpose. He respects the free will He gave you to operate as an individual. You are in a war not of your own making. The Lord protects, but he also wants you to stop walking around wounded in a war zone.

The Lord gave me a word picture to help me under-stand His desire to redeem empathy. What do I mean by "redeem empathy?" Jesus' death was the price, the ransom paid for your release from sin and its effects in every aspect of your life. However, out of respect for the free will He gave you, you must ask for that redemption to be applied to your gift of empathy as well. When you ask Him to redeem your ability to empathize, it means you ask Him to crucify it—allowing you to die to that ability. To redeem it means the Lord then resurrects that ability to empathize, even as He resurrected Jesus. It means that Jesus will be in charge of this resurrected ability.

When emotional, spiritual, and psychological freight builds up without discharge, weight collects until something breaks inside. You withdraw or block out awareness of anything more. For the sake of your relationships as well as your health, ask the Lord to redeem and be in charge of your empathy and your burden-bearing capacity. This ability, like all other aspects of your humanity, needs to come under the Lordship of Jesus Christ.

When He is in charge, you have access to His wisdom, light, life, and power. When He manages the functioning of your spirit, He will provide protection and direction. This ability is a blessing under the management of the Holy Spirit. Empathy operating without the safeguards of the Holy Spirit can result in burnout, depression, physical breakdowns, and can damage the relationships the Lord meant to bless and refresh. Empathizing can feel like a curse when you don't know how it works. Although you can "feel" a person's trouble, you alone can do nothing about it. Because you merely sit in the pain with them, after a time you come to resent people, for you know, on a subconscious level, that they are the source of your distress.

Working Together

Empathy and natural areas of strength work together. Some capacity for empathy is resident in everyone regardless of natural strength. Your natural strength is something you do well and easily, like teaching, mechanics, administration, music, etc. You easily channel compassionate responses to information from empathy into the area of your expertise. Empathy advises and compassion moves a mechanic, a nurse, or a doctor to volunteer their services. You are at ease using the information your spirit gives you to guide you into action in many areas of service. Though these "sensings" are quite subjective, you have used them so objectively for so long that you think nothing of acting assuredly on subtle nuances.

A trained speaker or teacher senses and reacts to subtle nuances of acceptance and rejection in audiences. It becomes so automatic he thinks nothing of it. He can easily sense when his audience is becoming fearful in reaction to what he is teaching or proclaiming, and check or counterbalance statements to ease their hearts. This is a function of empathy, to inform and guide him about how and what he says.

However, even though we trust and use empathy on a daily basis, most are woefully untrained and ignorant about what may happen when empathy turns to burden bearing. That same speaker, so adept at adapting to his audience, may become confused or frightened when the Holy Spirit begins to draw the fear of many in the audience through to Himself. The speaker has given himself to the Lord; therefore, he may feel the fears of the people streaming like a river through him to the Cross. If he is theologically, biblically, and experientially untrained, the fear that he senses has now become so much more intense than simple empathetic sensitivity that he becomes confused; he cannot understand it and begins to wear it. It may seem to him to be his own and causes him to tremble, or stutter, or lose his train of thought. Satan can take advantage of this situation to haul things up from bad memories to convince him that all the fear is his own, that he ought to quit trying to be a teacher for the Lord.

"Blessed is the man who finds wisdom...then you will go on your way in safety" (Prov. 3:13-23). "The fear of the Lord is the beginning of wisdom; all who follow His precepts have good understanding. He will have no fear of bad news" (Ps. 111:10; 112:7). We need God's wisdom to rightly understand and use our empathetic muscles to bear one another's burdens.

God's design is for your spiritual gifting and natural talents to work in harmony. When the Holy Spirit is in charge of your empathy, you find yourself drawn to a person or situation. The Holy Spirit connects you with wounds in another by empathy. If you train yourself to do so, you can pray specifically and intelligently because you feel what the person is struggling with. You may also be motivated into other appropriate actions. Compassion, born of empathy, can more easily move a person to action in the area of their natural gifting.

If I am a mechanic and I sense sorrow or pain in you, I want to help, so I ask if there is something I can do. How can I bless you? Can I work on your car and thus take a load off? On the other hand, if I am financially blessed, empathy informs me of need, and compassion moves me to respond by helping financially. Empathetic sensing works to call you into action through your natural gifts. God wants you to have compassionate, practical, and tangible responses to information gathered by empathy. He does not want you to stop with reading each other, with gathering information, absorbing and retaining emotional energy.

Rather, He wants to add to what you are currently doing. He is asking a new thing of you, but at the same time is repeating the call to the Church to "act justly and to love mercy," (Mic. 6:8) and to set captives free (Isa. 61:1). In other words, He wants you to lighten emotional and spiritual loads and connect people with Jesus in this way *in addition* to the practical helps.

I believe the Lord wants you to develop a *prayer reflex* to people's burdens and to be consciously aware and understand your responses to these burdens. The Lord wants you to know what you are doing and become skilled at it. When feelings, mood swings, and sensations come out of left field, He wants you to have an informed, intelligent prayer response, a burden-bearing response to such information rather than assuming all such things originate within you.

The human design includes empathy. It *will* operate, but if you are ignorant of this aspect of your being, you will not know "what comes over you" from time to time. You will respond as if what you feel is your own and you may cause hurt to others and yourself. You can inadvertently damage the very relationships you cherish, and the person the Lord wants you to help will not receive the aid He intended. Because it feels so natural, so full of common sense, you are probably not aware of God's heart at work in stirring you. Too often people respond inappropriately and miss the call to lighten someone's burden by bearing a portion or aspect of their burden to Jesus and on to the Cross. God does not want you to stop doing the practical; He is calling you to go beyond material help and bear a portion of others' loads to the Cross, be they spiritual, physical, emotional, or psychological. In this way you imitate Jesus and function as a child of God, which is what He designed you to be.

Sin separates and divides. Empathy connects. Burden-bearing intercession for another overcomes the division, clarifies the mind, and restores a person's capacity to see options and make wise choices. Burden bearing goes over and through the dividing wall between God and a person. Sin is defeated. Empathy connects, allowing you to know what others experience. Responding to what you perceive empathetically by bearing that burden to the Lord provides the opportunity to mature and develop into God's plan for your life—your destiny.

The ability to sense and identify with what is in another connects us in our spirits and makes us corporate beings. Without empathy no one can function optimally as a child of God, for empathy connects us to each other. It binds us together corporately as families and groups. It is our greatest hope because it enables us to be in relationship with God and each other. We have lost awareness of our connectedness—of our corporate nature. Empathy is our greatest resource to restore awareness, rebuild relationships, and reveal our sense of being part of something bigger than "me."

The next chapter is a word picture of a natural burden bearer. This picture provides benchmarks for those of you in the learning process by which you can assess and understand yourself and those around you. You need a general sense of how you are designed in order to co-operate with the Lord in any "spiritual tune-up" He might have for you. Living life according to design rather than against it results in peace and joy, life and energy. Now let's look more in depth at the characteristics natural burden bearers hold in common.

Endnotes

1. Your neural hardware determines your soul's capacity to communicate, soul to soul, but does not affect your human spirit's capacity to communicate human spirit to human spirit. This explains why those born with developmental delays, retardation, or autism can still have an amazing capacity of spirit. The human spirit does not have the same limitations as the soul. For more information see Arthur Burk's http://www.theslg.com for connection to Sapphire Leadership

Group, Inc. with its links to Plumbline Ministries (Tools to discover and develop your identity and express it powerfully in community) or Amthest Healing Concepts (Resources to Heal and Nurture the Human Spirit).

2. See Appendix B regarding the development of the cingulate cortex.

CHAPTER 2

Fearfully and Wonderfully Made— Portrait of a Natural Burden Bearer

Everyday Burden Bearers

What do natural burden bearers look like?

Meet Eloise, a natural burden bearer—redeemed in that she was born again, but with a temperament not yet yielded to the Cross in the area of burden bearing. She is one of those people you want to be with because you always feel better after being with her. However, Eloise is more than a bright spot in your day. For years, with little help, she managed the Sunday school department of a large, historical downtown church. In a college town with professors salted through the membership, there was no excuse for a slouching education department.

Although she had no job description, she *saw and sensed needs*, and without fanfare went about meeting them. She was very creative in the way she met the needs of the children and staff.

For example, she brought top-notch teaching materials to the classrooms by brokering and agreeing to host a large and successful day-care. She bathed everything in prayer. She resigned when, and only because, her husband said, "Enough!" She wanted to make things better, to lighten others' loads so she soaked up needs of the children, needs of the teachers, and needs of the pastors and *carried them—in her heart, mind, body and spirit.*

Some of the burdens and stress clung to her until finally her husband retired her. At first glance, you would think she was an overachiever who could not delegate; but she was, at a motivational level, a fleshly burden bearer who felt responsible for the needs she saw, sensed and felt. Two years after they hired the Christian education minister, he continued to find tasks no one thought to do because Eloise always did them.

Tony was fortunate. He learned how to cooperate with the Holy Spirit in bearing burdens as a kid. At age 12, his mother found him weeping over the newspaper, filled with grief because of the suffering of a family whose daughter was murdered. His parents taught him how to intercede for the family and pass on to Jesus the pain and grief he felt continually wafting off the pages of the daily newspaper. He learned he was not weird, but specifically designed for a purpose dear to God's heart.

Terry was not so fortunate. She lost her arts and crafts business because she could not force herself to put her business above someone else's need. If she could have done the art, the design, etc. and let someone else take responsibility for the business end of things, she might still have her store. However, when people complained about the prices, she gave them discounts. When people owed her money, she extended them credit. Putting a price on her own work nearly gave her ulcers.

Family and friends told her she should take a firmer stance with people and put the needs of the business first. She agreed. But when people came in to chat, not to shop, she was unable to "stick to business" and never made a profit. She absorbed the people's burdens. All the conflicting thoughts and feelings made her think she was losing her mind. Not only did she lose the business, the stress nearly destroyed her body. Her weight dropped until she was frail. She thought she was a failure, a nothing, a "nobody." She thought there was something inherently wrong with her; what, she was not sure.

She had always been "the different one," so she meekly wore whatever emotional or spiritual abuse came her way—and in her spiritual circle plenty did. She attracted it like a magnet! Then she learned about burden bearing, and how to bear burdens rightly. She learned that not all craziness she felt was hers. She learned to pass on the burdens, confusions, troubles, and distress to Jesus. She learned how to live within her boundaries, according to her design. She is healthy now and she has a career more suited to her personality.

Who Is a Natural Burden Bearer?

Natural burden bearers are those who, like it or not, have an unusually high ability to empathize. For them, sensing and identifying with others' emotional, spiritual, psychological, and physical freight is a way of life, it happens unconsciously, automatically, "naturally"—a natural burden bearer.

Natural burden bearers have a high level of sensitivity that enables them to receive or hear messages, see pictures, taste the flavors, and feel the intensities of what other people experience. It is like being in the other person's skin, experiencing what they experience. The Lord has so finely tuned some people that through the gift of word of knowledge (1 Cor. 12:8) they know not only that you are hurting, but where, how intensely, and sometimes why. The bulk of natural burden bearers are on a continuum up to this point.

However, to be complete, I have to acknowledge there are some who are even more sensitive. It is as if they have long-range sensors that reach across the country, even across the continent. Some see spiritual realities so clearly at times they cannot distinguish between the natural and the spiritual. For them reality is sometimes like being in an I-Max theatre and they are tipping out of their chairs! The majority of natural burden bearers, though, are not that finely turned.

Society teaches you to pay no attention to this "extra" incoming data. If you are unable to do that, you learn falsely that everything you sense and feel originates with you—making you weird. Consequently, many of you who are equipped with "Doppler radar" walk blithely out into the world and cannot understand why you come home all wet and covered with mud. Had you known how to read and interpret your data stream you would have worn rain gear—or at least grabbed an umbrella! On one level you are aware of the data you receive; but in time, you learned to block it out, to pay as little attention as you possibly can to it. You learn to ignore the radar screen in front of you.

Scripture states that God calls everyone to bear burdens at some time or another "Carry each other's burdens, and in this way you will fulfill the law of Christ" (Gal. 6:2), but not everyone is a *natural* burden bearer. Many people run, but not everyone runs like an Olympic athlete. However, until there is a turning to the Lord with the burdens, natural burden bearers, like everyone else, wear the burdens they absorb, which is *doing the work of the spirit with the strength of the soul.*

It is not the soul's job to bear burdens. Burden bearing in your own strength can affect every area of your life, causing havoc, even derailing the Lord's plans for your life. At a minimum, it can be tiring because of the confusion it causes. You can come to erroneous conclusions and judgments (Chapter 6 explains judgments further) that affect you in many different ways. Highly sensitive, empathetic people are in every kind of family imaginable and every walk of life. They bring sensitivity, creativity, and intuition to their calling, ministry, profession, or occupation. Highly empathetic teachers use their creativity and intuition to design innovative, interesting, and effective lessons and exercises. Through sensitivity they often intuitively "know" the students' areas of difficulty and identify students in need of more attention.

When I taught English as a Second Language, whenever the Lord prompted through the gifts of the Spirit, I was able to "get inside a student's head" and "know" what he or she wanted to say and provide the needed vocabulary. Burden-bearing engineers and scientists turn their creativity and sensitivity toward their work as well as toward fellow workers—it comes easily, it is part of who they are.

Gene Eby is one such example. He and his engineering department were exhausted from years of failing to find the right kind of porcelain insulator bushing capable of handling the megavoltage of electricity that would be generated from the yet-to-be-completed Grand Coolee Dam. He could feel his team's disappointment and feelings of despair. One night he surrendered the problem to God and the next morning "heard" God speak to him while reading his Bible, which had fallen open to the familiar story of when Jesus changed the water to wine.

As a Christian engineer, he suddenly realized that it would take millions of volts to change the molecular structure of water to wine, and yet those pottery jars did not explode. He intuitively knew this story had something to do with the Lord's answer—he just didn't know what! He shut everything down and sent his team on a month's vacation, praying that the Lord would refresh them—spirit, mind, and body. He passed their exhaustion of mind, spirit, and body on to the Lord. Upon their return, he talked with each one.

Mr. Cermak, in charge of porcelain clays, had visited the Middle East during his vacation. He told of visiting the newly opened tomb of King Tut in Egypt. He had a wonderful time and brought back a souvenir. That night Mr. Eby felt his spirit come to attention with a picture of the Bible story of Jesus changing water to wine in a ceramic pot. He called his friend at 4 a.m. and asked what the souvenir was—a pottery shard from a pot used for King Tut's feasts. They tested the 3,200-year-old pottery shard and made a bushing of the same composition.

Finally, they found the type of clay that could handle the voltage produced by the huge turbines of Grand Coolee Dam! Gene Eby was sensitive to his fellow workers, feeling what they felt, and did two things. He met the physical need that he could see by giving time off, but also came along side by lightening their load with intercession. Because the Holy Spirit enabled him to feel what they felt, he could pray intelligently and specifically. He also listened to God and acted on what he heard. This was "normal," the "logical" thing for him to do.[1]

How you think and how your mind and spirit work together may seem "normal" and "logical" to you. Natural burden bearers are often unaware that others do not operate the way they do and are quite surprised to discover that not everyone thinks and feels as they do.

When Does High Sensitivity Begin?

Empathy as a spiritual function begins even in the womb. From conception, you are like a little sponge, soaking up both negative and positive emotions. You are like an air filter filling up with spiritual smog. As a group, burden bearers tend to have parents and/or grandparents who were also highly sensitive. It raises the question of whether or not there is a genetic component to sensitivity that passes the characteristic through the generations.

Jesus' work on the Cross can keep this natural tendency from becoming fleshly. For we can pass our burdens on to Him. Beginning in the garden of Gethsemane, Jesus drew the burdens of all humankind into His spirit. It affected His emotions—He was overwhelmed with sorrow to the point that He wanted human companionship (Matt. 26:36-45). Isaiah 53:4 says, "He took up our infirmities and carried our sorrows." It affected His body so profoundly He could not stand. He sweat blood (Luke 22:44). On the Cross you can see that it affected His spirit and His relationship with His Father when He cried out, "My God, my God, why have you forsaken me?" (Matt. 27:46).

Reconciliation and the restoration of relationships is the high calling of every burden bearer. What better tool could the Lord provide to accomplish that task than high sensitivity, which is the essence of empathy!

Common Traits

So how do you know if you are a natural burden bearer? Natural burden bearers have common traits. If you have unusual empathy, if you are known for your unusual compassion, creativity, and intuition, you share the most important and prominent features of the natural burden bearer.

Natural burden bearers easily sense what others feel, in some cases, nearly to the point of mind reading.

Literature and film often portray spiritual truths. Remember Radar from the television series M*A*S*H? Radar was the epitome of an unrecognized and untrained natural burden bearer at work. His keen sense of empathy was such that he "read" the Colonel's mind. His compassion and sensitivity resulted in some laughable situations, but he was also the one who found and fed orphans, supported a widowed Korean lady, and patched up broken relationships between various M*A*S*H personnel. His character is typical of many natural burden bearers.

One of my fun stories about sensing what is in the heart of another is about David and me. I am not talking about ESP, rather being tuned in to the heart through the Holy Spirit and experiencing what another feels. In this case, the feeling was joy over what David was doing "secretly." He was asked to fill in for a pastor for a summer. With only one Sunday remaining, I asked, "Hey, David, when will you be paid for all the work you have been doing?"

He popped into the room and said, "Don't even think it! I have designs on that money so just don't even think about how to spend it."

I looked at him, grinned, "Oh, thank you! David, that is so sweet of you!"

Eyes wide he said, "You don't know what I'm going to do with that money."

However, I did know. Secretly, he was going to replace the diamond that had fallen out of my wedding ring. I felt the anticipation of joy in him as he looked forward to giving me a long-awaited gift. He finally admitted that I was right, and asked me to join him in choosing the diamond. It was fun.

This ability to sense what another is going to say or do enables people to work together smoothly, to finish each other's sentences, or "know" when someone is not telling the truth. It enables you to track and follow the twists and turns conversations take. This close association makes it possible for a boss to turn and ask, "Where is that…that…that…" and her assistant to reply without looking up, "To your right, under your dictionary." Empathy helps you modify your words, your mood, and behavior to be appropriate in the presence of grief or great joy. This is sensing someone's inner state, where they are emotionally. Empathy is also different from words of knowledge, which appear as a thought in your mind, often without context and do not necessarily have feelings attached. For a great many, this empathetic kind of "knowing" happens all the time.

Unusually Empathetic, Compassionate

Natural burden bearers are unusually empathetic and compassionate. You feel trouble and turmoil acutely and want to do all you can to "make it better." As children, natural burden bearers bring home all the hurt birds, literally and figuratively. As a child, you took on responsibility for keeping the peace at home, peace between Mom and Dad, peace between the siblings. You became a peacemaker at school, between your friends, etc. But God did not design a little child to carry the weight of the family. Nevertheless, little burden bearer that you were, many of you stepped in to "make it better" and sacrificed your childhood. This can happen to extreme burden bearers even when there is no major trouble or tension in your parent's marriage.

In my case, my parents had a very loving, stable marriage. However, a series of unfortunate events resulted in my family "barely getting by" during most of my childhood. My mother and I were reminiscing one day when Mom asked, "Were you ever a child?" I thought for a time and responded, "Yes, I think so, for about six or seven years and then I sort of skipped to being an adult." I was not keeping the peace so much as taking on feelings of adult responsibility for the family welfare—there were not enough hands to do all the work, so I jumped in. This robs those who do this of some of their childhood. Yes, I defended the weak and befriended the odd and outcast. As adults, the need or desire to keep the peace, or help make things better can cause you to be unwittingly overworked, or worse, create a vulnerability to being used and abused by those less sensitive.

David and I raised two children. As they entered school, they interacted with a wide variety of children and invited many of them home. There were far more visits from the ones needing intensive loving, attention, and training than there were visits from children from homes that shared our values and lifestyle—at least it seemed that way to me. Our eldest remembers bringing one little boy home and thinking, "Here he is, Mom! Love him—that will fix him!" I sensed what they were doing and sympathized on one level, but it drove me to distraction on another. Before I understood anything at all about discharging the weight of burdens, the constant additional load was too heavy for me.

More Creative

Burden bearers tend to be more creative than average. As David and I thought over some good friends of ours whom we know to be burden bearers, all of them fit this description. Mark is a gifted artist and cartoonist. He is also a writer; his insights into various spiritual and emotional problems have helped an untold number of people. Amy is a gifted poet and writer; another Amy is a gifted painter. Mary Claire and Caroline are outstanding photographers. Their sensitivity and ability to capture the sense of a person's spirit—or just life, causes you to catch your breath. Sometimes as I look at the artwork, I see each individual's zest for life as a reflection of the Lord's joy in His creation.

Lee is a landscape artist—she paints, she does not do lawns! The only one who can create better skies is the Lord Himself. Why shouldn't she paint well? Her Father taught her! Barry was a dancer in her youth; now as a grandmother, she catches the rhythms of life in clay. Her decorative pots command the eye to stop and give time to take in all they are saying.

Our late friend Martin was a pianist. The music that flowed through his hands took him to the concert stage during one period of his life. After he met the Lord, he understood his music as never before when he discovered that many of the classics were composed as worship music. The preludes he presented Sunday after Sunday were more fulfilling to him than the adulation of the concert stage. God became his audience of One, but he also blessed a small congregation weekly as his music lifted us into the Lord's presence.

When our children were small, their favorite stories were the ones I wrote. These examples are from within the arts, but the statement holds true for all areas of human endeavor.

Stan and George were both amazing in business. They made a bundle of money and invested it heavily in the Kingdom of God. Our daughter, Meilee, is in sales—her creativity in dealing with people and making sales makes me wonder where she came from!

I saw a documentary about a mechanical engineer who became paraplegic as the result of an airplane accident. He was unwilling to give up his active lifestyle so he brought together his training and his creativity to develop all sorts of mobility devices to enable him to continue flying and enjoying the outdoors.

Our sensitivity, creativity, and intuition serve our occupational needs no matter if you are an urban planner, pastor, lawyer, retail associate, aeronautical engineer, maintenance worker, builder, developer, medical researcher, waste collector, dentist, or a parent—especially a parent!

There are ways you use creativity "on the job," but creativity is also for your personal benefit and refreshment. The Lord knows you need cleansing, release, and restoration of energies after allowing life's troubles to coat and fill you up. He provides creativity as a way to release any tension remaining from your "on duty time." It is a way to narrow your focus, a way not to think or feel anything other than what you are working on. When my hands are in clay, on the keyboard or in the cookie dough, my mind calms and the last dregs of the burdens that came to me drain from my spirit and body. After the release comes the refreshment of being in touch with the Father's heart.

Psychic Gifts

Natural burden bearers occasionally have psychic gifts, which is confusing. Some burden bearers have sensitivity and empathy on the very high end of the scale. They do "see" and "hear" things often at great distances. These are the ones with inner long-range sensors, surround sound, and 360-degree view screens. They may also have some clairvoyant experiences. Mark Sandford, son of authors John and Paula Sandford, coined the term, "accidental psychic" to describe these very highly sensitive natural burden bearers.[2] These folks do not go looking for what can be found, but "accidentally" hear and see things in the spirit realm simply because their very high sensitivity gives them clarity of vision and accuracy of hearing.

There is much information floating around in the spiritual dimension. Some Christians stumble upon it accidentally, and find it confusing. Scripture teaches not to dabble in such things as divination, which is *searching* for information through supernatural powers other than God, having "unusual insight, intuitive perception."[3] (See Deuteronomy 18:10,14; First Samuel 15:23; Second Chronicles 33:6; and Leviticus 19:31 for Scripture support of the words divination and clairvoyance.)

What do you do when you experience unusual insight that "just happens"? Being this highly sensitive is not sin. It is, however, very important to ask the Lord to be in charge of this aspect of your being. I want to be very clear that you do not dedicate your psychic abilities to Jesus and use them in His service. Instead, come to Jesus asking Him to kill any tendency to misuse your sensitivities. Such misuse is part of your fallenness and needs to die on the Cross. You want to no longer be psychic. Then it is up to Jesus to resurrect your empathetic nature. If He does, it will be changed just as Jesus' body was changed and different after His resurrection. If the Lord resurrects and restores your ability to see, hear, and feel what is in another, He will also tune you in to Jesus only, through the gifts of the Holy Spirit.

Most accidental psychics, in the beginning especially, are naturally highly sensitive burden bearers who are untrained, uninformed, and do not know the Giver of the gift. They do not know any other way; they only know they want to help people and are doing so the best way they know. These people need an introduction to Jesus and His Lordship over all of life. Once introduced to Jesus, some accidental psychics are quite happy to place the Lord in charge.

Others, however, choose to be master of their abilities—at least that is their perception. A confirmed and dedicated psychic develops these abilities without the wisdom and training of the Lord. He/she chooses to do his own thing rather than the Lord's. This independent one would rather feel in control of self as well as in control of "spiritual power," than be a servant of the Lord with Him in charge of the "power" and development of ability. He does not want to be controlled by or submitted to the Lord's direction and timing. The sense of power and control is, of course, a delusion of the enemy. But the power that tempts him to resist surrendering to the Lord is often the heady, seemingly successful, control of others through his gifts, or controlling others by being able to help them.

Scripture forbids any clairvoyance done deliberately. "'Do not turn to mediums or seek out spiritists, for you will be defiled by them. I am the Lord your God" (Lev. 19:31). (Also see Leviticus 20:6,27 and Isaiah 8:19.)

Knowledge can be very seductive. People are born curious and tend to peer where not invited. You may be tempted to go looking for "what else may be out there," especially those of you who are incredibly sensitive. When you search by your spirit without the Lord's direction, you take yourself out from under His protection and may become a target of the enemy. Information you see, hear, or sense may in fact be accurate, but it is only information. It may be helpful; it may not. You do not have the wisdom and grace the Lord has. He knows the timing and the sequence in which each person needs to receive information that is presented. His timing and His ways lead to conviction and repentance, not pride in self-importance.

When the Lord shows you a thing, it is revelation and always brings good fruit when you submit to it. Information gathered from "out there" or read from another's spirit and blurted out prematurely can rip and tear because hearts were not properly prepared. Information without revelation can throw you off balance, into striving, condemnation, or depression, or it can galvanize you into unwise actions, denial, or rebellion. Peering in unrestrained curiosity, in a need for recognition, or significance, never leads to good fruit.

God is the only One who has the right, the authority to enable you to have access to someone else's inner being. Yes, each one is born with a measure of ability but because of sin, because of the Fall, humankind is sinful in every aspect, even this one. That is why Paul says we are both saved and are being saved (1 Cor. 15:2; 2 Cor. 2:15). When you accept Christ as Savior, your human spirit's eternal destiny is settled. You are saved from the ultimate penalty of sin. However, God wants to save you now, not just in the future. Therefore, salvation must also come to other aspects of your being so you can yield every part to God's will (1 Thess. 5:23).

Your ability to connect with others spirit-to-spirit must also come to the Cross, be crucified there, resurrected, and be "harnessed" or yoked with Jesus so you are restored to be the sensitive person He created you to be. Since you may accurately sense and feel other people's state of being, you must learn to hear from the Lord so you treat the information responsibly. Questions to ask the Lord:

Am I to share what I "know"?

Am I to intercede?

Am I to carry some of their load to the Cross so they are not overwhelmed?

Am I to intercede until the Lord brings people and circumstances together for a "sovereign encounter," or until they have strength enough to make wise decisions?

Am I only to send up a flare, asking the Lord to bring the person who is to help in this situation?

Lord, what do You want me to do?

Speaking out without the Lord's authority can result in harm. It can reveal the work the Lord is doing in a heart prematurely. When the soil is soft, a root comes out easily. When it is dry and hard, the plant breaks off and the root remains to grow again. Hearts are no different. *Knowing something does not automatically give you permission to speak it!* The Lord knows when a heart is prepared to hear with benefit and when a word spoken prematurely would strengthen a hardness of heart or galvanize a person's rebellion or denial. Wait and intercede until otherwise directed.

Seeking the Lord's heart on the matter is most important—until we are in Heaven, we will all have mixed motivations.

Clarity of vision into spiritual realms, like any gift of the Holy Spirit must also be under the Lordship of Jesus Christ, and brought to the Cross. The Fall changed human inclinations, reorienting them toward sin. Since then humanity has a "bentness," a propensity to veer away from God, to peer and go where we should not (such things as ESP, clairvoyance, telepathy, tarot cards). This is why you must ask Jesus to help you come to the place that, as far as you are concerned, your ability to see is dead. The Lord can reclaim and cleanse the gifts, talents, and abilities you give back to Him. The Lord can reclaim who you are as a sensitive person and restore your ability to hear Him. These abilities will not function safely unless He is directing their function.

There is safety in setting the will and the heart to be servant rather than master. As servants you can rest in the wisdom of His choices, knowing that His plans are for the good for others, as well as for you. He can redeem and return to you whatever you give Him, or He may replace one gift with other spiritual gifts of His choosing—such as intercession, word of knowledge, mercy, etc., which involve an empathetic and perceptive spirit. He does not take away without giving you opportunity to ask Him to replace with what He knows is best for you. The Lord does not want to leave you with a vacuum.

Shy, Quiet, Withdrawn

Often natural burden bearers appear shy, quite, and even withdrawn. Some may actually be shy, but a majority are not so at all. When comfortable and given opportunity, natural burden bearers can chat as well as the next person. But because of high sensitivity to the intensity of others' burdens, many tend to avoid crowds. Natural burden bearers do not necessarily enjoy being around groups of people. This is not due to any lack of interpersonal skills, but is a choice to be where there is less spiritual, emotional, and psychological freight.

The attempt to avoid noise, turmoil, and confusion that natural burden bearers sense causes some of them to withdraw, that is, until they learn how to release and find rest in Jesus. Does this sounds familiar? You may fall silent in groups and drop out of the conversation. You follow the discussion, but it takes so much effort to elbow your way in or shout others down with your contribution that you choose not to talk. Some of you work your way to the fringes so you can breathe! Your lack of participation is an attempt to counter-balance the noise, activity level, and intensity. This is also why you may choose not to be involved with people; you prefer still waters and green pastures—people, places, and activities that appear to some extroverts as subdued, and consequently, you may appear to be shy.

When I tell people I have a shy side many laugh aloud, they literally do not believe me. However, as a youngster I wandered in the woods or went off behind the barn when company came. I spent long hours walking our 280-acre farm and riding bareback on the old workhorse in an effort to escape spiritual as well as physical noise. Plants and animals were not noisy; they did not fight or talk back. They nurtured my spirit. People do not believe me because I have lived with an extrovert and learned many of his ways. I now enjoy people and group activities; even need that kind of interaction in moderation. *However,* I must always retreat to quiet, to nature, music, art, and books, and to the Lord to recover. The Lord renews my energies in quietness and stillness.

A friend told us she no longer enjoyed shopping. David and I were shocked because this woman used to say that shopping was her spiritual gift! She was outgoing and fun to be around. When she took you in tow, you knew to hold on tight! However, at the time she told us of this change she was a much more peaceful, quiet person. The difference came when the Lord brought healing to her life and called her into intercession as a way of life. In order to handle all the practicalities of life as a child, she learned to suppress the sensitivity that we now saw. She became so tuned to God that after four years there was a complete 180-degree turn around in relation to her ability to enjoy the noise and bustle of crowds of people! The Lord quieted her spirit so she was comfortable with the quiet. Although equally at ease in the crowd, she wearied of the busyness much sooner. And more surprisingly, she could become quiet in a group in such a way that she could *appear* shy or withdrawn.

Loud Noises and Speech Patterns

Natural burden bearers often avoid loud noises and develop understated patterns of speech. Have you noticed a tendency to hear noise, music, conversation, thoughts, and feelings louder and stronger than they register to others? You seem to need fewer decibels than most, for you a little goes a long way. Because you "hear" things as being forceful, you may speak softly, or in what others perceive to be understatements. When you speak without much obvious emotion or intensity, others perceive your statements as an expression of a preference, rather than a definite desire. The force with which you speak does not accurately portray to others how you feel. It sounds appropriate enough to you, but others apparently do not perceive it the same way. Because you tend to feel your desires are "less important" than others, you "fix" the situation by acquiescing. If you give up your needs and wants too often, you become resentful.

When a person speaks in a "normal" tone, you may hear it as loud or strident, as if the intensity of the speaker's spirit registers as increased volume. You are probably not actually hearing sounds more loudly, but rather, you sense the spirit behind what a person says, behind the music, behind the sermon. The person speaking, delivering the sermon, or playing the music has an intensity or "loudness" of spirit. The volume you "hear" may have more to do with the intensity in the speaker's spirit (or musicians') and less to do with actual decibels of sound.

If the speaker or musician is living a sinful lifestyle, your spirit may sense his or her rebellion and the Lord's grief over it—the hidden sin combined with the Lord's grief is what causes the intensity. Your eardrums may not be in as much danger as you think! People who do not hear the intensity of the spirit do not understand why people and sounds impact you so forcefully. They are mystified that misunderstandings, criticism, jibes, and rejection hurt you so deeply.

David and I were talking with a friend one evening. Feeling strongly about the topic of conversation, David shared his thoughts and feelings with some intensity, but not loudly by decibels. Our friend's grandson was playing on the floor in an adjoining room. He looked up at David and said, "Hey, you don't have to shout." His grandmother started to correct him for speaking disrespectfully but David intervened. "No," he said, "I wasn't physically shouting, but my spirit was."

A natural burden bearer went to a healing conference. One of the teachers/ministers was an older man with a classic older Pentecostal style of delivery. He, in fact, was shouting. My friend had to excuse herself from the session. The volume and delivery style was causing her to feel condemned. It felt verbally and spiritually abusive. She was reacting both to what she sensed in the man's spirit, and to what shouting meant to her because of her experiences. She called me at that point as a way of grounding herself. I suggested she ask the Lord to be in control of the volume and be a filter or buffer for her, to ask the Lord to allow her to see and hear what He wanted her to see and hear. She went back into the conference and had no more trouble. She saw and heard far differently than before and no longer felt condemned.

Atmosphere or Spiritual Environment

Natural burden bearers sense the atmosphere or spiritual environment in a location more than others. Marsha hates to ride the city bus—too much noise, too much pain, spiritual and physical. Like many of us, she is learning and being healed.

For Rosa, the four-block radius of downtown has a heaviness, or oppressiveness, that makes it hard to think. She will not go there unless several others go with her. She is learning to listen to God's direction and to live within the limits He sets for her until she is healed enough to go anywhere without picking up too many burdens indiscriminately. Jeremy does not like to visit his aunt Jen because she lives in a "sad" house.

The Mystery of Spiritual Sensitivity

You can probably think of a relative or associate that you would rather not visit because of the unspoken hurt, anger, or expectation that hangs in the air. You may have had the experience of going into a house and having the hair on the back of the neck stand up, or you feel a general sense of wariness. You are sensing the environment or the atmosphere.

David and I had friends who were renting a home that had been vacated because of a divorce. When we visited them, the entire house felt oppressive, but upon entering one particular room, I immediately became dizzy and lost my balance. When I left the room, the dizziness vanished, and we wondered. Our friends inquired about the former occupants and discovered that the wife was involved in borderline occult activity. The room in which I "lost my balance" was the meeting room. My reaction was a physical portrayal of a spiritual reality—an off-balance philosophy that went around in circles!

I once visited a church and nearly had to leave during the worship service because the music seemed loud to the point of being physically painful. The percussion was so forceful my eardrums felt as if they would burst with each beat of the drums. On a hunch, I leaned over to ask David if it was too loud. He said, "No, no louder than usual." By plugging my ears, praying, and holding onto Jesus I was able to stay; but it was an endurance test. Worship never hurt so badly. Later we discovered that the leadership of the church was in serious turmoil and distress. The beloved pastor had become too emotionally involved with a woman in the church. He refused to accept the caution of the elders about inappropriate familiarity, and later refused their correction entirely. He was eventually asked to leave.

I was touched by the distress of the leadership that day, by the illness of the pastor and the resultant stress upon him, and the stress of elders who were sick at having to confront a pastor they loved. I felt their concern for the people's reactions and their concern for a wife in turmoil as well as the grief of our Lord. In addition, He allowed me to experience what He hears when we come to Him saying, "I love you" but our hearts and lives are out of tune. It is so much "noise" to Him; it does not delight His ears. Our "out of order lives" grieve His heart. "If anyone turns a deaf ear to the law, even his prayers are detestable" (Prov. 28:9).

This was a case of sensing the pain in the leadership of the place—the physical plane, and the pain in God—the spiritual plane. The emotional distress and grief from the church leadership filled the physical environment, and the grief of the Father filled the spiritual environment. It was a double whammy and the sheer impact of that distress and grief registered in me as physical pain and nearly drove me from the building. Environments can affect us powerfully. Again, it is wise to ask God to keep you from picking up anything in the surrounding atmosphere He has not called you to feel through the gifts of the Holy Spirit.

Across Miles

Natural burden bearers sometimes know what a friend is feeling across a space of miles. An experience common to many is sensing when a close friend or relative is going to call. That person may have been popping into your thoughts for a day or two and then, suddenly, a phone call comes or a letter arrives. Many of you have also had the experience of waking in the middle of the night, aware of a friend in another city or state, in some kind of trouble. Parents often sense when children are in emotional need and seek them out to give support, or sense when a child is in danger and ask the Lord to protect.

David and I awoke from a sound sleep about 11:30 one night feeling that disaster was impending. As we prayed asking who, what, how, why, and when sort of questions, it seemed we were to make a phone call. We argued with God that it was far too late to call anyone, but He seemed to insist. Feeling very foolish and with great apology we phoned. We learned later that our call interrupted a spiritual encounter that would have had long-lasting ramifications! We were so grateful the Lord did not allow us to sleep, and did not allow our arguments to dissuade Him. After we were obedient, sleep returned quickly.

Another time the Lord called me to pray for three days for a friend in another state. I felt an intense sadness, a feeling of loss and grief. As I identified the feelings, I asked the Lord who to pray for because I knew the feelings did not belong to me. At the time, there was nothing in my circumstances to generate those feelings. This friend came to mind in a strong way, so I prayed for her, asking the Lord to come into her circumstances with His life, His answer. On the third day, I felt a pressure in the middle of my back as if the Lord put His hand there and escorted me into the bedroom to intercede for my friend. The prayer was so intense at times; I had no words, just the silent groaning of my spirit until finally the intensity faded. I immediately called her. She shared that she and her husband had a marriage crisis during the time I had been praying. While I was interceding in the bedroom, they experienced a breakthrough. Goose flesh appeared on our arms as we talked and laughed with delight.

They had been rejoicing and thanking the Lord even as I called. The Lord calls us to pray for people in other countries, and time zones—distance is no problem for God!

Burden Bearing Affects

This subject is treated in depth in Chapter 10, but let me briefly say here that an incoming burden can cause a change in mood, and exaggerate, or intensify your own feelings. However it affects you, it usually seems like the feeling originated with you and therefore you accept and wear it as your own. Far too many of us blame ourselves for being out of sync—we join the conversation two subjects late, we laugh when others cry, we cry when they laugh. We feel weird, and others are happy to agree with us. Consequently, many of us struggle with low self-esteem and self-worth when in fact we are highly creative and often highly intelligent! We just don't *feel* creative or intelligent.

God's Provision

The Lord provides empathy, creativity, compassion, and intuition as spiritual resources for repairing and restoring His people and building His Kingdom. You bless Him when you make practical use of it in your occupations. It blesses His heart and brings you joy when you use it for the personal release and refreshment of others and yourself, and for the restoration of physical and mental energies. Some may hide in their art or craft, in their intellect or laboratories and workshops, driven there by bearing burdens in a wrong way, doing the work of your spirit with the strength of your soul rather than doing the work of your spirit in concert with His Spirit.

In Summary

Exceptional sensitivity, creativity, and empathy—these are aspects of the cluster of characteristics common to natural burden bearers. Any one individual may not exhibit all the characteristics discussed here, and each of you will exhibit characteristics to different degrees. Although I have defined a natural burden bearer as a person with a high ability to empathize, that is on a scale from high to extremely high empathy. Additionally, an individual can be predominately creative or predominately sensitive to others and their environment. The predominately creative person is still sensitive to others. Our friends Lee and Barry are both very, very sensitive to others, but their vocations dictate that they operate mainly out of the high end of the scale for creativity.

Before going into the process of burden bearing, I want to establish the foundations of empathetic burden bearing firmly in your heart and mind. These early foundations are based on your family interactions as a youngster.

Endnotes

1. Richard E. Eby, *Caught Up Into Paradise*, (Grand Rapids, MI: Revell, 1990), 97-101.

2. Mark Sandford is also an author. John and Paula Sandford founded of Elijah House, Inc., Spokane, Washington. John was the first to teach on burden bearing. Mark then expanded that teaching. This book is an attempt at a comprehensive treatment of the subject.

3. http://www.m-w.com/dictionary/divination; retrieved 11/1/06.

CHAPTER 3

Life Goes Awry—Damage to the Portrait

The last chapter drew a portrait of the natural burden bearer as a sensitive, compassionate, creative individual. The problem is, you may not always come across that way or operate in those ways, right? Why is that? Why do many of us have no clue that we are sensitive and compassionate? Some of you know all too well, but still feel deep down that you are "wrong," "different," and not "normal?" Why can't we joyfully meet life head on and be ourselves? Why does life have to hurt so badly? Sensitivity, compassion, and creativity are such positive qualities, why do we feel so discontented, so unsafe? What went wrong?

You were born into relationship. Compassion, sensitivity, and creativity are relational qualities. Ideally the family should nurture and develop these aspects of your personality. If you did not have the good fortune to be born into a nurturing family, your ability to express sensitivity, compassion, and creativity may be spotty or undeveloped. For some, those qualities were downplayed or outright squashed. Some never learned the vocabulary that went with what they experienced.

Consequently, as adults they cannot separate the tangle of emotions they feel.

You learn to "do life" in the family. This is where you, together with parents and siblings, lay foundations for how you see, interpret, and experience life. It is within the family where you learn emotional fluency and flexibility; what emotions are called, what they feel like, which ones are appropriate to express, where they are appropriately expressed and where not, for what duration and intensity. You learn how others will respond to emotion and the lack of emotion—you learn how to relate. These learnings become your interpretative grid and the lenses through which you see, experience, and make sense of life—they form the template for future relationships.

Psychologists agree that the most important predictor of mental health is in acceptability of emotions and their expression.[1] To me, this sounds like remaining true to your design as you grow. This is the crossroad where you either embrace or start turning away from your original design. You need to be able to be sad, angry, frustrated, or confused without worrying about your status as a member of your family. You need to know that you can make a huge mistake and still be your father's child. You need to be able to be sideways with the world and know that you can still go home and be welcomed and loved.

However, not many lived in this type of family environment. If you did not develop an entire aspect of your personality or learn the acceptability or appropriate expression of a full range of emotions, how will you become the person God designed you to be?

Emotion is integral to sensitivity and compassion, to whom you are. Holding true to your design in these first years of life is incredibly important. A little turning from yourself early on translates into a gulf of separation from your "true" self as an adult. A building a couple degrees off plumb at the foundation is several degrees off at the roofline. The house will be unstable. When you become a stranger to yourself, not knowing who you are or what you feel, like a house off plumb, you become unstable and insecure.

When your parents and/or siblings did not allow you to be yourself, when the emotional, empathetic part of your personality was stifled and unappreciated, you did not learn what to do with what you saw, sensed, and felt—especially if your family members did not know either!

Current brain research tells us that the cingulate, the part of the brain responsible for emotions, copies the organization of, and develops in the same ways as the more mature brain of the primary caretakers.[2] Parents who received little to no nurture themselves are not likely to be able to lead their children beyond what they experienced. From time to time, it does happen, but that is the exception rather than the norm.

Experiences that do not tell you the truth about who you are sow tiny seeds of untruth like spores of mildew. Then roots grow and carve out little fissures in your foundations, producing telltale spots that damage your portrait. Life experiences make changes, and you become different, your life goes awry and little by little, you turn away from your design and destiny. Your original design was to be a reflection of your heavenly Father. Sin warped that design; life experiences further distorted it. Your destiny remains to walk like Him, talk like Him, live like Him—to be a child of God. It takes salvation, and a lifetime of walking with Jesus, to work His character and nature into your life and mine.

Jesus said, "Anyone who has seen Me has seen the Father" (John 14:9). If you are a burden bearer it means God put an aspect of His heart in you. You feel something of what God feels for His children. Burden bearing is one of the ways God works the character and nature of Jesus into you. High sensitivity is an aspect of His person that is built into you. Working *with* this design rather than against it is to row with the current.

You will be better able to understand what has tempted you to turn away from your inner design, or "true" self as a natural burden bearer, as you answer the following questions and think about the implications of your answers:

- Did my family suppress or support expression of emotions?

- How did they respond to "acceptable" expressions of emotion?

- Did teachers, friends, and family defend or accuse, did they empathize or belittle, minimize or mock?

- How much prayer, love, laughter, communication, and forgiveness were in my family?

You cannot escape sin in this life, neither can you avoid hurting others or being hurt yourself; it is a matter of degree. To the extent that there is laughter, good humor, communication, forgiveness, and love expressed in your family, you experience less damage, and to the degree that these were not present, you experience greater wounding. Negative responses from people outside the family build on the fissures in the foundation formed within the family and drive them wider and deeper. You may need to understand how you were hurt in relation to your sensitivity—or directly because of that sensitivity—and bring some healing to that before you can accept yourself for who and what you are. You also need forgiveness for your reactions.

Hurt within and from outside the family wounds and can warp your view of yourself and your sense of value. Assessing that a particular event was hurtful may be an accurate assessment that God would agree with. The most damaging part of a hurtful event is not the event itself but your own *sinful* reactions—angry condemning reactions, bitterness. Judging and condemning those who cause hurt is assuming God's role. He is the judge, a role which He does not share with anyone. These reactions cause trouble with the laws of God. These sinful reactions, explained more fully in the next chapter, cause you the most damage.

Although we are going to talk about hurtful things—at least they hurt you—this is not to lay blame. You need to know the facts of what happened to make a damage assessment. You need to find out how you were hurt and where to forgive, and ask forgiveness for ways you resented or looked down upon your parents or yourself. Any guilt on the parents' part is not to give children a "stick" to beat them with. Looking for facts of hurt is not for the purpose of condemnation, but for forgiveness. It is to give the hurts to the Lord for healing.

Common Family Experiences

Here we will discuss some common hurtful family experiences that may have separated you from your true self, but like most anything else, not everything applies to everyone.

Each of us is unique. Those who have had some of these experiences will be able to recognize the hurts and the life-altering affects. These hurts not only commonly occur in families in general, but, for reasons you will shortly see, families with burden bearers are especially vulnerable to them.

Stoicism

"Oh, it's nothing. Never mind, I'm fine...." "What I do has nothing to do with you." "I'll do it my way." "It only hurts if you let it...." are anthems of the stoic and the rugged individualist. Stoicism and rugged individualism are killers for the highly sensitive. When your family considers these belief systems virtues, it is even more devastating. These attitudes toward life avoid feelings and deny their value. Whether your family "believed" feelings were not important, whether they were overwhelmed by circumstances that did not allow the "leisure" time to process feelings, or whether your family actually made it unsafe to express feelings, the result was a denial of feelings and their importance. This denial can corral raging, crashing emotions and even create an impression of orderliness, but at great cost.

Highly sensitive children in a stoic family see no emotions and hear no admission of feelings (or very little), but are keenly aware of trouble or turmoil in the home. What you see does not match what you *feel* and *sense*. This dissonance causes you to doubt yourself and take false responsibility for the "craziness." "It must be me." You grow up feeling that you must be defective in some way. You are different from all the others.

Denial of Reality

Any time adults deny the reality of negative emotions and tell a child, "Everything is fine, Honey," they teach a highly sensitive child to distrust himself. That confirms self-accusations of craziness. As highly sensitive children, you sense emotional pain and trouble in others who deny its existence or who loudly deny the right for anyone else to talk about it. Denial of reality is painful; it twists your insides. Your senses say one thing and the family's words say another. Whom shall you believe? You soon doubt your own perceptions; by the time you are adults you may try to pay no attention to your own perceptions whatsoever.

Using Emotion

It is ironic to use emotion to deny others the expression of emotion, but it happens. Some use emotion to stop others from emotional expression as a way to avoid facing their own, like the woman who refused to cry and would not allow a grieving mother to cry for her infant son who died soon after birth. Volatile anger keeps others away from real but suppressed feelings, like fear, hurt, insecurity, and loneliness. Some burden-bearing children saw an angry volatile exterior, heard loud denunciations of feelings, but at the same time sensed the underlying pain and trouble, the fear, the insecurity, and loneliness. You quickly learned that asking Daddy why he was angry was not a good idea. No one addressed the real issues; everyone denied or ignored the truth. That was crazy making. You concluded that adults do not tell the truth, and not surprisingly, trust is a big issue for you as an adult.

Another set of emotions used to suppress others' expressions of emotion is intense hurt and sadness. When parents were intensely sad or intensely hurt all the time, you knew to give them a wide berth. You learned quickly that such parents did not want to face whatever was bothering them. The sad faces, the sighs, the tears, or emotional flatness—these warning signs told everyone not to say anything and to stay away. Subsequently, you could not be your true self in their presence. The cloud of gloom or hurt expanded their personal space bubble; smart people stayed away as much as possible. Those compelled by love to venture near were sent away or hurt.

Using the Child

When all the family members repress emotion, sensitive ones often become the family's emotional outlet. Your assigned task is to "emote" for the family. If Sister Susie does not make the cheerleading team, she comes home and picks a fight with Bonnie the burden-bearer. Bonnie cries and Susie feels better. Dad's boss yells at him at work so later that evening he yells at Bonnie when she walks into the room. Bonnie is hurt and cries—Dad feels better. Bonnie seeks out Mom for some comfort, but rather than receive comfort she ends up comforting Mom who is so stressed she cannot "see" Bonnie. Bonnie sops up her mother's distress and staggers away to her room but on the way she encounters big brother who calls her "sissy" and "cry baby" because of her tears.

No one verbalized it, but it was common subconscious knowledge that any given family member was free to pick on, bully, or confide in you until you expressed some emotion. Your expression made them feel better without their having to express the forbidden emotion. They retained their picture of themselves as "all together," "in control," and you again confirmed your role as "the weird one." They were able to walk away happy while you staggered off with their garbage, which flattened or separated you further from your original design! You did your "job," you lowered their inner tension. This was actually a pattern of projection, in which the family learned to project their own undealt-with emotions onto the scapegoat child—by nature the most burden-bearing one.

Therefore, you somehow felt responsible to process whatever emotional content you received, to do the emotional work for those who refused. No child has the emotional maturity or tools for processing an entire family's emotions. God did not design one little person to carry that kind of load, indeed, "for each one should carry his own load" (Gal. 6:5). The number of you who felt obligated as children to take on such a task is staggering. These are very sad examples of our corporate nature—what one does affects all!

Particularly deadly to "sensitive ones" is to have the misfortune of being "the favorite." Whereas the sad parent pushed most people away, but sometimes chose to draw in a burden-bearing child. The sad or hurting parent chose you *because* of your sensitivity—they could easily exchange part of their hurt and sadness for your life, joy, and happiness. The adult felt better with you around—you became a source of life and an emotional dumping ground. This is something of a parasitic relationship and gives only temporary relief to the parent, overburdens the child, and creates a very inaccurate identity for the child. If the parent dumps feelings but does not process them, and if there is no prayer, no healing can occur! Again, the result: nothing is resolved and the place and function of emotions denied.

Everyday Fare: Rebuke, Ridicule, Name Calling

"Not again!" "If you can't talk to me without whining, I don't want to hear it!" "Just dry up those water works." "I don't have the time or the energy to deal with this." "Hey, Stupid! (Whiney, Weenie, Woos) I'm talking to you!" It hurts to be the family target; it becomes ever more lonely. Highly sensitive children are sometimes blatantly "picked on," but more often they received continual and subtle undercutting. "Poor Joanie, that child! I swear I don't know if she's ever going to grow out of it...." Maybe you were the "black sheep," the "weird one," the one about whom everyone was "concerned," because "the kid is just not quite with it." "Well, you know Bobbie; something is not right, the child is odd!" "That child is going to be a juvenile delinquent!" This, of course, added to the sense of craziness that many of you felt. By focusing on you, talking about you, and being concerned for you, others blocked out and avoided their own emotions—meanwhile wrecking your confidence.

Continual rebukes for feeling and expressing the emotions of the unseen burdens you carried hurt deeply. Ridicule and others' perception of you as weak made you want to turn away from sensitivity. You did not want to be a "cry baby," "thrower of temper tantrums," "sissy," "grouch," "overly sensitive," "snotty brat," "grudge-holder." The list of names goes on, changing a bit as you age. Snotty brat and sissy become "that emotional one," "the neurotic." Rebukes, ridicule and name calling provided you with labels that gave substance, texture, and color to your negative picture of yourself.

In time, you came to accept these negative portrayals as the truth about yourself, which built and continues to fuel low self-esteem. Your acceptance of the role others put upon you justified their behavior. Your acceptance completed this "logic" built on false assumptions. Your portrait changed in subtle ways with each hurtful episode, while the basic structure of your life moved more and more off plumb as you turned away from yourself. When you begin to listen to your self-talk as an adult, in times of frustration, you will hear yourself use these labels.

"Don't Be So Sensitive"

Many parents did not take the time to search out and listen to what was behind our "odd," "different," or "excessive" behavior. Siblings did not have the inclination. Many times neither parent nor sibling knew how to express emotion themselves, so they did not know how to draw us out to help us understand what was happening. We felt unimportant, minimized, or dismissed. We heard phrases like, "Oh, don't be silly!" "There you go again, making things up." "Don't be stupid!" "Don't be so sensitive." "You don't know what you are talking about." "Just stop it. I don't want to hear it." "I do not have time for this right now. You are being too sensitive." "It's not all that bad." We concluded, "I must be wrong. It must be me." Sometimes it was not with words, it was non-verbal behavior such as shaking the head, rolling the eyes, or a pained expression on the face, but the message was clear.

When parents and siblings paid no attention to your emotions and put little importance on what you had to say, you learned to downplay and devalue yourself. As an adult, you continue to do to yourself what others did long ago. In the final analysis, no one really listened to you so you never told your story. "Not being heard" translates into "I am not important; what I think and feel is not important. If I am not important, I have no value. I am just taking up space. Why am I here; why do I bother? I am a bother." You can talk yourself into low self-esteem and depression, which are frequent companions for many burden bearers. By the time you are an adult, you rarely listen to yourself, and if you do, you have trouble believing what you hear.

"Excessive" Emotion

When you had an emotional response that was really over the top, and you could see it yourself, you embarrassed yourself! It was not only embarrassing, it was confusing when a fountain of tears or a volcano of anger followed a small hurt, disappointment, or trouble. This and other "excessively" emotional responses also chipped away at your self-esteem and self-confidence. The thinking part of you might have agreed that, "It wasn't all that bad" and you too wondered why your reactions were so "excessive." You could never be confident that your responses would be measured and appropriate to the situation; so you became tentative and indecisive. You did not realize your spirit was already full of other people's emotional baggage in addition to the troubles of your own life.

As turmoil pushed for expression, even a small slight could release growing inner pressure and create an avalanche of tears. If the tears were only for your own troubles, there would have been less. As a child, you were not aware of the accumulation you carried. You did not learn to express your own emotion because you took in so many hurts from other people—you never learned what was actually yours. The flood of tears was very confusing.

Embarrassment hurts. Embarrassing your siblings and yourself was bad enough, but when you embarrassed your parents, that was too much! They were as confused and embarrassed as you were by your displays of apparently excessive emotion.

No Blessing

If you grew up in a certain kind of family, no one bothered to give a positive picture of your character or your future.[3] Some families do not praise or notice the positive qualities of sensitivity, compassion, and creativity. Other families may feel appreciation, but do not verbalize it, or thank their children for acts of compassion. They do not compliment their children or tell them what they do right. The rationale comes from a fear that the children will become prideful or arrogant. Nothing could be further from the truth. Thus, no one told them that these qualities could "take them to the stars," that they could be an astronaut, a firefighter, poet, governor, or painter.

You need self-confidence and inner strength of character to take risks. You need to hear over and over what is right, good, and loveable about yourself. If you do not hear these things from early on, you may come to feel it is your place to be an emotional soccer ball, kicked around or cast aside, or ignored and never chosen in the first place. You become unsure of your worth and place. To compensate for insecurity of love and belonging, you may become overly responsible, the caretaker, the peacemaker, the servant of all with no one to care for you. You feel like Cinderella or the Frog Prince.

If these kinds of things happened in your home, you learned to repress and store your sadness, your hurts, confusions, troubles, and emotions. As you branched out from your family, your sphere of "responsibility" grew. You felt responsible for the emotional and psychological turmoil you encountered outside the home and did with that what you learned to do—repress, and store. In time, you may have become lost to yourself. You lost the sense of being a distinct individual and lived your life as though everything you felt originated from you. Now, as an adult you find it a daunting task to discern what is "mine," and what is not. You may not know where to begin.

One young woman who was coming into awareness of herself as a burden bearer said, "I am beginning to think that I have no idea who "I" really am. I have been everything to everybody for as long as I can remember. I have no clue who "I" might be apart from the expressed and unexpressed expectations of people in my life!" You bless a child when you teach him who he is.

When our grandson was about a month old, I saw his daddy hold him high over his head, look him full in the face, and declare, "You are Antonio. You are Spanish-American. First, you are Spanish and then you are American. Your heroes are Jesus, Daddy, and Sammy Sosa!"[4] That child will never wonder who he is!

The Lost Children

What are the outward effects of living in these negative types of family milieus? Think back to elementary school days. Remember big-eyed, sad Susie who was never too far from the teacher and who was always in tears over something? Rachel (the perfectionist) was mean to her. Little Joey pushed her. Leon stole her lunch—just to tease her and get a reaction. He got one. She ran too fast and fell...and so it went.

Remember Kyle, the classroom bully? He made one unfortunate child after another miserable. He wore a leather jacket in first grade and strutted around the playground, first making Ricky the object of his terror, then Billy—anyone who was somehow different. He did on the playground what his dad did at home. I know. I met his dad.

Annie, the only one with braids and glasses, avoided the entire playground scene. She chewed her food so slowly that the noon hour was gone by the time she finished. That is one way to avoid rejection.

Erin sometimes brought her jump rope and played quietly around the edges of the playground or sat on the swings or seesaw by herself. Carrie looked at her shoes when anyone talked to her. Sometimes she and Kristen joined Erin or the two of them had a quiet game of marbles out of sight of the rest of the class.

Then there was Johnny whose mom died over a year ago. He came to school looking like a street urchin. His dad was still in depression—came home from work, drank beer, and watched television. Johnny did his best to take care of the both of them, and looked old for his nine years.

And Lisa, the little go-between, always solicitous of Miss Teacher. Lisa tried to keep the peace—between the children and between the class and the teacher.

It is obvious, even at the elementary school level, the typical life stances that these children will increasingly adopt as adult approaches to life—the peacemaker, the caretaker, the scapegoat. In first grade it is easy to pick out the burden-bearing children who will attempt to *avoid* the trouble and pain like Annie, Erin, and Carrie, and those who try to *fix* the problems they see and sense like Johnnie and Lisa. No one taught these children how to pray, how to forgive and pass the burdens on to Jesus. The older they became without learning to do so, the more their lives went awry.

Distrust God

Regardless of the stance taken, to fix or to avoid, burden bearers can develop a deep distrust of God. When they see that for all the effort, that for all the laying down of life, troubles, afflictions, wars and devastation continue, they are tempted to conclude that God is cruel, disinterested, or heartless. They learned at home and church that He is all loving and all-powerful, and yet all manner of evil continues—this equation does not balance, especially for youngsters. We hear the temptation whispered to Eve in the Garden whispered again. "Does God *really* have humankind's best interest at heart? Looks like God says one thing and does another—can't really trust someone like that! Maybe you should go ahead and help yourself." We begin to believe the whispers. Mentally we may believe that God is good and trustworthy, but our hearts have learned to believe otherwise. For this reason Paul urges us to, "See to it brothers, that none of you has a sinful, unbelieving heart that turns away from the living God. But encourage one another daily, as long as it is called Today, so that none of you may be hardened by sin's deceitfulness" (Heb. 3:12-13).

The very people who should (and most often do) love you the most also have the power to hurt the most. Because you love, and because you feel so intensely, you also hurt deeply. You assessed life, people, and God, and at some point concluded, "No one is going to help me. I have to help and protect myself." You will run afoul of the laws of God when you add condemnation and bitterness to your assessment, when you move past the assessment and into judgment. If you go on to make inner vows (strong promises to yourself), you will continue to keep them. In this way, you begin to forge a suit of homemade armor. We will talk about homemade armor in the next chapter. With each piece of armor you forge, you disfigure your portrait. You participate in the damage by hiding your original image. Each whisper of the enemy you believe takes you another step away from your true identity.

Summary

You form your identity as a child. Emotions are important to your identity—as a child, what you feel, is "who" you are. You may have heard commands and admonitions such as: "No child of mine is going to...." "In our family we never...." "As long as you are a part of this family you won't...." You translate such statements as, *"If I can't be sensitive, what can I be, and how do I do that? If I can't be sensitive, maybe I can't be. Is being sensitive bad? Am I bad? I must be!"*

"Go to your room and don't come out until you can act like a member of this family." *"Maybe my mean older brother was telling the truth about my being adopted?"*

"Don't you bring that (anger, sadness, etc.) into *this* house!" *"Why is it OK to feel my emotions outside but not inside the house?"*

You learn more from modeling than from lecture. The experiences that created these kinds of questions produce a milieu of insecurity, ambivalence, and a disjointed picture of your "self." You do what you can to create your own security and stability. You connect the dots in the emerging picture of your "self." All children—not just you—all children respond by making decisions, taking stances, and coming to conclusions about life, God, and self that affect all relationships, thereafter. You become your own protector.

Endnotes

1. E. James Wilder, *The Complete Guide to Living With Men* (Pasadena, CA: Shepherd's House, 2004), 42.

2. See Appendix B.

3. John Trent and Gary Smalley, *The Blessing* (New York: Simon & Shuster, Inc., 1986).

4. Sammy Sosa played baseball for the Baltimore Orioles so well that in 1998 he was the National League Most Valuable Player and in 1999 was ESPY: Humanitarian of the Year.

CHAPTER 4

Homemade Armor

...each one is tempted when, by his own evil desire, he is dragged away and enticed. Then, after desire has conceived, it gives birth to sin; and sin, when it is full-grown gives birth to death (James 1:14-15).

The Scriptures explain how life works—they are your "engineer's manual." It is clearly stated that evil desire leads to sin and sin to death. How does that work out in your life and what does it have to do with burden bearing? When other people respond hurtfully and negatively to your sensitivity, you are tempted and nine times out of ten you sin. How, exactly? By making your own armor rather than depending upon the Lord to be protector and defender.

One "evil desire" is to protect yourself in your own strength. You forge homemade armor from hurt, anger, fear, and distrust; consequently, it interferes with relationships with God and others. It complicates life by making burden bearing needlessly burdensome. Homemade armor can prevent you from knowing yourself as a child of God and from coming into your destiny. You need a very clear-eyed assessment of when, where, and why you usurped the Lord's role as protector and defender. This is not to lay blame, but to determine how and where to ask God to forgive and heal.

Typical Childhood Reactions

From the youngest age, you and I are in the armor business. When you are a child, you react instinctively to protect yourself when someone hurts you. From hurtful experiences, you come to conclusions about God, people, and life. Anytime these conclusions are accompanied by bitterness or condemnation, you unwittingly activate God's laws. The hurt and the response to the hurt happens like this:

- Tom has his heart set on Dad coming to his Christmas recital but he never arrives. He is hurt and responds by thinking, "I can't count on Dad. He's never here when I need him." A wall begins to form around his heart to protect him from disappointment. He vows never to be like him, and he isn't, not exactly. For example, his father was an alcoholic and that is why he missed his recital. Tom becomes responsible, he provides for his family— he is nothing like his father. But, in taking on responsibility he becomes a workaholic and an absent father. His spouse says, "You are just like your dad!"

- Dad promised to help Larry build a model airplane, forgot, and chose to work late. Another hurt. Larry tells himself, "I do not want or need his help. Don't bother asking for help." He thinks to himself, "Never trust what Dad says, he doesn't keep his word." If he does not hope, he won't be hurt. Another wall goes up as he closes off his heart to keep out hurt and then years later wonders why he cannot be close and intimate with his spouse.

- Mother made Linda clean her room—to her specifications. Linda reacted in anger and yelled, "I hate this! When I'm a mom I am not going to be so picky!" True to her word, she is not picky. The children refuse to bring their friends home because their house looks like the county landfill.

- Lana tried to share her heart, but mom was too busy. Dejected, she determined, "When I'm a mom I'm going to listen!" She volunteers at the crisis center, she is on the ministry team at church. She listens all the time, and it hurts deeply that her teenager hurls the accusation that she does not listen. She thinks, "Child, you are not listening."

- When Lana's daughter did share and Mom did not hear because her mind was elsewhere, the daughter determined, "I'm not telling her anything anymore!" Lana is aware that many people feel close to her, but the ones she feels close to are few and far between. There is an immense inner loneliness, the feeling that no one really knows her.

With each bitter or condemning response, we forge another chink of armor, a chink of anger, hurt, and resentment that thickens over time, layer upon layer. The feelings of hurt, disappointment or anger are not sin. The sin comes in the condemnation, and the judgment. Scriptures say that at some point the sinful defense you made to protect yourself will itself become a source of destruction in your life. We will look at those Scriptures shortly. Either you do the very thing you hated or you "reap" by having someone in your life who responds to your powerful expectations by perpetrating against you the very behavior you hated.

Each time you added bitterness or condemnation to your emotional response (fear, sadness, anger, resentment, frustration, etc.), you added another layer to the armor you were making to protect your heart from hurt. Years later when you were grown, you forgot the anger and the harsh statements. As an adult, you cannot figure out why life seems to conspire against you—why your children do and say the things they do, why work situations go sour, why people you thought were friends betray you, why you make one bad judgment call after another.

Here is an example of making homemade armor. Morgan turns on the water in the garden hose and plays with it. Justin sees him, scolds his brother, and turns the water off. Dad walks around the corner as he is turning off the water and sees Justin "playing" with it. He punishes Justin but not Morgan—a clear misapplication of justice. Making this assessment in itself does not cause any trouble with God; He would probably agree. However, Justin went on to a condemning conclusion—the first step in forging homemade armor: "Dad is always unfair. There is no use trying to explain, he never listens."

Later as an adult, Justin used the word, "arbitrary" to describe Dad. This then becomes the lens through which he sees God—God too is arbitrary, and with Him there is no appeal. This condemning conclusion creates distance between Justin and God, between Justin and his father. Distrust takes up residence in Justin's heart. Inability to trust one person can generalize to an inability to trust anyone; this will complicate Justin's life. His inability to trust God will make burden bearing heavier, more burdensome.

For emphasis, let me say again, you run afoul of God's laws when you add bitterness and condemnation to your emotional response (sadness, fear, anger, etc.). Scripture is very clear that these are sinful attitudes. When you judge in the sense of condemnation, you usurp God's role and sit in His judgment seat. It may or may not *sound* like you are meting out judgment when you make statements, such as, "When I am a parent I will be fair." "When I marry, my spouse will not be like Dad. He will help out around the house!" Yet these statements do point to condemnation of parents, who they were or were not, what they did or did not do with you or for you.

The hurts we talked about in the previous chapter may have caused you so much grief that you did not want to repeat these experiences. Your responses to that hurt are your attempts to protect yourself. You made judgments and strong promises to yourself, most of which fall into your subconscious and you forget you ever made them. This is your armor. You wear your fears, expectations, and attitudes like a breastplate. You keep them in front of you like a shield in an attempt to prevent further hurt. The Law of God requires that you reap what you have sown, so years after you make the judgment, the reaping begins as you move into the role of the person you judged, completely oblivious of your armor (Gal. 6:7).

Consequently, as an adult, you bring wounds, judgments, strong promises, fears, expectations, and attitudes (the homemade armor) into *every* relationship. The normal grinding of life helps reveal these sinful protections. You pull out long lists of things the people you live or work with *should* be, what they *should* do, what and how they *should* think. You may have an even longer list of things they *better not* be, what they *better not* do, and what they had *better not* think. Most of the items on these checklists have an uncanny resemblance to your experiences growing up with the father and/or mother you supposedly left behind.[2]

As a child, you were not able or did not know how to depend on God to be your protector. You developed an "I'll do it myself" stance and will carry that stance through life until you learn differently. You make many, if not most, of these promises and judgments in your formative years, before you come to know the Lord. Like land mines, they lie dormant until you move into the very role(s) you judged.

For example, my husband, David, judged his father for his volatile, and unpredictable anger. He did not have an anger problem until he became a father. When it erupted he was shocked himself, not knowing where it came from and with such intensity. His mind told him his toddler's infraction did not warrant the blast he gave her. James 1:13-15 indicates that there is a time lapse between the sowing of the seed, and reaping the harvest. Because of the time lapse, you see no connection between your present experience and your past. You can't figure out why these things keep happening—authority figures are arbitrary, friends disappear or betray, etc.

How ironic that the very things you thought would protect you, blow up in your face, leaving you riddled with emotional shrapnel. They come back on you when you least expect it. You find yourself with a mate, a friend, or boss who manifests the very behavior you hate—and acts it out on you! You watch yourself act like those you could not tolerate. You observe yourself interacting with your children or other people in ways your parents did with you, the very behaviors you declared adamantly you would not do. You say things you determined not to say. You are critical or dismissive in ways similar to your parents. Some have the experience of saying, "Aaagh! I am my mother" or father. Why is this so? Let's inspect the homemade armor.

Judgments[3]

Judgments operate based on the natural laws of God and therefore have great power driving them. God's laws are absolute, impartial, and impersonal; they work whether you like them or not, believe them or not. His Word says that judgments will come to roost at some time or another, "Do not be deceived, God cannot be mocked. A man reaps what he sows" (Gal. 6:7). Judgments are those harsh, bitter, condemning attitudes and stances you took when you were hurt and then condemned and looked down on another.

Each time you judge, you plant more seeds—seeds of judgment that you *will* reap at some point. Like those who raised you, you find yourself being angry, critical, tardy, a poor housekeeper, a perfectionist housekeeper, absent because of alcohol, workaholism, or fleeing responsibility, etc. ... or, sometimes you find your mate doing the same or similar thing that you hated in your parent. Why? Scripture explains that that is how the universe runs. It is not God getting even, but the way the universe was created, with absolutes so there is predictability. Newton's third law says, "For every action there is an equal and opposite reaction." That absolute in nature makes it possible to send men to the moon and put huge telescopes in orbit. The same laws that work in nature work in relationships, and because of that, there is also the same kind of predictability.

In His kindness, God tells you what to expect.

- Exodus 20:12 says, "Honor your father and mother *so that* you may live long in the land the Lord your God is giving you." (Italics mine— cause and effect.) This Scripture implies an inverse corollary, which in the natural you recognize in the scientific law that states: For every action there is an equal and opposite reaction. The inverse corollary for this Scripture tells you that in whatever area of your life you did not or cannot honor your father and/or mother, you will have difficulty in your own life.

- Matthew 7:1-2 says, "Do not judge, or you too will be judged. For in the same way you judge others, you will be judged, and with the measure you use, it will be measured to you." Again, you can see from science: For every action there is an equal and opposite reaction. God does not have two different laws; the same law applies in nature and in relationships. If you judge people for their anger, you will become an angry person and life will bring you people who judge you for your anger.

- Galatians 6:7-8, "Do not be deceived: God cannot be mocked. A man reaps what he sows. The one who sows to please his sinful nature, from that nature will reap destruction; the one who sows to please the Spirit, from the Spirit will reap eternal life." This is plain old cause and effect. Be kind and people will be kind to you. Be a friend and you will have a friend. Be a grump and people avoid you. Greediness or miserliness will bring you loneliness. Choose to be generous and you will have an abundance of loyal friends.

- Romans 2:1-2, "You therefore, have no excuse, you who pass judgment on someone else, for at whatever point you judge the other, you are condemning yourself, because you who pass judgment do the same things. Now we know that God's judgment against those who do such things is based on truth."

According to this verse in Romans, when you judge another, you are just like him. In your heart, you are like the sinner; you cannot judge a murderer, for you have hated, and thus murdered in your heart (1 John 3:15). You cannot judge an adulterer, for you have lusted in your heart (Matt. 5:27). In some way, in thought or in deed, everyone has broken every commandment. The context of this passage says that therefore, if you judge, instead of receiving forgiveness for committing the same sin as the one you judge, you store up wrath for yourself. The sin remains in you, uncrucified. As long as that sin remains in you, it grows, for Hosea 8:7a says, "They sow the wind and reap the whirlwind." Therefore, as long as a judgment remains in your heart, you become more and more like the one you judge.

My husband's problem with anger is an example of this. Lana's mother did not listen to her so she judged her mother. Now she listens to everyone else but has little time to listen to her own daughter. Her daughter, hurt by the lack of attention, is repeating the pattern: judging her mother for not listening and then not listening herself.

You must come to a determination to forgive your mother, father, the people who raised you, for the ways they hurt you and kept you from developing according to your design. You must repent for ways *you* judged *them* and for ways you have participated in the same or similar behavior. Scripture says, those hurts will keep coming back on you until you do forgive. Forgive for your own sake, to stop the reaping.

The good news is that repentance and forgiveness invoke the same law. When you sow forgiveness, you will reap forgiveness and the Lord will intervene to stop the destructive reaping. You cannot compromise or escape these laws that work in both nature and relationships. Repentance and forgiveness neutralize a judgment. Anything short of that will only ensure that you will have to cope with the natural outworking of the judgment.

My husband, David, did not know he had a temper until he became a father. I did not realize I had condemned my father for being tardy, but I have a husband *I used* to refer to as "the late Rev. Brown!" Obviously, I sowed a seed of judgment and reaped that judgment in a husband who can become so preoccupied he is oblivious of the passage of time! I have forgiven my own father and asked the Lord to forgive me for having made such a judgment. Now I must also continually discipline my thoughts and reactions to David's promptness or lack thereof, lest I give in to the temptation to judge and it "drags me away and entices me" to anger and condemnation again, and a completely new batch of weeds spring up!

Inner Vows[4]—Strong Personal Promises

Judgments can become an inner vow over time. The child who resented her father for not telling the truth when he did not pick her up at school at the time he said he would, made a blanket judgment: "Dad is never trustworthy." In time she formed an inner vow. Such an inner vow is a judgment-driven set of the will. She makes a strong promise to herself: "I won't trust Dad to keep his word." The judgment formed into an inner vow that became more general and inclusive over the years. "Don't trust Dad," changed to "Don't trust men," to "Don't trust."

She will probably also come to not trust that God will provide or defend in a timely fashion. As an adult she can be aware of not trusting people without realizing that the lack of trust started in childhood. The current lack of trust that she holds onto is what God holds her accountable for. However, the lack of trust is only the surface manifestation; like a dandelion that grows back when you cut if off, it has a deep root. She could confess and ask forgiveness for lack of trust until blue in the face. The root *began* in childhood, and still draws from a pool of bitterness that formed at that time. It is reinforced each time she exercises a lack of trust. Bad fruit will follow until the vow to not trust is dismantled, the judgment against her father is repented of, and forgiveness is given and received. Repentance and forgiveness will drain the pool of bitterness and the root will die. She will have to discipline her reactions until trusting becomes a reflex.

Inner vows are the strong promises you make to yourself, especially during your formative years—most of them not made consciously. They set the heart and will. "I'll never be like my dad!" or "If that is femininity, *no thanks!*" "I will *never* compete. *No one* will make me compete." Or "I *will* compete— I *will* win!" "I will *never* share my heart." "I *have to* be good." "*Never* tell a woman (or a man) anything."

Inner vows are the "never," "always," "will," "won't," and "have to" statements you declare with such steely determination that it sets the direction of your heart and will. Some people are very aware of statements they made with venom in their voice. For most, these strong promises to self fall into the subconscious and are forgotten. If the vow was to never share your heart, you may wonder why it is so difficult to share at deep and meaningful levels.

Vows are even more intractable than judgments. You can suspect an inner vow when you find a seeming impenetrable barrier and, try as you might; you cannot get around or through it. When a behavior is stuck and you do not know why, you cannot change even when you want to; that is the time to see if there is an inner vow in play. You can locate these hidden, forgotten promises by how your life responds. You cannot see a black hole, but know it is there by observing the objects around it. A black hole makes objects disappear, and an inner vow makes efforts to change evaporate.

Dismantle a vow in the following way:

- Recognize from the behavior that you made a vow.

- With your prayer partner, ask the Lord to reveal the hurt underneath that tempted you to make such a promise in the first place.

- Forgive those who tempted you to make the inner vow.

- Repent for judging them and ask forgiveness for judging.

- Repent and ask forgiveness for having made the vow.

- Renounce it. (It helps to come to an approximation of how you worded the promise.)

- Ask your prayer partner to use the Lord's authority to break the vow, by His power. Ask Jesus to restore his original design of you and to take the place of the vow as your protector. See the prayer for inner vows in Chapter 12.
- Ask the Lord to replace the judgment and the vow with the Holy Spirit.

Judgments and vows affect all people, not just burden bearers. The only thing different with burden bearers is their high sensitivity. As an adult you may look at a particular incident and think, "That's not all that traumatic. How could such strong judgments and vows come out of that?" High sensitivity amplifies and intensifies experiences and feelings. It is why seeming "small" hurts hurt so deeply and affect you so profoundly, and why big hurts are overwhelmingly traumatic.

Let's look at two common problems: performance orientation and parental inversion. The complexity of these two problems is the result of the weaving together of judgments, inner vows, and the attitudes and expectations that develop from them, much like a tapestry. They become an integral part of your thought patterns and belief system by which you rationalize and justify your behavior, as part of your self-protection.

Performance Orientation[5]

Performance orientation is a life stance, a strong habit of thinking that if you are not perfect, if you don't "do it right," then you do not deserve love and belonging. Therefore, you perform to have those needs met—to *earn* love and belonging. Logic tells you, and your experience confirms, that love and belonging are conditional, doled out by significant authority figures based on how well you do. Performance-oriented people are great workers! You have plaques, pins, and bonuses to prove how dedicated, conscientious, and responsible you are. The trophies reflect the high value our society places on those who perform well. Some jokingly question the wisdom of healing this problem.

However, there is a dark side. Yes, a great deal can be accomplished, but at what price? You perform to earn love and belonging—things that you ought to receive unconditionally! When persons of authority or significance dole it out based upon your performance, you develop free-floating anxiety and insecurity. You must develop defense mechanisms to cope with the anxiety and insecurity and, voilá, you quickly react with self-protective armor: "You misunderstood me, you don't appreciate me, you are picking on me."

It is not always easy to see the fine line between a calling, such as "helps" or "servant" and a multifaceted deception such as performance orientation. The Kingdom of God needs workers, but workers who know that God loves them no matter what. It needs workers who serve from gratitude for what He has done, people who know that if they never do another thing for the Kingdom of God, He still values them. However, when you serve from insecurity about your place or value, from the insecurity of having to earn love, good is accomplished but at great cost. The fuel for the accomplishment comes from an exhaustible source. It is only a matter of time until you burn out.

Insecurity of place and value may push you to become competitive. You want to secure your place so you hold things close to the chest. It is difficult to confide, to share ideas, or be part of a team. It makes job reviews terrifying. Bonuses and promotions, although welcomed and desired, only make a job more exhausting. You may push yourself to collect trophies, volunteer to take on more responsibility or take on classes so you can hang another degree on your wall. If your sense of value comes from the number of zeroes on your paycheck, then your value is precarious, which adds to the insecurity. Remember that high sensitivity exaggerates or intensifies what you feel. In this case, you don't just *feel* insecure—you *are* insecure!

Performance-oriented burden bearers may be so sensitive that suggestions, or someone "thinking out loud," becomes a command. My father was a carpenter and I inherited his love of old buildings. I enjoy remodeling and updating them. David is not so inclined. I loved to talk about this or that improvement on the wonderful old home David and I owned. I grieved that he hated the house. After several years, we discovered that he heard my "castles in the sky," "my air houses," as demands, at least as very strong suggestions, to implement the improvements I imagined. His performance orientation pushed him to think he *had* to do the work, and do it well.

Building air houses was window-shopping for me, but it made him feel as if I was asking him to make my "dreaming out loud" happen, or he would not deserve love and belonging. He never felt he did enough, fast enough, or well enough. He felt stupid and clumsy. It hurt him that I continually asked him to "embarrass himself." When we finally realized what we were not saying to each other, he blessed me to work on the house and I agreed to ask specifically when I actually needed or wanted his help. Now he listens to my "castles in the sky" guilt free! When you sense hurt underneath another person's words it takes great courage to plunge in and talk about what you sense—but it is worth the effort!

You feel your own insecurity intensely, but you also feel other person's insecurity. If you assume all you feel originates with you, other people's insecurity adds to yours. You have a double portion. Feeling that "something must be wrong," you typically assume it is your fault. The next step is to heap blame and condemnation upon yourself, and put even more effort into doing more, doing better, being better. You either screw yourself into the ceiling as your inner tension builds, or into a downward spiral of anger or depression. Unsuccessful efforts to please and make life better adds fuel to the fires of low self-esteem. Performance-oriented reactions do not help relationships and high sensitivity has the effect of fueling performance orientation, making it worse.

The creativity of a highly sensitive person not only makes it possible to see unfinished tasks, but how to complete them as well. We see solutions to problems at work, church, and at home. Some of us volunteer or accept additional work that the Lord may not be asking us to accept simply because we see the solution as well as the need. In addition, we tend to want to "do things right." As a result, we sometimes refuse help when we need it, and do not delegate because of fear others may not do the job "rightly." Performance orientation tempts us to set the bar too high. When we focus on helping the Lord to conquer or heal the world, the usual outcome is neglect in another area—we neglect our bodies, spirits, and relationships. Those closest and the most loved pay the highest price for our "perfect performance."

Parental Inversion[6]

As a highly sensitive burden-bearing child, any vacuum of need in your family easily drew you into parental inversion. Simply stated, the parent-child relationship is inverted—the child takes care of the parent, or fills the parental role in the family by being the "man of the family," or the "little mother." It begins in childhood when one or both parents are absent or ineffective for whatever reason. The parental figure(s) either caused, or allowed us to carry too much of their adult pain, troubles, and worries. The parent depended upon us, which made us feel better about ourselves. In time we came to need the parent's—someone's, anyone's—dependence on us to feel good about ourselves. Eventually, some of us took on the identity of "the dependable one" or "the rescuer" and have carried this identity into adulthood.

These directives push us to seek out the over-burdened, ill, or ineffective. Thus, we are vulnerable to co-dependent relationships in which we can provide stability or rescue and nurture. Our original design does include compassion and nurture, but this inverted relationship introduces a discordant hue to our portraits, a shading, or intensity that moves us away from our intended identity.

Lest you think I am saying that parental inversion is all the parents' fault, let me say that burden bearers can be parentally inverted even if parents do nothing to solicit that from them. The burden-bearing child is a "natural"; he or she sees need, and in the case of parental inversion, steps forward to meet the need, to lighten the load, to make things better. Parental inversion is an orientation a caring child can pick up on his own, with no encouragement from parents.

The parentally inverted perform for love and belonging like those who are performance oriented, but with an added burden of anxiety that *unless I "do it right" (perfect) something terrible will happen to others and somehow it will be my fault!* If you must be perfect so that nothing awful will happen to someone, you must also control those in your sphere so they do not do something "wrong" or perform incorrectly. As an adult, sometimes almost compulsively, you try to either "fix" or control those within your sphere of influence—family, co-workers, and church family. The condition is not unique to natural burden bearers, it afflicts those less sensitive as well; but because of high sensitivity, you are even more vulnerable to stepping into a nurturing parental role.

Remember, you can easily sense or see needs and solutions. Your internal wiring is such that you want to lessen pain, bring peace and reconciliation, and lighten others' loads. Parental inversion creates a situation for you to do what you do best—nurture and care, but unfortunately, you do it in your own strength and to your own hurt. You give away your own life rather than laying it down and giving away Jesus' life. You see needs in a community so you develop programs and outreaches, and then wonder why there is little response after all the time, effort, and money spent. However, you may never have asked the Lord what He wanted you to do in any of these things—you give away your life. When you have God's heart for His people, you lay aside your life and serve up Jesus' life, in His strength.

Parental inversion often is a condition underlying co-dependency. Adult co-dependent relationships become a continuation of a pattern that began in childhood. When you "need" an adult to depend upon you when you are a child, you become an adult who needs people to be in a dependent role. Some parents are aware of the sacrifice you make, acknowledge it, and do as much as possible to lessen the pressure on your life. Other parents, if aware, don't acknowledge contributions, which adds to your martyr sense of invisibility and being taken for granted.

Many grow into adulthood with self-esteem issues. When your needs are not met, whether because of financial difficulties, family size (too many children so no one receives much) neglect, ignorance, or simply because you were not seen at some point, you resign yourself and accept that life will be this way. You agree that you are not worth attention and that what you want does not matter. You determine to not need or want anything. To protect your heart from the disappointment of hope, you become needless, wantless, and very angry but do not know why. High sensitivity does not create the condition, but it does intensify, magnify, and energize all of its aspects.

The high sensitivity of a natural burden bearer makes it possible for a parentally inverted mother to meet a child's needs so well and so completely that the child does not develop proper life skills. A parentally inverted husband may keep house, or cook better than his wife does, making her feel inept, a burden, and shut out. If a husband has to or can do everything, where is the wife's place, and vice versa? People under a parentally inverted person's ministry often become weaker, not stronger, and thus more dependent.

A parentally inverted pastor may feel driven to be emotionally present for all the church people. If he does not or cannot release that emotional load to Jesus, it so fills his human spirit that his wife may feel second-class; she receives only the dregs of his energies. The church becomes the other woman. She feels she must compete for her husband's affections. She can become angry at the church and even God—how can she compete with God? Talk about futility!

The unredeemed sensitivity of a natural burden bearer can tempt you to want to help too much, in ways that enable or enmesh. Having compassion, insight, and solutions to problems is good. However, the lie "unless I 'do it right' something bad will happen" intertwines compassion with fear, and can push you into behaviors that strain rather than build relationships.

Your reactions to experiences in your families of origin form your view and interpretation of life. If your parents listened to you and mended your hurts, you probably found it more easy to judge that they and other authorities in you life will listen and respond to your needs. If that was your response, you will also tend to see God as listening, caring, and acting on your behalf. Conversely, any way in which you judged your family for being untrustworthy you will have difficulty trusting God with your hurts. To the extent you will not be able to trust God with your own hurts you will not trust Him with others' hurts. Therefore, you step in with your armor on, and become the needy person's savior, the one who gives, who rescues, but rarely receives. The armor you have dressed yourself in to prevent hurt also keeps love out.

Unlike broken bones, people cannot readily see the hurts and emotional lacerations that happen to a highly sensitive person. When parents are unaware of the need to "debrief" you as a child, and do not help you sort through your empathetic load, the pile grows—some never dissipate. It takes time for the armor to cause you problems. Hurt piles upon hurt without attention. Emotions start to leak. You begin to have difficulties coping. Your portrait takes on a somber cast and your life seems to run in a painful track. We will discuss how to heal this hurt in Chapters 11 and 12.

The homemade armor you made in childhood, the judgments, vows, expectations, and beliefs, is woven into an interpretative evaluative grid. It tells you the meaning of what you see, sense, and experience. Beliefs, attitudes, and expectations further refined it. All combined, it provides the rationale, motivations, and justifications for your interactions with and reflections on the world.

I trust that you have a feel now for your design and how the very thing God created in you to bless your life can also harm you. When you dedicate this empathetic capacity to the Lord He can redeem it, repair you, restore your design and bring you into your destiny as His child. Jesus came into the fullness of His life as He bore burdens and brought life to all. You too can come into your destiny as you bear burdens and bring life. Now let's turn to the nuts and bolts of the solving the mystery of spiritual sensitivity.

Endnotes

1. Scripture regarding anger and bitterness: Matt. 5.22; 1 Cor.13:5; 2 Cor. 12:20; Eph. 4:26; Eph. 4:31; Col. 3:8; Col. 3:21; 1 Tim. 2:8; James 1:20. Scriptures regarding condemnation: Matt. 7:1; Luke 6:37; Rom. 2:1; Heb. 12:15; James 3:14.

2. This point can also be made of siblings, teachers, and other authority figures.

3. John and Paula Sandford, *The Transformation of the Inner Man*, (So. Plainfield, NJ: Bridge Publishing, Inc. 1982), Chapters 1, 11, 14.

4. Ibid., 191-206.

5. For more on this topic, see *Transformation of the Inner Man*, Chapter 3.

6. More on this topic in *Transformation of the Inner Man*, Chapter 17.

CHAPTER 5

Foundations

God's purposefully designed three foundations to burden bearing:

1. *Centrality and work of the Holy Spirit.*
2. *Importance of the Cross.*
3. *Corporate nature of humanity.*

What does it mean to have a corporate nature? Plainly put, if you are corporate, you are one of many making up "the one." We all affect one another (see 1 Cor. 12:12-27). Like spokes in a wheel, springs in a mattress, struts on a car, you either strengthen the whole or weaken the whole. If you separate yourself and isolate yourself, you do not have access to the strength of the whole and therefore weaken yourself. You are the strongest and the most uniquely individual when you are safely part of the whole. You may readily categorize yourself as a social being; you choose to seek out others of your kind and be part of a group. It is your nature to be corporate, to be one of many making up one—one family, one group, one tribe, etc. Empathy is what makes being a responsible part of the group happen.

The Mystery of Spiritual Sensitivity

Being part of the whole gives you the strength and confidence to be a strong individual. You see it with children. In the safety of family, they can be outrageously funny, amazingly creative, or stubbornly persistent. However, among strangers where they do not feel safe, they may become mute and unresponsive.

The concept of corporateness in reflected in our English language. We speak of church "bodies," governmental and judicial bodies, and bodies of work, but often we do not make the connection as to how institutions and language reflect our nature—or do we? Could it be that we feel our connectedness but have not made the intellectual association between what we feel and what we understand with our minds? If you think about it, you connect more with a person who speaks your language than one who does not, who comes from the same country, or ethnic group within that country. Ideally, you experience the greatest connection to the primary people in your life and a bit less so with secondary people, etc. Even science fiction buffs are much more connected to a perfect stranger than to a one-eyed alien, say from the planet Romulus III. I dare say that people generally are more aware of their corporateness subconsciously than they are consciously. I believe the Lord wants us to move into living more consciously corporate.

Empathy is the glue that makes connectedness possible. Unity, being of like mind and spirit, is the visible outworking of your corporate nature, and unity does not happen without empathy. Empathy is essential to healthy relationships, and without it, intimacy is impossible. Salvation is all about the restoration of intimate relationships between God and man. Burden bearing is integral to that restoration process, and sitting squarely underneath burden bearing is your corporate nature. It is this corporate nature that the Holy Spirit taps into when calling you into empathetic burden-bearing intercession.

Have You Heard?

When I had received some relief from the load of burdens I had unknowingly accumulated and carried for years, one question plagued me. Why had I not heard of burden bearing before? Why don't churches teach about corporate nature? Why don't we know about our connectedness? Why doesn't someone teach these things?

The most obvious reason we don't know is that the apostles and the early church leaders did not think to teach what "everybody knows." They did not have to make a point of teaching corporateness. Middle Eastern children lived corporately; it was one of those unwritten cultural things that are imbued, learned by "osmosis" if you will. The most obvious biblical example of corporateness is how Adam's sin affects everyone. Another is the story of Achan's sin. Because of one man's sin, an entire army was defeated (see Joshua chapter 7).

Paul is the only apostle who enunciated the concept as he taught the Gentiles—Romans, Corinthians, Galatians, and Colossians—culturally *Western* people. He taught that Jesus' sacrifice was sufficient for the salvation of all who come, even as the sin of Adam brought about the separation of all humankind from God. The actions of the one affect the many (Rom. 5:15,19). He taught the Corinthians the same thing. The church in Corinth permitted a member involved in gross sexual sin to remain an active member of the church. They allowed sin to be a part of the church body much like yeast in a lump of dough. Before long sin affected the whole church.

Paul taught that you and I are members of the corporate Body and when one member suffers, we all suffer, even as when a toe is hurt, it affects the whole body (1 Cor. 12:26). Roman Catholic tradition refers to this oneness as our being part of the "Mystical Body of Christ."[1] Apostle Paul also taught that we need each other to function properly, that Christians are to come alongside those who struggle under an overwhelming, crushing load and help them through it. Consequently, the early Church was careful to teach that the sacrifice of Jesus was sufficient for all time, but did not put much emphasis on how what one does affects everyone else. They did not think to teach what "everybody knew."

Not the Only Cultural Difference

Even though you might logically agree with the idea of corporateness, you may not fully "get it" because Western Christians have not understood what we read in the Scriptures. Western culture elevates individualism above communality, so the concept of corporateness slipped through theological cracks. With The Age of Reason, came a modern heresy—what the individual does, does not affect the group. The concept of solidarity, corporateness, unity, or oneness is an Eastern concept foreign to our culture. It remains a foreign concept, because when it comes to corporateness, Westerners do not make the connections between the corporateness they read about in the Bible and what they experience in life.

Second-language speakers know that whenever you translate words from one language to another emotional impact is lost. They translate fully *only if* there are matching categories to carry emotional experience. Every word, every concept you learn, has an emotional component. Your brains have neuro-connectors that associate words with experiences and emotions. The word triggers the association; this is how you build meaning. If your society does not have a matching cultural category, if your emotions are not piqued, corporateness will remain an intellectual construct without texture or passion.

A Saudi student once asked me what *fog* is. I told him. He furrowed his brow and shook his head—he heard and understood the words but they were without meaning. I smiled and said, "You wait, Faris. One day we will have fog and then you will know." That day came. He smiled from ear to ear! "You were right, Mrs. Brown! It was like you said; but I had to see it and feel it. Now I know what is fog."

For the Western mind, the concept of corporateness is an abstract, intellectual concept with little emotion connected. For the Middle Easterner, "oneness or connectedness" evokes deep, strong emotions regarding family, extended family, tribe, etc. It evokes love, passion, duty, and responsibility for the life and reputation of a host of people at a depth that is nearly impossible for a Westerner to understand. Westerners have little to no background experience to associate with the word. You may have heard the word "solidarity" as part of the battle cry of the resistance to and subsequent fall of communism in the late 1980s. Briefly, some experienced corporateness. As a burden bearer, you struggle against your entire culture which drives you to individualism and independence. But, the concept is there, in Scripture.

A Scientific Mind-set

Where would you be without science and technology? For the past 300 years, the benefits of civilization have been too numerous to count, and in the past 50 years achievements have multiplied exponentially. Nonetheless, the scientific mind-set of Western culture has moved us ever further away from understanding our connectedness and unity (corporateness) than the Galatians were! Like the "foolish Galatians," (Gal. 3:1) we are "bewitched" by the thinking that holds empirical knowledge to be the one and only source of truth. This thinking has made the gulf between mind and spirit widen. Western logic has Greek roots, and we, like the Galatians, find it difficult to move outside that logic. Today if something is to be above suspicion, it must be reproduced or proven in a laboratory. Even with the recent research[2] connecting portions of the brain to empathetic functioning, it is not easy to quantify the experience of empathy or measure the benefit of empathetic burden bearing.

Unlike science and technology, empathy, the essence of corporateness and unity, also has to do with our spirit. The Lord repeatedly calls His Body to unity in each era. I believe He calls us at this time, in this era, to bring to conscious awareness the operation of our human spirit.[3] In each era, the enemy tries to bewitch us and drive a wedge between people, between God and people, and in some way divide an individual from himself or herself.

Additionally, people generally do not know about burden bearing, corporateness and unity because the prevailing philosophy of individualism cuts them off from others. Western society has become so individualistic that this concept of oneness or corporateness, of how what you do affects those around you, is lost to consciousness. Nevertheless, your corporate life is real; the way you live your life *does* affect those around you.

However, people generally have lost the sense of being a part of something bigger than they are. Generally speaking, we live our lives in the moment and for ourselves, unaware that what we do and how we live affects others both now and in the future. That lack of awareness can lead you as an individual to feel that what you do and who you are does not matter, to feel as if you are not part of a community.

Love of what is new and different now outranks the values of permanence and stability. In a society of change and mobility, with its accompanying lack of roots, it is difficult to develop community. In families with absentee parents, or in families that break and blend again with divorce and remarriage, it is all but impossible to maintain the permanence and discipline needed to build the skills of corporateness. This is sad, for corporateness was very much part of society in biblical days. The sense of solidarity, unity, being a part of a family, group, tribe, and nation was and still is much stronger in Eastern and Middle Eastern cultures than it is in Western culture. In these other environments, the language of relationship and emotions is more conscious, alive, and well than in Western society. Granted, these same unified, close-knit emotional relations also produce zealots who seem to unquestioningly follow leaders determined to destroy what they believe threatens their group/tribe/nation. But the point is, in Western society the sense of solidarity, unity, and being part of something bigger than "me" is felt less powerfully, and for some, not at all.

Empathy has the power to revitalize and maintain a vibrant relationship with God, as well as build unity of heart and mind in families, communities, and people groups if we actively, consciously use it as the Lord intended.

Humanism and relativity have further widened the gap between the mind and the spirit for Christians born since World War II. They come to the Lord as adults, and then into the church. They wrestle with a kind of thinking that lacks absolutes. They tend to read Scripture's absolutes, such as the Ten Commandments, as suggestions rather than absolutes from the Engineer's Manual explaining how life works. Without absolutes, it is difficult to make the connection between cause and effect, between actions and consequences. If you truly are corporate, and if what you do affects others, the consequences of what you do are huge! You need absolutes to ground yourself, to pull you back when you drift.

An Old Heresy

One final reason Westerners have lost the sense of interconnectedness that burden bearers feel but do not understand, is due to the influence of a long forgotten heresy—Docetic Gnosticism.[4] Gnostics taught that the body was evil and the spirit was good, that you should seek to be a spiritual being and avoid the body, the natural or the secular. The effect of Docetism upon Western culture is that it has created an artificial spirit/body split, which has led to a sacred/secular split. That mind-set is with us today and has led us to emphasize the secular and physical world and deemphasize the sacred and spiritual. Thus, burden bearing seems oddly "other worldly" and out of place in our culture. Burden bearing doesn't occur to us because it is outside our paradigm—outside our way of thinking.

This philosophy incited huge debates in the early church and was declared a heresy by the Council of Nicea in a.d. 325. However, the belief system permeated the culture and as people became Christians, they brought their ways of thinking with them into the Church. It remains with us today, in both the church and society, as one of those informal cultural things we all learn because "that is the normal way to think—everyone thinks that way!" Well, yes and no. Burden bearers from Western cultures feel the connectedness. For them there is no split between the spirit and body, but few understand what they sense and feel, why or what to do with the information. (For a discussion of the current influence of Gnosticism, see Focus on the Family's response to *The Da Vinci Code* at http://go.family.org/davinci/content/A000000049.cfm.)

The Fall

Empathy is to the spirit and emotions what words are to the mind, a language, and a means of communication. The Fall dealt a severe blow to the language of the spirit; spirit-to-spirit/heart-to-heart communication was impaired. Humankind re-routed these essential communications through the mind, which is very good at finding ways and reasons not to listen to your human spirit or the Holy Spirit.

The Lord calls you to wholeness. He wants to reconnect the spheres of the natural and spiritual. He declared all things good upon creation, and that included, not just the mind or spirit, but also the body where you experience the sensations and emotions you absorb through empathy. His call is to join Him in the task to "restore all things" (Matt. 17:11). To be part of this plan, you must regain your identity as a child of God. From that will flow a restoration of your capacity for empathy and the ability to learn to recognize, respect, and respond to the language of your spirit, in subjection to His direction and control, through the gifts of the Spirit, as outlined in Scripture.

Will I Ever "Get It"?

Given that you do not have a cultural category to help you with an emotional understanding of corporateness, how can you learn? Mark 10:15 sheds light on the question: "I tell you the truth; anyone who will not receive the Kingdom of God like a little child will never enter it." Primary learning comes from concrete experience. Children are concrete learners. They learn by experiencing—touching, smelling, feeling, tasting, and hearing. This is the level at which you develop emotional meaning. That is why small groups, when facilitated well, are so important in churches today. You need to see, feel, taste, sense, and in so doing experience oneness before you can "know" on an emotional level that you need it. Like my Saudi student learning about fog, you need to experience the Kingdom of God to truly "know" it. The Kingdom of God is here—it really is, but you cannot "experience it" until you become concrete about it.

My Theory About the Garden

I have a theory that I will not be able to prove until Heaven, but I think Adam and God reached out in their spirits, read each other's hearts, and knew each other by means of empathy. Empathy may have been their primary means of communication. When I think about the way God constructed our brains, to learn empathy long before words, it makes me wonder if God's intention was to have empathetic communication as a primary means of communication. I am not suggesting that God wanted Adam to evolve to where he didn't use his vocal chords and just beamed thoughts at God telepathically as in science fiction shows. Rather, I am suggesting that greater empathy would have made vocal communication even more fruitful. The two work together!

Empathy involves more than just burden bearing; it is also observation of body language, vocal tone, etc., intellectual assessment of what is observed, imagining oneself in another's shoes, and perhaps even other elements. A mature Adam would have grown to where there was a perfect marriage of all of these. Burdens would not replace, but rather enhance the other elements.

God yearns for you to be able to read His heart, to know that your heart delights in what delights Him, and that what devastates Him, devastates you. He cries out, "Oh, Jerusalem, Jerusalem, you who kill the prophets and stone those sent to you, how often I have longed to gather your children together, as a hen gathers her chicks under her wings, but you were not willing" (Matt. 23:37). God desires relationship with you, but if you or I possess the empathy skills of a stump, something vital will be missing from the relationship! You can humble yourself; you can learn. You must accept the fact that, at this point, you are handicapped.

The Road to Rehabilitation

Our former son-in-law left a Wall Street job to come to Idaho for an opportunity to "be" with our daughter before they married. He looked for work endlessly. Racial prejudice was such a problem that the only work he could find was in a sawmill doing manual labor—he was Latin. At one point, he slipped on some ice and a saw nearly severed his right hand. God was gracious—one of the best surgeons in the country, as well as the doctor's special therapist, had a practice just five minutes from the mill.

During Rodmy's recovery, the Lord began to teach me about empathy, how He designed people with this capacity, and the ability to read and communicate with each other's heart and God's heart. My theory is that Adam was on a learning curve, like the rest of us. By the time of the Fall he had not matured, he did not have full usage of all the talents, abilities, and capabilities he possessed. The devil knew this. He also knew that if humanity fully developed oneness with God through empathy, so that empathy was the dominant means by which people interacted with God, he would never be able to drive a wedge between God, you, and me.

If you could, at all times, sense the heart of God, there would be no way you would allow yourself to hurt Him by sinning. Satan knows that the most hurtful thing to the Lord is to cut you off from Him and damage your life. The Fall did to the human race what that saw did to Rodmy's dominant hand. *Our awareness of our capacity for empathy, that primary emotional means of "knowing" was nearly severed.* Since the Fall people have had to re-route communication of state of being through the mind, which has a limited capacity to comprehend what the personal spirit comprehends. We are all handicapped.

Rodmy is a body-builder and brought that discipline into his recovery. He worked diligently at his therapy. Three months after the accident, he began writing lessons, driving, and opening doors. He worked hard not to give in to despair and depression and to be satisfied with incremental progress. All during therapy, he was a month ahead of schedule because he was obedient, faithful in discipline, and willing to push beyond his comfort zone.

Your spirit can also be rehabilitated. With spiritual and personal direction, discipline and accountability (such as can happen in a healthy small group), your capacity for empathy and your awareness of it can be restructured, reconnected, and restored to its proper functioning (2 Cor. 7:1).

Sin is a fact of life. Just as Rodmy's hand may never be able to do some of the very fine or complex movements it was once capable of, yet in other ways it will be stronger than it was before. Sin not only damages our nature but also our spirit. When the Lord restores us, we may not function 100 percent according to His original design; however, we change and are stronger in new ways. We can *develop* the oneness God intended for us, but we must be obedient to our Great Physician (the Lord), faithful in discipline, and set our hearts and will to push or stretch ourselves beyond our comfort zones! For many people, being involved in a small group stretches us, but where else can we, like little children, see, hear, feel, and taste the Kingdom of God?

Why You Need to Know

You need to know about this empathetic functioning of your spirit because what you do not know *can* hurt you. Rather than creating connection, caring, love, and under-standing, the enemy turns empathy into a source of harm, creating division and wounding many. Empathy, one of those "good and perfect gifts," often becomes an instrument of destruction. Unredeemed empathy can and does fuel feelings of low self-esteem and low self-worth. It intensifies perform-ance orientation, which can end in burnout and severely limit what you can do. It can make you think you are losing your mind rather than contributing anything of value to the Kingdom of God.

Empathy is not something you can choose to have or not have. However, you can, and must choose to be conscious of when you are empathizing, and subsequently absorbing burdens, if you are to change your reflexive responses.[5] This uniting, absorbing quality of your spirit is a function of your humanity as much as walking and talking. We all absorb burdens—not all of us bear them to the cross of Jesus. Just as you learn to walk and talk, you must *learn* to be aware consciously of what your spirit does naturally. You must *learn* to bear burdens rightly so that you do not wear them as your own.

You must learn conscious awareness of what you do intuitively so that when "something comes over you" and you are "not yourself" you can call on the Lord for His help. Then even as you are absorbing burdens empathetically and carrying them to the Cross, you can receive His wisdom and the strength to do what He asks of you. Conscious awareness will help guard against the confusions that can come with or as a result of empathetic connection—you will be able to intercede for a depressed person, be with them in their pain without falling into their depression, thinking it is your own.

For example, I worked for a man with an anger problem. He radiated anger constantly and periodically erupted, smashing file drawers closed and slamming doors. I found it difficult to be in his presence. At that time, I was learning to allow the Holy Spirit in me to bear the burdens I encountered in the office. At lunch I saw him coming to my table, face all red and neck veins bulging! I thought, "Oh, no!" and braced myself. I could feel the anger coming toward me but suddenly it went up and over me, as if I were encased in a bubble. No more than a light mist came through the bubble. I felt enough of his burden to pray, but it did not hurt me in the way it had before. Lunch was almost enjoyable that day. I felt very secure being "in Jesus" (John 17:23).

When you are able to recognize when you absorb emotional, spiritual, and psychological freight via empathy, you will be able call on the Lord *in the moment.* He draws the burden through you, lifts it up and out of you and onto His Cross. Thus, the weight does not accumulate and crush you. When you are cognitively aware of when you are burden bearing, you will be able to more quickly listen and hear His direction for how and where to direct prayer, and for instructions about how to relate to a person in a way that is strategically helpful. When you are consciously aware of empathetic burden bearing in the moment, you can choose to participate, to be proactive rather than reactive. You will also be able to avoid beating up on yourself for missing the Lord when you do not recognize His signals. You will be more able to avoid kicking yourself for being so blind and not living up to your values when in retrospect you see that you did not come alongside someone who needed you.

Conscious awareness of when you empathize and bear burdens will mean that you will more consistently do the Father's will and miss fewer opportunities to act as a child of God. This awareness will result in wiser, more gracious and judicious prayers and interactions with other people. Knowing you are burden bearing will make it possible to receive more grace to restrain knee-jerk reactions that arise from the content of the empathic burden, such as the grace to refrain from flashing with rage absorbed from a friend. With the Lord's wisdom available to you, it is more likely that you will do less damage to relationships that are important to you. Knowledge and understanding will also be a safeguard for your physical and spiritual well-being.

You have much to gain from learning how to operate with your design rather than against it. This corporate nature is what the Holy Spirit taps into, or activates in some way that results in bringing burdens you absorb to the cross of Jesus where they are consumed, no longer able to affect you. Exactly how this happens is a mystery. We do not know how the Holy Spirit does it, only that He does!

Centrality of the Holy Spirit

High sensitivity is core to empathy, and empathy core to burden bearing—but burden bearing rightly, as I believe the Lord designed you to do, only happens through the agency of the Holy Spirit. When you invite the Holy Spirit to be in charge of the empathetic functioning of your spirit,[6] He directs that sensitivity appropriately, and protects you so you do not exhaust yourself. The Holy Spirit in you works with your empathy, gathers up the burdens you absorb naturally, and takes them out of your spirit, body, mind, and emotions. He neutralizes them upon the Cross and makes a way for the healing, restorative love of the Father to wash over you, renewing, rather than exhausting you! Again, how He does this is mystery.

Importance of The Cross

The Cross is the destination. This is the place you want the Holy Spirit to take you because this is where the weight of burdens comes off. You hear admonitions such as, "Take your burdens to the Cross," "Leave your burdens at the Cross." You cannot do that on your own. Only the Holy Spirit in you can relieve you of burdens cleanly and effectively— that is His job. To urge you to "go to the Cross" with the burdens is to urge you to turn to Jesus in prayer. I think the phrase helps us form a mental picture of a spiritual reality. Jesus' sacrifice on the Cross is our spiritual continental divide. On one side of the Cross sin reigns, on the other side Jesus reigns—the Cross is the place of decision.

When I refer in this book to "taking burdens to the Cross," I'm acknowledging the work Jesus did there. If Jesus had not freely given His life as a sacrifice for sin, there would be no way to approach God. There would be no relationship with Jesus or the Holy Spirit, and no connection with the Father God. The cross of Jesus is the stopping place of all sin, all pain and distress. Burdens left there cannot have life or power over you. When burdens follow you back from the Cross there is a reason which is discussed later.

Jesus allows you and me to participate in His ministry of reconciling and restoring people to relationship with God, with others and themselves (2 Cor. 5:18-19). You participate with Jesus as you voice a prayer that catches up the burden on the Father's heart, a prayer that invites Jesus into a suffering individual's situation.

Do not misunderstand! You can and do bear burdens without the Holy Spirit, but you do so in your own strength. This means that as you sit in the pain of another, and absorb a portion of their burden empathetically, you have no means of discharge other than distance and time. If you distance yourself from the source of pain, over time it dissipates. However, it leaves a residue in you if the Holy Spirit does not "clean you out." Residue collects more readily on already sensitive areas, especially when the burden's content is similar to your own tender spots. Collecting there, it weighs down your spirit, exhausts your body, and confuses your mind. More and more catches and slowly builds, like a corral reef. Little spiritual reefs combine to form a Great Barrier Reef, which muffles your hearing and blocks an ocean of life-giving love from your heavenly Father. You receive only the lip of the wave that sloshes over the barrier.

You are eventually overwhelmed, used up, and burned out. You question God's nature, and have no desire to allow anyone to be close. You withdraw to protect your spirit, body, mind, and emotions—you are little help to a suffering friend when overwhelmed. Your withdrawal feels like abandonment to them.

Now that you understand your design, let's look at the mystery of the burden-bearing process so that you understand what you are built to do!

Endnotes

1. Catechism of the Catholic Church, articles 790-795 with reference to Fathers of the Church.

2. See Appendix B.

3. Arthur Burke and Sylvia Gunter, *Blessing Your Spirit,* (Birmingham, AL: The Father's Business, 2005). This is an excellent resource for developing the human spirit.

4. "...the Gnostics took over the idea of a redemption through Christ, not the full Christian doctrine, for they made it rather a redemption of the philosophers from matter, than

a redemption of mankind from sin..." (Early Church History to a.d. 313, II, 20).

Retrieved on 12/14/07 an online copy of The International Standard Bible Encyclopedia found on StudyLight.org; http://www.studylight.org/enc/isb/view.cgi?word=gnosticism&search.x=0&search.y=0&search=Lookup&action=Lookup.

5. Daniel Siegel, *The Developing Mind* (New York: Guildford Press, 1999), 136.

6. See Chapter 12 for explanation and prayer.

CHAPTER 6

The Mystery of the Process

You can do something with the spiritual and emotional freight you absorb via empathy. The first step is to understand the process of burden bearing and how bearing burdens affects you. Understanding can prevent becoming overburdened, alienated, and broken, of little use to God, others, yourself. The focus of this chapter is the process of burden bearing.

The ability to be an empathetic burden-bearing individual is not a "special" or mysterious gift. It is not listed as one of the spiritual gifts alongside healing or prophecy in First Corinthians 12:4-11; however, *it is a quality which **enables** and **motivates** the use of spiritual gifts.* To say you are a "gifted burden bear" is to use the word "gifted" as we speak of giftedness in general—as a gifted musician or athlete—as having a greater capacity, as being on the high end of the scale. When I hurry a little, I call it running. A real runner might call it something else! Anyone can pick out a little tune on the piano. Not everyone performs in Carnegie Hall. In this same sense, we can say that some are "gifted" burden bearers—they are "naturals." Hence, the term natural burden bearer.

Nonetheless, everyone is capable of burden bearing. Not only are you capable, Jesus calls, even commands you to do so in Galatians 6:2. All Christians can encourage and inspire, or speak a word of correction—even without the prophetic calling on their lives—so also, all Christians can and do bear burdens without a full-time calling. Those who do have the giftedness of the "natural burden bearer" will find themselves in intercessory prayer in a much higher frequency than others.

When Needed

When is an empathetic burden bearer needed? The Lord calls you to bear burdens for others when they are experiencing overwhelming, crushing burdens, but (they can also be physical, financial, and spiritual:

- The circumstances of life disable them.
- They do not know they need to call out for help.
- They do not know they have the right to ask for help.
- They forget what they know about themselves, God, others, and life in times of trouble, confusion, and distress.
- The enemy of their souls comes to rob, steal, and kill.
- They are so loaded down with pain that they are unable to acknowledge it or face it and go into denial.
- The pain is so great they are sinking beneath the weight of it and cannot carry it to the Cross on their own.

Interceding for Others' Hearts

Many types of prayer originate with humankind. When you are thankful and grateful you express prayers of thanksgiving. When you praise, it is because your heart is full toward God, unless you offer the sacrifice of praise. You give sacrificial praise when you really do not feel like praising but know that it is right to do—you praise as an act of obedience. When you need something from the Lord, you petition. When you pray for someone's healing or salvation, you intercede; you go before the Father on someone else's behalf. You plead their case, but you initiate the prayer. *You* see the need and *you* beseech the Father.

But in burden bearing, the prayer originates in the heart of God. He wants to do something. He sees a life being overwhelmed, troubled, tormented, or confused, and He moves to do something about it. God Himself finds someone to alert, someone who is willing to connect to another's trouble, a person who can empathize and pray on another's behalf. He looks for someone to voice a prayer inviting Him into the situation—someone to make a prayerful response to the information received through empathy.

Without empathy, you could not sense the heart of God, and burden bearing is all about the heart of God. Empathy enables you to be receptive to the desires of God's heart, to His purposes for another, and then to express prayers inviting the Lord to come into a given situation. The Holy Spirit in you gathers up the burden for Jesus to do with it as He sees best. As you read previously, you can have empathy, and even, for a time, carry another's burden in your own strength. With prayer though, you have access to the endless strength of God to connect the other to His healing strength by lifting those burdens up to Him. Without prayer, however, your strength soon fades and you are of no help.

God Works Through Us

"Why is intercessory prayer necessary? If God wants to do something, why doesn't He just do it?" The answer is that God is true to Himself; He does not change. At the time of creation, He decided to delegate the running of planet Earth to humankind. He gave humankind authority and committed Himself to respect your will. Intercession is necessary because of your free will. It is your life, so most often God restrains, or limits Himself to work within your free will. Intercessory prayer is inviting God to act in another's life. With invitation, God can gently soften a person's heart to receive advice, to see God move on their behalf or hear His direction. Without an invitation, He waits.

God sees every hurtful thing before it approaches; every trouble people have and every sorrow. He wants to help more than anyone else; but if He helps too much, He would reduce a person from a son or daughter to a robot. He wants fellowship throughout eternity, not only with you but also between people for the sake of unity. When unity is lacking, intercession is needed to restore it. He prompts a burden-bearing intercessor to pray the desire of His heart. When asked in this way, He is free to act.

As a burden bearer, you may often be in the position of interceding, or asking the Lord to act on someone else's behalf. Intercessory prayer opens the door for the Lord to wash over the person with love and mercy, clearing the mind, softening the heart, and helping them remember who they are in Christ. Invitation makes it possible for the Lord to step into the situation and lift the overwhelming portion of the load without violating a person's free will. With some of the burden lifted, the person can think clearly, make wise choices, and pray their own prayers. Intercessory prayer helps prepare and soften a heart to hear and receive advice, to repent, or reconcile. It holds back the forces of darkness that would crush and destroy.

Intercession is important for another reason—we believers do not even know how to pray as we ought, for ourselves let alone for others! James 4:1-3 says that we ask amiss and out of wrong motives in the heart. People often confuse needs and wants. Your true needs, known to you and unknown, will more likely be met with better timing and strategic sequencing if the Holy Spirit is guiding the prayers, interceding on your behalf. Jesus' words from the Cross, "Father, forgive them, they know not what they do," resonate the truth of our lives. Far too often we do not know the ramifications of what we do. Most assuredly, we all need intercession.

Because many do not know how much they need God, some fail to ask for His help. Some do not ask because of unbelief, assuming, "God could never forgive what I have done." Sometimes, you become so overwhelmed with life, so confused with the magnitude of your problems that you forget what you know. You forget who you are, the new standing that salvation gives you. You forget who God is, and do not call on Him. In those times, I believe your loving Father sees your plight and prompts a burden bearer to ask Him to act on your behalf, to lift the overwhelming portion of your burdens so you can believe, hope, and think clearly again.

Go To the Bible

Christians must ground beliefs in the Word of God; your knowledge of burden bearing can be no exception. Several

Scriptures show burden bearing as a form of intercessory prayer.

Isaiah prophesied that Jesus would identify and empathize with humankind, but also go on to make the only substitutionary sacrifice needed, "Surely He took up our infirmities and carried our sorrow, yet we considered Him stricken by God, smitten by Him, and afflicted. But He was pierced for our transgressions, He was cursed for *our* iniquities; the punishment that brought *us* peace was upon Him, and by His wounds we are healed (Isaiah 53:4, emphasis added).

Paul states the effectiveness of Jesus' sacrifice in Hebrews 7:25, "Therefore He is able to save completely those who come to God through Him because He always lives to intercede for them." Jesus lives to intercede for us. He lives in you and intercedes continually for you. You join Him in His work of restoration and reconciliation as He calls your attention to trouble in others; you feel it and put words to the desires of His heart. If you do not intercede for others, you fail to allow Jesus to live His intercessory life through you—He is still in you, but in this area, dormant!

Paul explains further in Second Corinthians 5:15,17, "And He died for all, that those who live should no longer live for themselves, but for Him who died for them and was raised again. Therefore, if anyone is in Christ, He is a new creation; the old has gone, the new has come!" Your ability to identify and empathize with others will never be as complete as that of Jesus, but through His Holy Spirit in you, you can bear burdens effectively. He is the only Lamb of God, the Supreme Burden Bearer. But we would not be able to lay our lives down for each other at all or to love each other at all if we were not able to feel, sense, or know something of what another individual experiences.

Just as you can see the positive effects of corporateness and burden bearing in Scripture, you also see the negative side portrayed—the effects of sin on the "body," or the group as a whole. In these cases intercession opened the way to remedy a negative situation.

In Genesis chapter 20, Abraham lied to Abimelech, telling him that Sarah was his sister rather than his wife. Abimelech took Sarah into his household and the next thing he knew all the wombs of all the women in the kingdom were closed. No babies! He went to Abraham with "What have you done to us? How have I wronged you that you have brought such great guilt upon me, and my kingdom? You have done things to me that should not be done. What was your reason for doing this?"

Abimelech understood that the actions of one man affected the entire kingdom—the wombs of all the women in the land were closed! All the people of the land were bearing the burden of one man's sin! Abraham confessed and then interceded for the people and the Lord restored them (Gen. 20:17).

When you read the history of the judges and kings of Israel, you see repeatedly that what the leadership did or did not do directly affected the people and the land. The people and the land bore the burden. And when intercession happened, the Lord stopped the famine, the plague, etc.

Given that a spirit-to-spirit connection exists, given that we all come into the world with the physical equipment for empathy (the cingulate cortex),[1] and given that your empathy does function to whatever capacity you develop, what are you to do with what you "know" about each other? What are you to do with emotional, spiritual, or psychological burdens that come to you?

The Better Way

The burden-bearing response is a relational response that is simultaneously vertical to God and horizontal with your fellowman. Although the response is primarily relational, wonderful things flow from it—relief, healing, companionship, normal developmental things, discipleship.

To help your linear mind deal with a "global" experience that may take only seconds, here is a linear synopsis of burden bearing.

1. You sense a person's emotional state—empathy draws you.

2. Ask the Lord if this is a burden you are supposed to deal with.

3. If not, then immediately ask the Lord to lift it off of you.

4. If this is a burden you are supposed to deal with, turn to the Lord in prayer; the Holy Spirit draws the burdens of others through and out of you.

5. The Lord responds with loving comfort and healing for the person you are praying for (in the process you experience those blessings vicariously).

Empathy Draws

Empathy draws you to feel or sense people's emotional state. Empathy establishes a horizontal relationship; it connects you with someone else. Empathy is the language of the spirit and emotions; therefore, you become aware of a feeling, sensation, or emotion; sometimes a thought may be attached. If you are where you can physically do so, attempt to engage that person in conversation directly, over the phone or e-mail—someway. Then you can correct, clarify or confirm what you sense, which further informs your prayers.

Many times, you will help people in profound ways you never know by loving kindness that seeks after them, inquires about, and listens to them. Information flows back and forth between you. God adjusts your own inner state to match a hurting individual—He brings you into sync with them—and in this way "experience" their experience. You also feel what is going on inside them, which informs your prayer. It allows you to accurately identify the problem and intelligently call on the Lord to do something about it. You can pray eloquently and with passion when you feel intensely and acutely what someone else is experiencing!

Empathy also appears to siphon off a bit of the load so people can begin to pray and function for themselves. If the process stops at this point, *you wear* the burden rather than let the Holy Spirit draw it on through you to the Cross—you bear the burden wrongly. It might help the other person in the short run, but in time wears you out and tempts you to bitterness and cynicism.

Turn To Jesus in Prayer

Initiate a conscious connection with God. Now you have both a horizontal relationship and a vertical relationship. *The Holy Spirit **in you** gathers up the burden from all levels of your being and pulls the stress, trouble, and grief through you like thread* *through a needle to the Cross—the stopping place for all sin, pain and grief—where Jesus takes responsibility for it.* When the Holy Spirit is in charge of your empathy, you experience only enough of the other person's trouble to pray intelligently and effectively so that the Lord can restore their ability to pray their own prayers, see options, and make wise choices and godly decisions.

The Lord Responds

As you turn to the Lord you can cry out to God for what the person needs, giving voice to the prayer the other may not be able to pray. The Lord responds. He draws the burden through you, off, and out of the other. His healing love flows toward the hurting person. He comforts and cleanses you both—you because you have been sloshing about in someone else's "stuff." He releases to both of you joy and the kind of power and energy that raised Jesus from the dead. You return to the mood that you were in before the burden came, only better. It may be that the urgency to pray for someone is just not there anymore. Or, you may become aware of God's love pouring over this other person and yourself.

However, such relief is rarely instant. You cannot always expect to sit across the table and watch a person go from despair to joy. However, a person is far more likely to return to joy more quickly when you let God synchronize your inner state to match theirs. When He puts you in touch with another's distress so that you experience it, you siphon off a portion. This allows them to return to joy more quickly than when you resist the Lord's prompting or do not learn how to share another's pain and bring it to Jesus.

Your prayer connects you with the Lord, which is a healing relationship for you as well as the person for whom you intercede. As a burden bearer, your intercessory prayer leads others to Jesus by helping bear their burdens to Him. You intercede in that you speak on another's behalf, but you are not a mediator; that is Jesus' role. First Timothy 2:5 says, "For there is one God and one mediator between God and men, the man Christ Jesus," You and I are not that kind of mediator—more on this in a bit later.

Release from the burden comes to you, not from empathy, but when the Holy Spirit in you draws the burden through you to the Cross and exchanges the pain, trouble, turmoil, or oppression in the one with whom you empathize for *the Lord's healing touch*. A measure of relief may come to the other person as a portion of their load comes to you. However, relief through empathy alone is not true healing, nor is it lasting. He restores you as His life flows on, over and through you on its way to the troubled person. Your relief may come quickly because you have done what He asked.

At other times, the Lord allows the burden to continue because He wants you to remain in intercession for the other—one prayer may not be enough. The person may need intercession over a period of time as the Lord prepares hearts and brings people and circumstances together. Relief may come quickly to the troubled person, other times only partial relief—just enough to get them on a path to the Lord and to relationship with Him. His long-term goals are to develop deep, loving relationships, to grow up each individual to be like Jesus, and to work the nature and character of Christ into us all. In His wisdom, He knows what is best for you as well as the person He asks you to pray for, so He may or may not ask you to remain in an ongoing relationship. It may or may not be appropriate for you to be involved in the other person's ongoing process of becoming more like Jesus, but it is always appropriate to be a friend. It is your responsibility to ask Him for specifics about what to do beyond the intercession.

Now, What Am I Doing?

The job of intercessory burden bearers is not to fix the problem. I cannot say that often enough or emphatically enough! Our Lord is the "fixer"—you simply become the connection between Him and a person having a problem. After you have expressed the prayer of invitation, you must listen closely to God for any directive about further involvement. You must not assume that you are appointed to speak to people, or to come alongside to help or support in some concrete way. Initially and throughout the process, you must never assume that you are to do anything more than be a friend and pray.

However, you must listen to the Holy Spirit and ask if there is more He would have you do. The Holy Spirit knows the heart and mind of God as well as your frame—what you can and cannot bear. He knows when a burden is or is not for you to carry; when you are either ill suited to bear a particular burden, or when it is for someone else, and your carrying it would take away what the Lord wanted to do in that person. Additionally, He knows when to bring others in to help, and when your services are no longer needed. To step back and not "help" God can be hard for some.

The Holy Spirit in you then draws you to turn to Jesus and you find yourself making your way to the Cross, filled up with the burden. In prayer, you "give" it to Him; the Holy Spirit draws the burden through you and onto the Cross. Jesus assumes responsibility for it from that point. Jesus does not necessarily remove the problem from a person's life but He does deal with the overwhelming part. He lifts away enough of the pain to make it possible for the person to face the situation, to do the task at hand. Galatians 6:5 says, "for each one should carry his own load." You bear a burden as long as the Lord calls you to pray. Jesus takes only enough of the burden off the other person to make it possible for him to bear his own load.

Your part is to be available to the Lord, to be willing to allow Him to connect you with others and, in that connectedness, to call out to Him. He is the one who directs; He is the one who decides which of the other's needs to touch, when and how. Let me repeat, the burden bearer is merely the connection between God and the person in trouble.

Some readers may object, saying that Jesus is the mediator between God and man. I agree, Scripture says so in First Timothy 2:5, but remember all those reasons intercession is needed? When you are overwhelmed, you forget to ask—you need someone to ask Jesus for you. Examples from the Gospels: Jairus came to Jesus on behalf of his daughter (Mark 5:21-43ff). The friends of the paralytic let him down through the roof so that Jesus could heal him; they did something on behalf of the man (Mark 2:1-5). And Acts 9:36-40 tells that Dorcus, a woman known for her good deeds, had died. Believers sent for the disciples to pray on her behalf and she was raised to life.

Circumstances of life can become so debilitating that you feel unable to pray, you don't know how to pray or are "paralyzed." When you are overburdened, crushed, or broken you forget to ask or forget that you have the right to ask; you don't know how to ask. Some never knew in the first place.

Remember that a burden bearer brings a portion of the over-whelming portion of the burden to Jesus, to the cross of Jesus. Jesus lifts enough of the burden to allow the person to think their own thoughts, feel their own feelings, and pray their own prayers. Jesus is still the mediator between God and humans.

Some individuals have been hurt by Jesus' representatives and will have nothing to do with Him, yet need Him desperately. These people need someone to pray those prayers of invitation so Jesus can respect their free will while at the same time gently begin the healing and reconciliation needed. When the burdens of life are lifted sufficiently, the person can pray directly to Jesus for themselves.

When you invite the Holy Spirit to redeem your empathy, your heart is better able to accommodate His wisdom, light, life, and power. When you ask Him to be in charge, He will draw burdens through you that are appropriate for you to bear, and He will provide protection and give direction.

"That's All Well and Good, But..."

In one sense, that is the theory—it sounds simple enough when you lay it out in a linear, neat and tidy fashion like this. However, as you read previously, the *experience* of empathetic burden bearing is "global" and can be quite another thing when you are in the midst of the process. When you fill up with another's trouble and confusion, it feels as if it is your own. You may become as confused as the one you empathize with!

You must learn what your signals are, those subtle inner changes that indicate that the Holy Spirit has connected you with another. You need to know what it feels like when Jesus

draws a portion of a burden into your spirit for you to experience so that you may pray intelligently and passionately
about it on your way to Jesus and His Cross where He draws
it out of you. When you are learning these things, you very
much need a few trusted people who can speak into your life
and tell you when you are not acting like yourself not thinking, or talking like yourself.

What if I Don't Know How?

If an empathetic person does not move forward with the
burden-bearing process, the energy of transferred emotions
will dissipate only after time and distance from the source.
Even then, a residue, like plaque on teeth, can remain. In the
meantime, the would-be burden bearer will likely respond by
acting out or *acting on the information as if it were my own, for
example...*

- I absorb anger, but do not pass it on to Jesus, so I
  "rip strips" off the people around me.

- I absorb depression, so I become morose, curl up
  and eat chocolates.

- I absorb and feel the adoration of someone I have
  helped. Assuming the feelings are my own, I
  respond *as if* the intense adoration I feel is mine
  for the other. (This is trouble if it becomes
  romantic!)

- I absorb stress and distress and isolate myself,
  often blaming others for my feelings.

- Absorbed emotional freight overwhelms me and I
  numb myself to make the pain go away. Or, I
  behave in self-destructive ways to make the

numbness go away—with alcohol, drugs, sex, cutting, or engage in high-risk sport to distract myself.

• I absorb too much pain or too much shock and become so numb that I behave in self-destructive ways to feel high, to feel something, anything.

• I try to "fix" the problem in my own strength and wisdom.

• I pray, but because I think it is my own problem, I only ask the Lord to make it better, to "take this off me!"

Acting without understanding is not yet the fullness of relationship the Lord wants for you.

Coming into Your Own

Learning how to bear another's burden to the Cross is an aspect of learning to be fully human; it is part of the revelation of the children of God. Romans 8:19: "The creation waits in eager expectation for the sons of God to be revealed." Learning to act, walk, talk, and live like a son, "one who inherits" is the ultimate destiny of every Christian. That is your position when you accept Jesus as Savior; working the character of Jesus into human nature is what happens next. You and I will spend a lifetime doing that. Burden-bearing intercession can speed up the process because you partner with Jesus in His ongoing ministry of reconciliation. You feel Jesus' heart for people. Reconciliation of all humankind was what Jesus did not finish, that is what His affliction was for! (See Colossians 1:20.) Positionally and legally reconciliation is finished; but practically, in peoples' lives, it still needs to happen. "We implore you on Christ's behalf; Be reconciled to God" (2 Cor. 5:20). You are part of that! Being part of that ministry wears off your rough edges so you look, walk, and talk more and more like Jesus.

One of the great temptations in broken humanity is to over-spiritualize anything and everything, or go the other way and deny reality. I want to present burden bearing in the context of your humanness, as a part of the revelation of who and what you are in God—sons and daughters. Jesus was *the* Son of God—the first fruit. He is the most fully human being to have ever lived, and you are to learn to be like Him. He is the Supreme Burden Bearer, albeit not the only one depicted in Scripture.

In Good Company

I believe Daniel was "deeply identified with" the spiritual turmoil of his people, and that was why he was able to voice that great intercessory prayer in Daniel chapter 9.

Ezekiel was a burden bearer who acted upon his connectedness with his people. Ezekiel 4:4-6 records that he spent 413 days incapacitated as a prophetic act of burden-bearing intercession.

Listen to Paul's empathetic response as he writes to the churches in Galacia and Corinth. Galatians 4:19: "My dear children, for whom I am again in the pains of childbirth until Christ is formed in you." Second Corinthians 11:28-29: "Besides everything else, I face daily the pressure of my concern for all the churches. Who is weak, and I do not feel weak? Who is led into sin, and I do not inwardly burn?" Paul empathized with these people, felt their struggle, and brought that to the Lord! Again in Philippians 1:7-8 "...I have you in my heart;…all of you share in God's grace with me…I long for all of you with the affection of Christ Jesus." You can see that the Holy Spirit connected Paul with the people across great distances, especially in the Second Corinthians chapter 11 passage. In bringing the cares of His people to the Lord, Paul felt the affection of Christ Jesus for them in addition to his own human affection for them.

In addition to the Bible, there are stories of godly men and women throughout history. The Lord identified the legendary Reese Howells with the burdens of the Welsh people in such a way that he was able to intercede for that nation. God's loving response to his Daniel-like repentance was the Welsh Revival of the early 1900s.

These examples are rather high profile burden bearers—most of us go unnoticed. Throughout this book you read about daily, run-of-the-mill burden bearing—the kind that happens every day in homes, churches, and workplaces. People have been bearing burdens all along. Some have worn them, not realizing they did so. Some, when they did not understand, hardened their hearts because of the unrelenting, unmitigated pain and turmoil they felt, and refused to carry burdens. Others brought them to the Cross because they realized there is no other place to turn.

In these days, the Lord wants you to be consciously aware of yourself as a burden bearer—for your sake, so you need not be retired early from "Kingdom action" because your bodies, emotions, or spirit have been overwhelmed, crushed, or broken.

The Lord in His wisdom knows that you are ready to take on the training and the good works He designed for you to do. It is time to learn how to live as a son or daughter of the King. Ephesians 5:1-2 (NASB) exhorts us, "Therefore be imitators of God, as beloved children; and walk in love, just as Christ also loved you, and gave Himself up for us, an offering, and a sacrifice to God as a fragrant aroma." Genesis 1:26-27 says that God made humanity in His image. Jesus, the model of what God intended humanity to be, calls you to imitate Him who has born the burdens of all humanity.

This is not to say that burden bearers are to bear the burden of all humanity. This is a call to learn to bear burdens *as the Holy Spirit initiates* and to do so with confidence in the adequacy of Jesus who is the Burden Bearer of all burden bearers. You are to imitate, and only bear to the Cross as much as the Holy Spirit indicates is appropriate for you. As you learn to bear burdens rightly you become more like Jesus **and** more fully human. As your Lord's image is revealed in you more and more, you see and the world sees the children of God. The whole of creation longs for you to know yourself as one who inherits—and to live like it. When you consciously live as a child of God, you will find your prayer more efficient and effective. Consciously living as a child of God, you will live as "first fruits"—becoming like Jesus in nature and character.

Christians, as the Body of Christ, will stand with and even carry each other more and more as the last days before Christ's return approach. Not only will the frequency of need to bear each other's burdens increase, but also the intensity of need will increase. I believe you will need to learn to deliver the burdens to the Cross quickly and cleanly as the volume continues to grow. Hosea 4:6 says, "My people are destroyed for lack of knowledge." It follows that knowledge can be a protection to the ones who have it.

Do you identify yourself as a burden bearer? Are there ways in which your life is terribly different from the characteristics of a healed burden bearer as presented here? Are you overwhelmed, weighed down with the residue of burdens you do not know how to off load? Do you struggle with low self-esteem, feelings of questionable value? Are you dogged with depression or feel your life is not working? If so, skip to Chapters 11 and 12, you will find help there and begin to come into your destiny as an effective burden bearer, a friend of God, an imitator of Jesus.

It is my hope that by putting this global experience into linear terms you will be better able to understand it. To further bring understanding the next chapter examines burden-bearing dynamics in the two most foundational and formative relationships you have.

Endnote

1. See Appendix B for an explanation of the physical basis of empathy.

CHAPTER 7

The Mystery of Burden Bearing in Marriage

"For this reason a man shall leave his father and mother, and be united to his wife; and the two shall become one flesh. This mystery is great..." (Ephesians 5:31-32 NASB).

Your first, most important, and formative relationship is your relationship with your parents, your "family of origin"—the template for all future relationships. The second most important and molding relationship is that of husband and wife. These two relationships are foundational in nature. High sensitivity and burden bearing have the potential to facilitate unity, harmony, understanding, and communication. They can be a catalyst for healing wounds from your family of origin and facilitate building happy, healthy relationships—or fuel distrust and division, withdrawal and destructive, or dysfunctional behaviors and attitudes, which create destructive dysfunctional relationships.

As the push and pull within marriage challenges you personally, and as a couple, you have the potential to continue to mature, develop, and move into your destiny—or not. You can choose to allow the challenges and blessing of marriage to work the nature of Christ into you—or resist. To make this choice you must bring certain qualities to the marriage. You must possess strength of character adequate to the challenge; you must have some basic trust, and enough life skills to persevere, to keep trying, to continue communicating, and above all, you must be flexible.

You come into marriage with the template for relationships that you learned in your family of origin. You relate to your spouse according to these "rules," but what happens if your spouse does not respond the way he "should"? Are you rigid and inflexible? Do you insist upon the "proper" response, or do you have the inner strength and trust to persevere to find out what does not fit and why? Are you willing to change? If you can be flexible with a spouse, you have a relationship template that allows for change, an essential for relationship with a God whose very Presence changes you. A rigid relational template limits the potential, and you risk missing the depth, breadth, beauty, and variety within relationships. A flexible, open-ended template allows for depth of intimacy, excitement, and variety in relationships, both with your spouse and with God.

Willingness and openness to change allows God to use the challenges and blessings of marriage to work the nature of Christ into you. You are more likely to use your high sensitivity to facilitate the healing of old wounds, the development of growth, unity, intimacy, and all those good things you want if you look at change as a good thing. If change and flexibility makes you fearful, you are more likely to use high sensitivity to manipulate your spouse into giving you what you think you want and into being the person you think he or she should be. Again, you can choose to allow the challenges and blessing of the relationship to work the nature of Christ into you—or resist. Something will break—either in the marriage or in you—if you refuse to change, or your template is rigid and does not allow for change.

The high sensitivity of the burden bearer can both facilitate the marriage and can complicate it. High sensitivity helps by enabling you to read each other accurately so you feel "met." Loving, accurate empathy provides support, brings healing, amplifies good and positive traits and characteristics, and helps create a positive picture of your future and destiny. Burden-bearing intercession on behalf of your spouse and marriage opens the doors of Heaven!

On the other hand, high sensitivity can hinder a marriage by accurately identifying weaknesses but then responding to them in a critical spirit rather by intercession. Accurate empathy hinders a marriage when one spouse interprets a mood swing or elevated tone in the other as "my fault," "I must have caused it." High sensitivity amplifies and intensifies whatever each partner brings to the marriage, positive or negative, and consequently either facilitates or complicates the normal grind of two people learning to live together.

Some choose to find a comfortable rut and venture no further, like the servant who hid his talent (Matt. 25:14-30). Another way to say "nothing ventured nothing gained" could be "nothing gained because nothing risked." If you settle for less than your spirit "knows" you could be, you do so because you lack the tools to confront or the know-how to struggle, negotiate, compromise, and come to mutual understanding— such working through has not been modeled or taught. You may have damaged self-esteem that tells you that you do not deserve any more, even though your heart says otherwise. You may have a fear or anxiety-based outlook on life. You may have damaged trust, with little to no confidence in the commitment of the marriage covenant; or strength within yourself to persevere.

The concepts of commitment and trust are only abstractions because you have had little to no experience of them. Abstractions cannot move you. High sensitivity amplifies every inadequacy or deficiency you bring to your marriage. It can muck up your natural development and maturity by what you tell yourself the feelings and experiences you have mean. You arrive at erroneous conclusions when you assign inaccurate or inappropriate meanings to feelings and experiences and by that come to question your mate's motives—especially if you think all you feel and think originated with you. Questioning motives erodes relationships.

Empathy functions in the covenant relationship of marriage as it does in other relationships. You sense, feel, and absorb some of your mate's emotional, spiritual, mental, and physical freight. As in other relationships, you can either wear it or bear it. You can carry it to the Cross in prayer and invite Jesus into the mix, or shift the weight and carry it in your own strength. The difference between the impact of empathetic freight in a marriage and other relationships expresses in the potency, immediacy, and constancy of the marriage connection. Burden bearing for others can move you, turn you upside down, and stir you like a big wind, but burden bearing for a spouse can move you like a seismic event! Over time, you become familiar with what you feel ebbing and flowing from your mate and can miss each other, assuming once again that "everything I feel originates with me." When that happens, you miss opportunities to lighten each other's loads, to grow in intimacy and become more like Christ.

Covenant Relationship

Potency, immediacy, and constancy of connection between spouses arise out of the *covenant* relationship of the marriage. Covenant connection is at the core of your being. Covenant, as you see it in the Bible, is something far deeper, more profound than you think of it today. Covenant, according to Scripture, is a relationship between one who holds all power and one who does not. The greater power binds or obligates itself to the lesser. God set up the agreement, set the terms, and obligated Himself to Abraham. Abraham simply agreed to God's terms. When you enter into marriage, you agree to live together on God's terms, not yours. One of those terms is that He will make you one flesh. This is not a metaphor—it is a reality, as you see in Genesis 2:24, repeated in Matthew 19:5, Mark 10:8, and Ephesians 5:31. Apostle Paul asserts that even casual sex results in a one-flesh reality (1 Cor. 6:16). If "being joined with a harlot" has this effect, how much more powerful is a joining before God and under covenant!

When you enter into the covenant of marriage, you enter into a binding agreement, the husband and wife together form the lesser "partner" with the Lord God as the greater. God considers the husband and wife as a unit, with two members making the whole. God joins a couple in such a way that it has a physical effect even though you cannot see it. How He does this is mystery—complete mystery.

In North America, the word *covenant* is often a synonym for contract or agreement. However, a covenant with the Lord is not a legal contract between business partners—you cannot dissolve it if things do not work out to your satisfaction. Dissolving a business relationship might be messy, but it is possible. A legacy of the scientifically oriented Western mindset is, "if I can't see it, it does not exist." You cannot see the joining that happens as God sees it, so people tend to view vows as some nice religious way of saying, "We commit to cohabit, raise children, and share expenses!" God does not see it that way.

More happens with marriage than with a business agreement. Unlike business agreements, dissolving a marriage is much more messy and devastating because it affects a person on every level of being—physical, emotional, spiritual, and psychological. Some describe divorce as being like an amputation, surgery, or dismemberment. When you rip apart what God has joined, you create a kind of living death—indeed, the marriage, as a living entity, dies. Because people cannot see the joining that exists, far too many blithely enter into marriage, and divorce.

When two people exchange vows (solemn and strong promises) "before God and these witnesses," they enter into a covenant with God, not just each other, and agree to live according to the terms of the vows they take. These solemn promises spell out the particulars of the covenant. Vows do not disappear in the wind like a vapor trail if you forget them or choose to disregard them—and God never forgets them. He obligated Himself to be part of the relationship.

Before going any further I need to point out that the Lord made provision for divorce—not as part of His plan or design for your life, but as a concession due to the hardness of hearts (Matt. 18:8; Mark 10:5). It is to be the exception, not the rule. As He says in Malachi 2:16, "I hate divorce says the Lord God of Israel, and I hate a man's covering himself [or his wife] with violence as well as with his garment...." It is not my purpose to open a discussion of divorce. Here, I simply want to acknowledge that caveat.

Metaphors of Marriage

Several metaphors help illustrate the reality of the "one flesh," and the immediacy and potency of what burden-bearing husbands and wives do for each other.

• An electric circuit...

The Lord hard-wires your spirits when you say, "I do." In saying, "I do," you forfeit the on/off switch. Current flows back and forth between husband and wife and you cannot turn it off! Unless the Lord intervenes, when the emotional state of one fluctuates, even if hidden, the other feels it. Important to note is that you can absorb a feeling of numbness when your spouse is totally blocked and disconnected from feelings.

• A three-legged race...

Taking marriage vows is like entering a three-legged race.[1] The Holy Spirit binds the husband and wife together as surely as two legs are in one sack—whether you believe it or not, whether you come to dislike each other or not. When a husband goes one way and the wife another way, both will fall. It behooves couples to mutually decide on a direction and adjust as quickly as possible to each other's gait and rhythm. Otherwise, you will spend much of married life in a heap on the ground. When you trip each other, the usual reaction is to curse the other rather than reflect upon what caused the crash. Was it a difference in rhythm, gait, or direction? Did the difference occur because of miscommunication or bumping into each other's wounds and baggage brought into the marriage?

- Twins…

The connection between a husband and wife is so real that the sharing is more like a set of twins in a womb of the Lord's making, sharing a common amniotic fluid. They maintain separate bodies, separate digestive systems, receive their nurture and sustenance individually, but share their environment intimately.

Safeguarding the Covenant

As well as indwelling each believer, the Lord's presence can be invited into and flow through this new entity of the marriage. When you spend time with the Lord together, as husband and wife, a flow of purity comes from the Lord's presence that cleanses, refreshes, restores, and renews. Prayer together, for a couple, is not an option if you want to maintain a healthy marriage. You must go to the Lord together, and regularly pour the lean water of the Holy Spirit into your relationship.

Christians generally have not understood the reality of the legal spiritual entity created in a covenant relationship, how literally two do become one spirit and one flesh. Because of the lack of understanding, husbands and wives live as separate individuals who share life, home, and family. The Body of Christ has not comprehended our shared oneness—we have only an inkling of how we affect each other. The Lord wants us to understand and move into the fullness of joy that He designed marriage to be.

Marital Burden Bearing

When you know something about your spouse that wasn't communicated out loud, you generally chalk it up to familiarity or being "weird." Usually this kind of knowing comes to you as a thought or an urge; there is generally little if any emotional impact and it is easy to claim as your own. Examples include the time that I knew David was going to fix my wedding ring. I felt his joy in thinking about my surprise. Or, to have been thinking about him, or my mother, only to have the phone ring, and there they are. There were many times when I would be thinking about David's day at work and have the sense that I needed to prepare in the event that he was bringing company home with him. And I often know ahead of his coming home when he needs extra consideration because he had a particularly difficult day because I have felt his feelings throughout the day. There is no particular emotional flavor to this "knowing." The thought or urge was suddenly "there," as word of knowledge.

We are all familiar with spousal connectedness of this variety. Sometimes the knowing truly is from familiarity and habit, but other times it is because of sharing the content of your human spirits as sensing flows back and forth through the spiritual gates the Lord has opened. Familiarity grows because of this flowing back and forth between partners. It may seem as if it is nothing special, everyday, or mundane. It sometimes feels no different than self, and in a way it should not because God joined you. You are one, and this is one reason you may not realize how much you lighten each other's loads or increase them.

You may miss the everyday expressions of marital burden bearing because they are so common. You finish each other's sentence...and do it correctly! You sense what the other needs or wants. You know when to serve, offer to help in some way, or allow for time and space. This kind of sensing or needs and wants can feel like it all originates within you rather than from those around you. However, when the Holy Spirit directly connects you with anyone else through empathy for specific purposes, such as to warn, give help, direction or information, it has a different feel to it.

One particular week while working on this chapter, I *felt* busy and pushed by other people's schedules and needs, but I was not! My first reaction was to ask the Lord why I felt so "put upon." The distinct thought went through my mind to "read what I was writing." I was writing about husbands and wives! When David came home, rather than "laying a diagnosis" on him, I questioned how he was feeling, how his week was going. He described the very feelings I was having. We chuckled and lifted his week to the Lord, but then I could pray for him very specifically. I was able to draw out and listen to pent up frustrations, to give thought to ways to help him vent through exercise, or soothe with music, and thus lessen tension. As I did this, my week miraculously became peaceful. His burden had flowed through the open gates of my spirit and I experienced some of what he was experiencing. Those unpleasant feelings called me to awareness of what his experience was so I could lighten his load. As a portion of what was in him was drawn through me to the Cross, he was better able to carry on with his work. Sharing of common experience, if you allow it to, helps intimacy grow. This, I believe, is what God had in mind with marital burden bearing—to divide the burden and multiply the joy.

Before I understood burden-bearing dynamics, I would have assumed that all the tension I felt was my own. When pushed to my physical limits, I have less grace and can verbally snap at anyone nearby. Growing up as a "lightweight," my only defenses were my feet and my tongue. I could run, or and I could riddle—ridicule. Neither of these skills is helpful in a marriage, but when under stress you revert to old ways. Now that I understand burden bearing, I have learned to check my schedule, and if the schedule does not validate the whirlwind I feel, I know David is having another one of those weeks! During these times I try to be kinder, more patient with others and myself because I realize tensions or confusions of my own are likely being amplified—it may not all be mine! I know that as I pray and hold David up, the excess will flow on through me to Jesus. Understanding how we affect each other, I catch myself sooner and revert to the old ways less often.

Sharing Emotion

Burden bearing in marriage through the sharing of emotion and states of being is a way you walk in each other's shoes. When you are aware of this dynamic and have a mindset of prayer, the "knowings" easily flow into prayer, and without thinking, you bear the other's burden to Jesus! In the one-flesh relationship, you share your emotions, your energies, your workload, and the natural consequences of the other's actions or lack of action. God meant this sharing to bless and to be a help—to divide the negative and multiply the positive.

However, because of the high sensitivity of the natural burden bearer, burden bearing can feel like a curse when one, or both, is ignorant of burden-bearing dynamics. When we act out what was absorbed, when our own wounding drives us, when we actively refuse to bear burdens to the Cross or are consciously rebelling against God, we wear the burdens and walk around like a magnet in a pin factory—attracting pins and needles!

Resisting your design can even have physical consequences. Resistance creates stress, and you know the results
of prolonged, unmitigated stress. Whatever you do with your
own stress, you will do with the stress you absorb from others. If your stress reveals itself in knotted shoulders,
headaches, or ulcers, the stress you absorb from others will
find those same places to lodge. The stress from the work of
taking burdens to the Cross that registers in your body, and
the spiritual residue you do not wash off, will cling to these
places. In time, you break at your weakest link—as in this
next example.

Melissa was going through some stressful experiences,
but because of the sensitivity of her spirit, she also felt the
stress her husband was carrying on his job. Out of her love for
him and her tendency to do what she could to make things
better, she did not share her troubles with her husband. She
tried to hide her burdens.

He, on the other hand, became more and more burdened
until he woke up one morning and did not want to go to work
and did not know why. She recognized that he was depressed.
He had done with her stress what he did with his own—he
pushed it away from consciousness, shared with no one, and
attributed the pressure to his job.

They talked, trying to discover what brought on the
depression. As they tracked it, they realized that his depression started at the time she began to withhold her troubles in
an effort not to add to his. But the more she withheld the sad-
der she became. Her trouble bathed him with her downcast
thoughts. Like most burden bearers, he wrapped himself up
in her sadness and assumed he was the one who was sad and
out of step—"wrong." He did have stress at work that he was

not resolving; that stress was not depressing either of them—it was her not sharing about her own stress that sat on top of his work stress and weighed him down. His conscious mind, noting his inner sadness, cast about for a cause and *assumed* it must all have to do with work.

As they talked, Melissa shared her troubles. They prayed about her situation and his depression evaporated! Withholding the trouble was a greater weight of oppression on the husband than her sharing that she had been missing him and trying to lighten his load. The sharing strengthened their marriage as they saw how closely they were connected. She felt cherished that he cared enough to draw her out, and when she shared, he felt loved and honored. This was blessing multiplied and burdens divided. If she had angrily spewed rather than sharing carefully and quietly, he would not have felt loved or honored. Love or honor that comes from demand is not nearly as sweet as that freely given. The incident added to their intimacy and unity; they knew more fully how each other felt.

God designed us to have the gates of our spirits open wide to our partners and to Him. Whenever a spouse withholds, there will be constriction. Constricted, our spirits do not flow at capacity, the Holy Spirit is not available to capacity, and since the spirit gives life, we have less life available. When the withholding registers, we run the information through our personal grid, interpret, and assign it meaning according to the family experiences of our early years. If we think we should withhold because you love, we are mistaken. The results of withholding or keeping secrets actually become oppressive to our mates. What both need is to communicate with love, and lovingly communicate! Secrets are deadly!

Sharing Energy

David's wiring is such that he struggles with wanting to save the world. Because I have MS, my energies are very limited. I have maybe $10 of energy in my personal account. David has more like $100 in his account. He can handle a lot more than I can—do more, go more, and recover more quickly. However, there are times when someone's pain is directly in front of him and he cannot or does not say, "I am sorry, this is my personal time and I cannot give it away." He gives time and energy to people when the need is directly in front of him—he sees and feels their pain and bears their burden. He wants to make a difference; he wants them to have relief.

However, he forgets that I continue to be connected and feel the exhaustion he ignores when he goes beyond his limits and gives away his recovery time. If he continues to give away time and energy, it becomes physically and spiritually painful for me. My body begins to scream at me. If it goes on long enough, I begin to scream at him. One Sunday afternoon David sat in his chair fighting sleep. I took a nap and he felt rested. What can I say.

Sharing Work

Kathryn's husband, Don, reached out to hug her. Simultaneously she felt feelings of revulsion and the thought, "dirty old man," went through her head. Because those feelings and that sort of thought was so foreign to their relationship, they knew the Lord allowed the sensation and the words to give direction for prayer. In conversation with a co-worker, Don learned that he was having marriage problems. It was as though feelings from his colleague clung to Don and he brought them home. The sensations were in or on him, even though he was not consciously aware of them. Kathryn sensed the wife's reaction to whatever was "dirty" about her husband through Don. The Lord identified her directly with the other man's wife because He knew the wife would not talk about it on her own. In this case, the sensations informed intercession and gave direction for ministry. Yes, the couple received help.

When David travels to teach for schools and workshops, the Lord often allows me to experience sensations that are student reactions to things that are happening. Sometimes it results in a spiritual warning to David and the ministry team, a direction for prayer for the school or an individual, or brings to light a dynamic among the students that needs attention. Even though I am not physically present, I still share in my husband's work.

There have been times when women who have had abusive fathers are attracted to my husband's gentleness of spirit; most of the time it is a clean yearning for a father who would be just like David. Other times the yearning is not clean, it is of a sexual nature, and the Lord allows me to feel the uncleanness. Our oneness allows me to be "present" in a way; it is a spiritual for protection him.

Sharing Natural Consequences

When David was in the height of his workaholism, I suffered. Relief came only when I asked the Lord to put the Cross between us to filter out the excess, to be a gentle but firm boundary to prevent me from subconsciously trying to carry David in ways He was not asking of me. I wanted to carry what the Lord asked me to carry legitimately, as a helpmate, but to reflect to David the tiredness that came from his excess so that he would feel and understand the damage he was doing to his body and mind. I did not want to enable a harmful addiction.

When I did this, within three days, he was feeling his own tiredness. This was a rather immediate effect with very physical consequences. Wearing the overflow of a spouse's excess is not the kind of burden bearing you want to be doing because it can enable a dysfunctional or destructive pattern of behavior that can lead to living parallel lives in the same house, sharing the children and the bills. Any such pattern does not build intimacy or unity!

David and I have seen many times that when one spouse will not face his or her own emotional tasks, the other spouse endures the consequences. Because a husband and wife are one flesh, what one mate does or does not do affects the other. A husband who refuses to cry may find his wife cries very easily over the slightest thing and does not know why. She is doing his crying for him. He cannot feel the pain she is crying about but when she cries, he feels better. John Sandford's Indian mother trained into him that, "Osage Indian boys don't cry." That shut him down. His wife, Paula, found herself crying unaccountably again and again—until they saw what was happening and stopped it in prayer. Now, John does his own crying—and Paula feels great.

Sarah found her eating addiction, which she had held under control for some time, spiraling out of control. Munch, munch, nibble, nibble! Unknown to her, her husband had a secret addiction he had never confessed, nor sought treatment. Later, after he shared his trouble with her, she saw that her addiction escalated at the time her husband's addiction flared up to the point that he found his silence more painful than confession, and sought help.

In some instances, partner A may be able to cope with stresses generated from partner B's excesses because of a strong constitution and good genes. Partner B may appear to be unaffected by the sin, but partner A may find dormant propensities activated because of being bathed in the stresses created by the other's excesses. In some cases, one spouse literally carries what the other refuses to face. One spouse can quite literally soak up enough stress that it enables the other to go on sinning or abusing the body in one way or another. This dynamic supports the dysfunction of one at the expense of the other, rather than the relationship strengthening and lifting both individuals. It is bearing burdens, but not as the Lord designed.

You do genuinely need to take excess stress to the Cross so your spouse can continue to function during times of great stress—for example, from tragedies in the family such as illness, financial strains, or a series of losses with no time to recover before the next arrives. You need to be able to endure and continue to function when there is nothing you can do to change the situation. Burden bearing allows you to divide the burden. However, these should be *periods of time,* not the normal state of affairs. If crisis is the norm, it should not be. *Continual crisis is not a normative state!* Ask help to get off the merry-go-round! I believe the Lord designed oneness of spirit within marriage to pick up each other's excesses *as long as* that leads to comfort, healing, and wholeness. If it does not lead to comfort, healing, and wholeness, ask the Lord to help you see what is awry with your situation and seek His directions for what to do about it.

Burden bearing, based in empathy, is an ability everyone has to one degree or another. It carries the powerful potential either to be a blessing or a curse to your relationships. When you understand it and work with the Lord, burden bearing within the context of marriage is a great blessing. When you do not understand it, you live with confusion, a sense of oppression, of heaviness, of being used and abused.

Burdens Compound the Weight

Burdens bound back and forth, compounding the weight. Without understanding, you sop up each other's tensions and compound your own, thus complicating relationships. It is a difficult dynamic to capture in words, but as common as peanut butter! A husband comes home with increased tensions, and the wife feels and absorbs some of the tensions without realizing and therefore does not turn them over to God. The husband, sensing her newly acquired tension without realizing what he is doing, absorbs some of her load, adding to what he already carried. Because he does not realize what he did, he does not turn the burden over to God. This interchange can repeat several times, each time compounding the load instead of dividing and decreasing it. Then, even if the husband manages not to be grouchy or impatient, he is now more vulnerable to being inpatient and snapping because the outside tension adds to whatever tension he carried from the day. If the wife is verbally sharp, acting out the tension she picks up from her husband, it can push him over the edge. The wife is short, sharp, or critical, not realizing that the impatience came from carrying and absorbing some of the extra tensions that the husband brought home.

If not trained by the Lord, both carry burdens in their own strength. The spouse who came home with a load of tension creates a huge emotional/spiritual withdrawal from the spiritual/emotional resources of the other spouse, whether intended or not. The other spouse then has far less inner resources with which to be gracious. All couples do this!

When both husband and wife are highly sensitive burden bearers and are determined to be positive rather than negative with each other, either can still sabotage the other if they do not understand burden bearing. Run the scenario again: Spouse #1 comes home with increased tensions, which spouse #2 absorbs. Spouse #1 manages by force of will not to be sharp or critical. However, spouse #2 is now tighter with the tensions that spouse #1 brought home. Spouse #1 feels the increase of tension within #2 and absorbs some of it, which adds to the previous tensions, so now #1 is wound even tighter! Then #2 absorbs more and so on, back and forth.

If they do not go to the Cross with the tension, each time one absorbs tensions from the other, they are added to previous tensions. Tensions continue to escalate until someone loses control and makes a sharp verbal jab at the other, who is also so tense that a terse exchange takes place. Both wanted to bless the other, but instead they hurt each other, and neither knew what went wrong.

Too Full to Take on More

Recall that you "hear" from the Lord in various ways. One woman who hears from the Lord through pictures asked Him to show her what happens when she and her husband try to come close to each other. She saw a picture of two water glasses three-quarters full. As the two glasses came closer to each other, they both began to boil, until both boiled over. She understood that the glasses represented the two of them and the water represented their individual emotional and spiritual pains. Both she and her husband were highly sensitive burden bearers. Each was full of pain, some of it their own, and the rest they had absorbed from others, and had not yet discharged at the Cross.

When they came closer to each other, they filled up with each other's pains, and boiled over. That is when they were impatient and hurt each other. It helped so much for this woman to understand what had been happening. She was able to ask the Lord to be a filter and shield between them so they could have closeness while continuing to seek the Lord's healing for all those stored-up emotional, spiritual, and psychological pains.

Attributing Meaning Without Clarifying

You can react to burden bearing when you attribute meaning to what you sense, without clarification. David says many times that if I really meant what he *thought* I meant, he would be very angry! Thankfully, he has a well-practiced habit of asking for clarification. Attributing unintended meaning can lead to erroneous conclusions, even wrongly questioning the motives of your spouse, which complicates and exaggerates the normal irritations, disappointments, and discomforts of marriage. The normal everyday grinding off of rough edges causes pressure that irritates. Normally you are able to bear such irritating pressures without difficulty. When someone lightly bumps a bruise you cannot see, you can assume the bump caused the great deal of hurt you felt.

Normally a light bump is not a difficulty. But the constant pressure of bearing your spouse's burdens can bruise your spirit in ways you may be unaware. Then, when a burden from your mate unexpectedly hits your spirit, you may over-react because your spirit is already tender and sensitive from daily on-going unprocessed burden bearing. It can "feel" as if the burden is a sharp, purposeful, and intentional hit. Making such an assumption without clarification can lead to wrong conclusions about your mate. This dynamic can also happen with others outside the family.

You can absorb the bitter thoughts and feelings of a friend who is experiencing marriage difficulties. If you do not identify the burden and empty it onto the Cross, when you collide with *your* spouse without realizing how deeply your spirit is carrying something of that bitter bruising pain of your friend, an ordinary irritant is magnified, causing you to feel maligned.

Cherri (names changed to protect privacy) spent an hour on the phone listening to Susan's tale of woe. Susan had no one to talk to; no one understood what she was going through. She felt abandoned by her friends and was unsure of God's agenda. There was no light at the end of her tunnel. She had no hope. There was no sense trying. Nothing would ever change. Feelings of anger, bitterness, self-pity and futility flowed for an hour before Sherri was able to bring the conversation to an end. Later, when Sherri's husband came home, she lashed out at him with bitterness over his neglect of her and spewed out her futility over ever changing her situation. She had absorbed her friend's feelings.

Cherri had some unresolved frustrations of her own, but much more mild in nature. However, because the feelings were unresolved and in the same area (abandonment), Susan's mountain of intense, overwhelming feelings bonded onto Cherrie's feelings, and she spewed bitter anger and overwhelming futility. She forgot to take the burden of the call to the Cross in prayer. She forgot to ask Jesus to cleanse and lift the burden out of her. When her husband came home, late, *again*, that ordinary irritant was magnified. Her husband bumped into the bruised feelings of Cherri's friend that sat on top of her own irritation, her own feelings of not being valued.

When feelings are already bruised and our mates bumps them, we think they intentionally and purposefully chose to make us feel badly. We can surprise ourselves by how upset we become. We find ourselves thinking, "What's the point, he doesn't care," or, "I'll never measure up to her standards." We do not realize how much is not our own feelings and thoughts, but the bitterness and despair of our friend's. We may assume what we feel is only our own feelings. Then, we can even forget, or push aside, what we know to be true about our spouses and our feelings toward our mates. We can even bitterly question our mate's motives and not realize that what we feel is the echo of our friend's bitterness that we absorbed. It is not our bitterness, until we make it ours.

Another scenario is also possible. Suppose that Cherri was devalued and abandoned as a child, and had not resolved that hurt. Then when her husband comes home late, *again*, if she spewed intense anger, bitterness and futility, the overwhelming intensity is *not necessarily* from the feelings she absorbed from her friend. She already had a stored up supply of intense feelings of her own, which were pushed by judgments she made from those early experiences. "He knows that punctuality is important to me! He doesn't care about how his tardiness affects me." If she absorbed some of her friend's anger and futility, failed to identify it as such and take it to the Cross in prayer, it added to her own. Her husband was the blessed recipient!

You must be careful, to the best of your ability, not to excuse hurtful behavior on your part as coming from "burden bearing." Cherri's husband cannot hide from his part, blaming it all on her bitter roots. His tardiness was a present and ongoing irritant that he seemed unable or unwilling to address. His tardiness tempted her to lash out. Her judgment that she is not valued drove her to lash out, and the burden she picked up only added fuel to an existing fire.

Performance Orientation

Performance orientation fuels burden bearing wrongly. If your sense of worth is dependent upon your performance, you are vulnerable to pushing yourself too hard, too long, which uses up your physical reserves. Everyone, at times, is caught in situations in which the pace is unchangeable. As you continue to overwork and further use physical reserves, you begin to experience either emotional flatness or raw emotions. You may then work even more frantically and become rawer and flatter emotionally. You may isolate for protection from people's pressures, but then you miss sources of nurture. You stop doing the things that refresh. You no longer have the energy to feel loving or happy feelings.

However, you are still a sponge! You still bump into and absorb other people's troubles. Now, your feelings and others' feelings are even more jumbled, but with less energy to think, sort, or perceive clearly. The more tired and jumbled you become, the more likely you are to forget what you know. You forget who you are and who your spouse is, and lash out at the closest source of unhappiness, making your mate pay dearly should she dare to suggest you are about to crash and burn.

In this scenario, you are looking at burnout made worse by not understanding the weight and the crushing of the spirit that can happen. Performance orientation pushes you, and you bear burdens wrongly. It is easy to lose sight of the sources of difficulties and to assume that your mate has caused them. Burnout is a multifaceted problem; we can not deal with it here. I mention it because it has its source in performance orientation, affects your marriage, and makes burden bearing more burdensome. If you think you, or one you love, may be dealing with burnout, I urge you to consult a physician or a counselor.

Negative Reactions to Marital Burden Bearing

You can have negative reactions to marital connectedness. Negative reactions because of your own wounding or lack of understanding, reinforce and make worse the baggage you bring into marriage. Negative reactions lead to wrong conclusions, especially concerning motivations, and tear at the very fabric of marriage. Rejection or refusal of marital burden bearing builds misunderstandings, divisions, and disunity. It creates distance and can lead to living parallel lives. It results in a lack of intimacy and unity. It can feel like a curse.

A friend shared that when she was growing up, her father would become emotional, teary, anxious, and indecisive. He would lose his way in emotion and not know how to return to himself. Her mother's response to him was, "Pull yourself together!" She needed and wanted him to be strong and decisive. As a child, my friend, and her mother, was afraid of her father's emotionality. Her mother's response was to control and shut his emotions down rather than help him sort and process them, which only made the situation worse for him.

However, my friend, even as a child, was aware that her mother's response was not appropriate. She wanted her father to have more emotional control, because, after all, he was the father. Fathers are supposed to be strong and hold the rest of the family together, right? In this case, when overwhelmed, the reasoning part of his brain shut down. He became anxious, emotionally paralyzed, and unable to discern which response was appropriate, fight or flight. This would have been a wonderful time for his wife to drain off a portion of his emotion and pray with him so he could come back to himself and provide the strength, security, and emotional stability the family needed.

Redemptive burden bearing, an appropriate and helpful response, would have been to listen to his tale of woe and prayerfully pass the confusion, pain, distress on to the Lord. Being helped to release the distress to the Lord, he needed further help, to think, talk, and sort through things to find out what were valid concerns and what were mere feeling reactions that came from outside himself. He needed help to sort what he needed to understand and what he needed to bring to Jesus. He needed prayer support to bring those burdens to the Cross. Feelings sometimes give accurate information, to which you need to listen. Other times, feelings give inaccurate information (or you interpret your feelings wrongly) so that you should not act upon, nor long entertain them. If my friend's mother had made a prayerful burden-bearing response, the Lord could have redeemed the situation. The parents would have modeled for the children how to bear burdens and how to process or "do" emotions. As it turned out, my friend adopted her mother's reactions to emotions. Pack them away. Shut them down. Turn them off. Do not have them.

From this negative modeling, she reacted to her husband's angers with rejection. It could be anger over anything; it need not even be directed at her! Anger or any negative emotion felt to her like loss of control. Now as an adult, even the appearance of loss of control rattles her sense of security, causing a negative reaction. She did not allow negative emotion to come in the house, and she was unable to lighten her husband's load. When she learned not to be afraid of his emotions, but to share them with him and help him process and pray through them, angers could pass in a half hour rather than taking two or three days to dissipate as they had in the past. She learned that having emotions is not a weakness but part of being a complete human being. She learned how to bear her husband's emotions without becoming overwhelmed by them. She learned that that was one way she could be a help mate.

Unfair Usage

Some burden bearers are so sensitive that they unconsciously "read" people but respond in an unredeemed fashion. Because of their own wounding, judgments, and lack of instruction, rather than interceding for the weaknesses and bearing the burdens to the Lord, they gather information and use it to build up themselves, to control, and to manipulate for their own purposes. This type of burden bearer ferrets out weaknesses, files these nuggets away, and exploits them later. Husbands and wives must guard against any tendency to use "inside knowledge" to take advantage of their mate. This is the way of the world, but as followers of Christ, we are learning a new way. Some, though, instead of allowing sensitivity to lead to intimacy, they build walls around their hearts for protection and hoard the information they sense in order to control others and keep them and their troubles far away. They believe the wall will keep pain from touching them.

In spite of their best efforts, hurt still finds its way through. Self-protections create burdens rather than lighten them! The wall does work in a way, but not the way they want. It keeps love out. People walk carefully around them and mind what they say. Those who use information to control and manipulate have serious areas of unbelief, areas in which they do not and cannot trust because of past wounding experiences. They are masters of the double bind and use "I" frequently, theirs is the noble martyr role—they have a black belt in the use of guilt and manipulation.

Mates of people like this do not have to worry that anything they say can or will be used against them at some point—they *know* it will! These people drive others away; they hurt the ones they love but know no other way to be. This is very unhealthy use of high sensitivity. It poisons a marriage; it destroys rather than builds up. This is a serious problem that requires much repentance and forgiveness. These people need very strong, emotionally stable friends who will lovingly not allow them to continue in the old way, but will call them to account every time they use sensitivity unfairly.

We all need to learn how to bear burdens rightly so we can become the people the Lord designed us to be.

Benefits of Marital Burden Bearing

Despite all that can go wrong by confusing what you absorb by empathy with your own emotional, psychological, and spiritual freight, and despite not realizing that you live, move, and breathe in a shared spiritual environment—what are the benefits of marital burden bearing?

*You are better able to understand
and appreciate your spouse's struggles.*

MS has affected my vision—the condition is called a nystagmus. The visual image is in constant motion. It makes reading difficult. David experienced what it is like for me when he rented a video that would not run properly. The image kept flipping. After about 10 minutes, he was irritated and changed the movie. I said, "Welcome to my world." He was astonished! It gave him a completely new appreciation of what I contend with, constantly.

You may have a similar reaction when the Lord connects you in ways that allow you to experience the edges of your mate's struggles. When you feel or sense their trouble, anguish, or temptation, you have much more compassion and appreciation for how well they do. It is easier to hold my tongue when I know by experience what David is going through and I am able to extend more grace.

Due to my eye condition, I do not drive, so I am homebound much of the time. My social interaction is on the phone, or at an event when David can take me. David's time was full of people and activities, and I began to worry about our marriage. We had so little time together. I began to feel sorry for myself—I was on the shelf, rejected, not part of life. All fat and dumpy and who would want me around anyway...and then I flirted with anger at David and anger at

God. Suddenly a thought went flying through my mind—what if these feelings were not solely mine! What if God was enabling me to experience some of David's feelings but I was adding my own details?! I asked the Lord to comfort and assure him of my love and commitment, but then felt the most loving thing I could do was to talk about what I was experiencing. When I drew him out, I found that indeed, he was feeling those same feelings but not verbalizing them. His concern touched me deeply and added to our intimacy. I was able to feel his love in a way I had not experienced it before. Some time later he shared that he was glad that I "felt" his love because he thought he did not do a good job of expressing it as he would like. I felt I knew him better—and this happened after 30+ years of marriage!

You can be practical help and protection for each other.

The Lord often gives me ideas that reveal another angle of ministry, a caution, or a new direction for David. I have learned to share with him what I sense and feel, regardless of whether it makes sense to me or not. If my sharing does not have any immediate significance, it alerts him to be watching for direction or understanding as events unfold. When the knowing relates to David personally, he feels cherished and honored. When it relates to his work, he not only feels loved by me in that I am willing to share his load, but also loved by the Father that He cares enough to provide a helpmate. The same is true when he bears a burden for me.

Marital burden bearing develops
trust and intimacy with your partner.

When you have shared experiences, you develop a unique companionship. There is a bonding that happens, if you allow it, that can come no other way. Foxhole buddies or fellow prisoners of war share a bond of common experience that others cannot know because they did not experience it. In the marriage relationship, this kind of intense bonding through shared experiences from burden bearing can be an open door to intimacy. Granted, if either partner has problems with trust, it will be more difficult to keep the heart open. Some are quick to rebuild walls around the heart after they lower them, after love melts them, or after our sovereign Lord, "shares your heart" with your partner without asking you! Intimacy is always a risk, but it is a risk worth taking. Developing intimacy is the only way you can ever feel met in the deep places of your being, where so many are profoundly lonely. What develops is not just marital intimacy from proximity, but intimacy with the Lord and each other, which is the deepest, most profound intimacy you can experience.

A Final Word

The Lord has been teaching me through pottery, through things I make on the wheel. For some time I was asking the Lord to share what was in His heart regarding this chapter, because I felt I was missing something. One day every ball of clay I put on the wheel fought me; it did not want to center. Rather than give up in frustration, I asked Him what He wanted me to see, what He was trying to teach me. At one point, I decided to do a "left-handed compression"—a way of taking a partially formed piece back down to a cylinder shape to correct the place where it went off balance. When you do a compression, you let the clay know who is in charge. The clay must submit to your hands and accept your design—"*I* am in charge." The clay does not dictate what it will be. Once it is compressed, you reform it.

Marriage is like that. Your spouse is often the instrument in the hand of the Lord shaping you, revealing the wobbles in your design as an individual. The Lord also shapes you together as a pair, and there is a design to that shaping as well. Most of the time a potter's touch is gentle, guiding the clay, but becomes firm and supporting when the clay takes on a mind of its own. When you react to your sensitivity and fight against it, you resist the Lord's design. When you build defenses and shore up your separateness, you resist the development of intimacy with each other; you resist the design for your marriage and the design for unity with Christ. You may force His hand to become firm with you. You can put strains on the relationship that it was not designed to bear. That is when the centrifugal forces arrayed against you can literally pull you apart. You can become so out of balance that you collapse like a clay pot.

In Summary

When, as married folk, you live together long enough, you mutually submit to each other, and negotiate your way to the place where you are in harmony; you think alike and have like values. You grind on each other until your differences wear off, or something breaks (the former being easier than the latter)! Those who live out of passion may take exception, feeling that the grinding and sparks can lead to love and life that is never dull! Just as you come to talk like each other, think like each other, and some say even come to look like each other after many years together, the same is true with Christ. He wants you to become so familiar with Him, so attuned that you walk like Him, talk like Him, think like Him, and even come to look like Him.

This spiritual connection between husbands and wives develops familiarity, intimacy, and unity. The Lord places high value on all these things. When you look at the best that marriage can be, you have but a flawed picture of the relationship and communication the Lord wants to have with you. The best that marriage can be is only a reflection of the unity of the Godhead.

You cannot achieve perfection. That is true, but a truth that need not devastate. You can stop striving for perfection and let the Lord bring you along. It is not all up to you. Life and transformation into the likeness of Christ are processes that end when you are with Him, face to face. Your responsibility is to put yourself into the process rather than resist it, and to keep yourself there. The Lord does not condemn you, so you must not condemn yourself either. When God looks at your marriage, He sees it covered over with Christ.

God knows your frame, with all your imperfections, and loves you perfectly. He loves you through all of your life's lessons just as you love your children through theirs. You are to *imitate* Him, like children imitating a beloved parent. He is a loving Father and gives you all you need. You have the equipment for relationship with Him. You have the capacity for empathy and the provision of salvation. In marriage, you have all you need. You have empathy and the additional help that comes from covenant.

Burden bearing within a marriage can open the door to and facilitate the development of intimacy with God and each other, as well as build into you the character of Christ.

You need only the courage and commitment to walk through the door.

Burden Bearing and the Single Person

Although I have approached the topic of burden bearing from the viewpoint of a married person, the dynamics apply to the single person as well. Singles will find burden-bearing dynamics playing out in the workplace in relation to bosses, co-workers, professors, fellow students, friends, and acquaintances.

What may be more difficult for the single person is to find relationships that can be family for them. Everyone needs family, so if you do not have one, my advice is to create a spiritual family composed of people the Lord chooses for you. God sent us into families; we speak of the Church as family. Unfortunately, many of us were, or are currently being, wounded in families and churches. Your family, natural or extended, may not be a safe place to grow in the Lord. Nonetheless, you are corporate and need to find brothers and sisters, fathers and mothers, aunts and uncles who are safe and nurturing. Those who are married would do well to include a single person in your extended family life. Ask to be part of their lives and for them to be part of yours. Yes, all the burden-bearing stuff will happen, and unresolved issues from families of origin will rear their ugly heads—but in a committed supportive environment. A single person needs to be part of a family for the nurture that comes through that avenue.

Singles without family struggle with loneliness and can be tempted to seek relationship in unhealthy ways or places. Family is a place to go; it is company, companionship, and a place to bounce around ideas. Loved ones tell you when your ideas are off base or on target. Family the Lord puts together has no dues or tests of membership. It is *'Ohana*,[2] where all are included and no one is left behind.

Closing Prayer

Lord, I acknowledge that I fear intimacy because I believe that if I trust You, and my mate, the same kinds of things will happen that happened to me as a child when I trusted.

Father God, forgive me for being afraid of You and show me the truth about my fears. With my head, I know Your nature is different from those who raised me. You said, "Love casts out fear." I ask You to love me so that I do not fear You in the wrong sense of fear. I set my will and my heart to trust You and I commit to the hard, scary work of keeping my heart open to You and to my mate and others. I know there is risk and that I may be hurt, but by faith, regardless of my feelings, I choose to step out of my safety zone. I cannot see the end from the beginning, I am not in control, and that is scary...so meet me Lord Jesus! Amen.

(Make a list of your fears and confess them to the Lord.)

Endnotes

1. For those unfamiliar with this game, a three-legged race is a common activity at picnics and other outdoor events of a light-hearted nature. Two people make a team. Both individuals put one leg into a sack, which is fastened shut. Each has one leg free. The object is to run, hobble or otherwise be the first over the finish line. The quicker a team is able to

adjust to each other's gait and develop a smooth rhythm, the faster they can move. Many move awkwardly or trip and fall.

2. *'Ohana* is the Hawaiian word for "family."

CHAPTER 8

Parenting a Highly Sensitive Child

Train a child in the way he should go, and when he is old he will not turn from it (Proverbs 22:6).

My circuits used to sizzle when I needed the family to hustle, get dressed and ready for whatever, and they acted as if they had all the time in the world. When I needed them in the car in about five minutes, I would put the "head 'em up, and move 'em out" tone in my voice. One time was making one last pass through the house to make sure no one remained behind, and found Michelle and her tender heart collapsed in her room. One sock and shoe on, the other sock half on and the shoe over by the bed. Her nose was running and her tears had made a big wet spot on her knee. "Honey, what's the matter? We need to go!" She could not or would not answer; she just shook her head.

I did not have time for the 20 Questions Game so I put on her sock and shoe and carried her to the car, belted her in, and drove off. She often dissolved into tears, even when playing with her friends. Half the time I never figured out what brought on the tears. It was hard to know what would set her off—many times I had to treat her with kid gloves. After a while it became tiring. It was not that I did not care, it just happened too often and at the most inconvenient times.

And it drove me to distraction when my child insisted upon playing with the pugnacious, smelly, foul mouthed, unkempt street child down the block because "Johnny doesn't have anyone to play with. His mommy died and his daddy doesn't take time to play with him. His Dad comes home from work and sits around drinking beer and yelling at Johnny. That's all he does!" I knew if I forbade her to invite Johnny over to play, it would galvanize her desire to do so. Forbidding the friendship would force the issue, and "Sunshine" would become Johnny's champion! I wanted to help the child, but at the same time, I did not want my child to pick up Johnny's ways. I wanted to preserve her angelic qualities for as long as I could! Aaargh!

And I always found it difficult to have a godly response when my gentle, loving child, possessed with an appropriate vocabulary, came home acting, walking, and talking like the one child in her class I "knew" would be sent to reform school?! Such a foul mouth in such a small child! The way she relates to her mother made me want to reprimand not only her, but her mother as well for allowing it.

Then there was the time when I spent the day washing the outside windows, climbing up and down the ladder until every muscle and bone in my body was shrieking at me that it was time for a hot bath and bed. Mind you, it was a ranch style home, not at big two-story, but still, all I wanted was bed. Then I heard deep, heaving sobs coming from my child's room. I went to comfort. She told a tale of woe about being rude to her daddy, slamming a door, and hurting Daddy's feelings. For the life of me I had no idea what she was talking about. I called Dad, maybe he would know. No. Nothing happened that hurt his feelings. When I told her, "Honey, you didn't do anything to hurt daddy," she was overwhelmed with a new wave of grief. Nothing I said helped. Everything I said made it worse—now she was convinced that I was not telling the truth. At the end of my rope, I said, "Look, it's OK. There is nothing to cry about. Daddy is not hurt. Now, dry your tears and go to sleep." Maybe you can relate a similar story?

A few years later, our budding teen took up the cause of yet another group of down-and-outers destined for detention. "But Mom! They should be able to publish their alternative school paper. At least they should be able to have an editorial column that really expresses an opinion. The teachers censor everything! You can't publish any opinion that differs from the administrative line. My friends have a right to their own opinion, and the principle should not be able to tell everyone what they can or cannot think and do! It's not right! Dad always says we have the right to express our feelings, hurt, or disagreement. That's all they want to do!"

"Well, yes, but with respect. Did they appeal to authority, or flip authority off?"

"But that's just it! The principle isn't respecting them or their rights!"

The Scripture flashed into mind, "In as much as you have done it to one of the least of these, you have done it to me." Suddenly I had a headache. Why? Because my child was immersed in another defense of "the least of these." How does she find all these hurting kids? Why defend the underdog so fiercely? Ah, well, she is like her father—doing what she sees her father do. You silently turn to God and groan, "Oh God. How do I deal with this! This child you gave me!"

One part of your head tells you that this push and pull is the nature of all teens, potential burden bearers or not, to question, test and sort through parental values and in so doing make them their own or reject or change them. The other part of your head reminds you that someone said children are God's little spies. They put their podgy little fingers on every flaw in our character. Highly sensitive children seem to have uncanny, unerring accuracy! Why is that?

Viewing Sensitivity

We all want our children to be sensitive—to each other, and certainly toward us as parents. You do want them to be sensitive toward rejected or bullied children; you value that. On the other hand, when you struggle with performance orientation and parental inversion you will probably want to shut down their sensitivity when it inconveniences or embarrasses you. Inconvenient and embarrassing expressions of high sensitivity require time and parental commitment. You value helping the motherless child—as long as he does not track dirt on your clean floor or sit on the new sofa with his filthy jeans. You value someone befriending Salty Sally who is friendless, but you do not want to make the time commitment required to love such a wild child to life, nor do you want your child to be negatively affected by association.

We value someone coming alongside teens trying to find their way without tough, loving adult guidance. However, we fear our own budding teen will not be strong enough to lift the whole group up, and will sink to their level. We value the sensitivity of our little wailing angel and are glad that she is concerned about her father's feelings—just not nooow! Right now, when we feel half-dead, sensitivity is a problem. We are too tired to deal with it so, "Don't be that way!" Again, let me state clearly that our own struggles with performance orientation and parental inversion will intensify these feelings and reactions. Our tiredness level will also affect the amount of grace we have available at any given time. Regardless, of your struggle, shutting down a child's emotions teaches the child the wrong thing.

Sometimes we have no solutions to our children's dilemmas. Sometimes we do not even understand the problem. The pain of helplessness combined with the pain in the child is often more than we can bear. We do what we have learned to do to make pain go away. By our reactions, we tell them, "You can be sensitive, but when it causes me a problem, you are too sensitive, so shut it off!" Alternatively, when we ask them what is bothering them and they tell us, impatient reactions quickly let them know that we cannot or do not wish to bear their pain. We teach them to find a little compartment in which to stuff it. These kinds of subtle, or not so subtle, double messages teach children not to trust themselves, or us, and by inference, God.

Importance of Family

Within the protection of a safe, healthy marriage, (not necessarily perfect) a child learns how to trust, and take risks in ways that build self-confidence, strength of character, and self-esteem. With these qualities, a child will be much more able to respond in a healthy way to empathetic information originating from outside of self. These qualities will make it less likely that he will "lose himself" when filled up with someone else's troubles. He is less likely to be confused about his own identity. Spiritually aware parents who are also knowledgeable concerning how high sensitivity affects a child can equip the child even further with prayerful responses, thus helping the child grow into burden bearing naturally and rightly.

Recognizing a Highly Sensitive Child[1]

How do you know when your child is highly sensitive and when the child is just marking your character flaws with peanut butter and jelly? You may not be able to tell right away, but as you study your children, the Lord makes it clear. In the meantime, you can modify your parenting so to avoid many of the hurtful behaviors outlined in Chapter 3, Life Goes Awry.

Recognizing a child as highly sensitive and potentially a burden bearer can be one of the greatest gifts you give him or her. Recognition is the first step on the path to raising a spiritually and emotionally healthy child. The following inventory may help you determine if your child is highly sensitive: (The more checks you mark, the higher the probability the child is highly sensitive.)

Characteristics of a spiritually highly sensitive child:

1._____Cries, or tries to intervene or comfort when another child is hurt or tormented.

2._____Needs "alone" time away from stimulation, noise, activity.

3._____Sometimes asks pointed questions about things that make adults nervous.

4._____Has a vivid imagination. Sometimes needs help in sorting physical reality and spiritual reality.

5._____Has visions, sees angels.

6._____Attuned to family needs and moves to help by helping with chores, or passively by not expressing needs.

7._____Attuned to and affected by others' moods.

8._____Overwhelmed by too many people, lights, noise, etc.

9._____Has times of excessive emotion—responses seem extreme whether it be grief, anger, sadness, or tears over physical hurts.

10._____Has times of uncharacteristic behavior, when he/she does not act like himself.

11._____Tender feelings, easily hurt.

12._____Appears shy and quiet.

13._____Vulnerable to sadness or depression.

14._____Drawn to strong personalities or weak personalities.

15._____Drawn to help in situations where there is intense inner turmoil and trouble.

16._____Is a chameleon. The child comes home acting like the last child he/she played with. She is belligerent or whiney, swears, kicks, and hits—acting out the behaviors characteristic of the playmate, but not characteristic of herself on a daily basis.

17._____Is spacey—doesn't hear when spoken to, forgets, may walk around oblivious to the rest of the world, seems absorbed in own thoughts—off in another world.

18._____Is often used as a scapegoat.

Some extremely sensitive children may:

19._____See things adults cannot see such as the inner state of another.

20._____Know or sense things ahead of time, such as when Grandma is coming, or that the neighbor child is going to fall out of a tree.

You have observed that even infants are able to respond to the emotional climate about them. Burden bearing is not a child's job, but children do what comes naturally. Their sensitive little spirits sense trouble and reach out to help make it better. It is your job as parent to recognize what is appropriate for children at each stage of life, to provide understanding and training, and, as much as possible, make children's boundaries clear so they learn not to take on too much or carry burdens too long. You want to delineate children's emotional responsibilities from yours so that they do not assume your responsibilities. This is where sorting becomes important. By sorting out the boundaries and responsibilities before confusion sets in, you create a solid foundation upon which children can build later.

Rob, a father of two, spoke to his 18-month-old son instructing him not to take on responsibility for the argument he just had with his wife. He explained that it was his responsibility because he was "Dad" and dads take care of problems because they love their families. He could feel his son relax in his arms. Of course his son's brain was not yet capable of understanding, but a child's spirit seems to sense and know things even before the brain, or the conscious mind, is developed.

Strength of character, self-esteem, and self-confidence give a child a solid foundation to build upon as he learns to define his own boundaries and develops discernment as he moves into the stage of initiative, interacting with other children, and beyond. Making it clear to a child where he stops and someone else starts, and who is responsible for what, helps a child define his own sense of self. Knowing who you are is essential to keeping your balance and your bearings in burden bearing.

Remember my theory about what happened in the Garden of Eden? It was important to satan to separate you from your knowledge of who you are (child of the King—one who inherits) and why you were created (for relationship). He knew that *if* you fully develop your ability to read the heart of God; you would be unable to sin because you could feel what sin does to God. God designed humankind for relationship, with capacity for empathy. Empathy is what connects you to the heart of God, and sensitivity is integral to that connection. You are born with "enough" sensitivity—enough to relate to God and others—enough for relationship. It is in relationship with family, or those who raise you, that your sensitivity is either honed or dulled.

Recall the parable of the talents in Matthew chapter 25. The first servant received five talents, the next two, and the last received one. From this, you see clearly that some receive more than others—different portions. It is a neutral fact, neither positive nor negative, and applies not only to sensitivity, but to all traits in general. Parents, you are to help your children develop their potential fully, whatever that may be. You can do one of two things: you can teach and train your children to be "all they can be," and teach them to use their talents to accrue the riches of relationship that come with that measure of sensitivity. Or, by negative reactions to their sensitivity, you can dull or warp whatever capacity they have by training them to fear and distrust. Thus, they become less than they can be.

In light of how high sensitivity amplifies and intensifies everything, how are you to approach parenting? You can assume all children are highly sensitive and potentially untrained burden bearers. Then you will be attentive and able to tailor your responses to each child's needs. That way, whether a child is a five, two, or one-talent kid, you will respond in ways that will hone and develop the capacity, rather than dull it.

Before going any further, I want to relieve anyone who may have the notion that I am advocating that parents take all their cues from the child in such a way that the child runs the show. Nothing could be further from my heart and mind. Parents must always be parents, providing loving nurture, guidance, training, boundaries, and discipline, with one ear attuned to the heart of the child and the other to the heart of God.

Common Parenting Task

"Train up a child in the way he should go and when he is old he will not depart from it" (Proverbs 22:6). This verse has been interpreted as meaning that Christian parents should know the way a child is to be raised so that he will keep the faith throughout his life time—a "one size fits all" approach. It would be more accurately rendered from the Hebrew as, "Educate and train a child according to the way God designed *him* to be, and when he is old he will not stray from it." You are to make sure the child is educated and trained. If a child grows up knowing who he is, of course he will remain true to himself when he is old—he knows how!

This is *the* parenting task in a nutshell, true for parenting any child. We are to listen to the Lord and listen to the child, and reveal to the child the path the Lord designed for him to walk. It is the parent's task to educate him, and to equip him to go that way, to learn to be himself by means of modeling and instruction. If you cannot do the job yourself, your responsibility is to find someone who can teach, model, mentor your child in the area you are not equipped to do so. The overall responsibility for parenting remains yours—you do not turn over the task of parenting to someone else. For a highly sensitive child, part of the modeling and instruction will also relate to burden bearing, so that the child learns to bear burdens to the Cross, rather than wound or destroy himself and others by wearing them.

When raising a highly sensitive child, the parenting task does not change. It does take on added emotional intensity, and has the additional task of teaching and training the child to bear burdens in a manner the Lord desires.

The added dimension of intensity and the additional task of teaching and training how to bear burdens properly are unique in raising a highly sensitive child—but that is a lot!

How do you accomplish the common parenting task?

By watching and listening...

You must become students of your children. You must prayerfully listen to the heart, and watch relationships and interactions to discover the way for each child to live life. Look for the design the Lord built into the child by which the child will accomplish those good works the Lord had in mind for him to do from the beginning (Eph. 2:10).

By giving your blessing...

You bless your children by giving abundant appropriate touches, by telling them the truth about themselves and their value to you and to God. You bless them by speaking abundant words of love, encouragement, and affirmation, and by giving them word pictures of a positive future. It is not that you do not see weak areas in their lives, but rather that you focus on the good and come alongside to strengthen the weak areas. You do not focus on the weak points and deride them for weaknesses to the neglect of the strong areas. You bless them by providing for physical, emotional, and spiritual needs. A blessed child will be able to trust, risk, and venture in life. A blessed child has strength of character and a sense of identity. He knows who he is. (For an in-depth discussion of parental blessing, see *The Blessing* by Gary Smalley and John Trent.[2])

By teaching and modeling...

In Bible times, a child learned the parent's craft or business by working alongside. When and where that is still possible, it is best because of the bonding and the modeling that happens between the two. When a parent cannot instruct a child because the child shows an obvious interest in areas outside the parent's expertise, the parent's task is to find someone who can! This models for a child that being "me" does not have to look like the parent—it is OK to be unique. If a father is a fisherman, but the son wants to be a carpenter, find the son a shipbuilder with whom to apprentice! It is the parent's responsibility to release a budding engineer to develop, and not insist he be a professional football player. If a boy is an artist and the father a mechanic, the father may be unable to teach the child how to be an artist, so he must provide proper instruction. He can still teach his son to fix his own car! The son's wife will bless him later on! When the father blesses his child with art lessons and does not insist he become a professional mechanic, his child's heart can remain open. In gratitude for freedom to walk his own path, he can *choose* to spend time with his father under the hood. Often when not so blessed, a child is tempted to close his heart toward his father, and is tempted to view him as cold and unloving by pushing him to be what he is not.

A mother, who is a professional, at a loss in a kitchen, may find herself with a daughter who is a gourmet cook. Applaud your children and cherish their uniqueness. I heard of one man who wanted to go into the ministry, but whose father, a businessman, insisted that he obtain a college education before attending seminary. At the time, the young man resented his father, but later on saw his father's wisdom and was grateful. Sometimes you may see a preliminary step a child should take before launching upon "his way" because it strengthens character and builds a solid foundation, essential components of properly equipping a child to follow the design the Lord built into him.

Sometimes the Lord reveals the way of a child in a moment, a flash of insight, an epiphany, or sometimes slowly over time. At the age of five our oldest daughter was walking around the house singing from a New Testament she carried. In a moment, the Lord opened my ears to hear the music He heard. It was mature, with depth, and I "knew" in that moment that He was saying that it was through music that this child would find her way. We immediately began searching for a piano instructor. Meilee now has a career in sales. Did I miss something? No. Through the discipline of music, she learned how to persevere, to push through difficult places. Whatever else she learned; God wanted that built into her character. Playing piano has now become one of the ways she releases tensions and burdens, and finds nurture and refreshment for her spirit.

Our second daughter's way was a mystery to us. She played soccer and injured her knee, was on the drill team, in the band, and then a cheerleader. She became a lifeguard. We helped her in all these things, always asking the Lord what this had to do with His design for her. We never saw or heard anything, so we kept persevering with her. Toward the end of her secondary education, we began to see her moving into a role of "soft" leadership. Because of her sensitivity, she intuitively knew how the other girls felt; she became both a mediator and leader among the cheerleaders. We saw strength of character and a willingness to take risks—but always that sensitivity to others. Now? She has a career in the military—a place where being able to see and sense the heart and intent of others is essential to avoid being hooked by superficial behaviors. Certainly a place for the Light!

I know a woman whose daughter is not sure what she wants to be when she grows up so she is trying everything! So far, she has had cooking lessons and French lessons from Mom and Dad. From outside instructors, she has received sewing lessons, horseback-riding lessons, and skating lessons. One of these days that child will find, by process of elimination, her calling in the natural, what it is that the Lord designed for her to do. Her calling in the natural and burden bearing, will together become the process by which the Lord builds the character of Christ into her. When she finds her way, she will experience feeling, "Ah, for this I was born," and pursue it with passion. She knows she can learn; she knows how to risk, how to fall, and how to fail—but she also has the experience of parents helping her pick up the pieces, learn, and move on. As her relationship with the Lord matures, she will have the same expectations of God.

In addition to helping a child discover her calling in the natural, (such as doctor, teacher, lawyer, merchant, Mom, businessperson, etc.), our task is also to help a child discover their spiritual giftings, and teach her how these become heart motivations—prophesying, serving, teaching, encouraging, contributing, leading, showing mercy. Include a look at the pastorate, music ministry, intercession, or mission work as possible occupations, which allow for the full use of natural gifting as well as spiritual. (See Romans 12:6-8.)

Spiritual gifting should fit with the occupation or profession in the natural. If one precludes the other, the result is frustration, unhappiness, and stress. Regardless of the secular work focus or spiritual focus, those who have a burden bearing or highly sensitive personality will discharge the burden-bearing function of their being within the context of those other callings. This appreciation of the uniqueness of a child, and training and equipping the child to be all she can be—that is the parenting task common to all.

Parenting Challenges

Highly sensitive children, of necessity, must learn all the developmental tasks other children must learn. They will need to go through the process of discovery of interests that may develop into occupations or professions. However, in the normal process of growing up they may respond more subtly, requiring closer attention to nuances in mood.

Over-the-Top Emotion

Keep heightened sensitivities in mind. In the busyness of life you can inadvertently run roughshod over a tender violet. You do not treat crude pottery and fine china the same. Some children can take the rugged treatment a pottery vessel can, but some are fine china, or fine crystal that requires delicate touches. What seems to be blatantly obvious to the highly sensitive may not be to others. To a child's way of thinking you, the parent, should know...and of course, when you do not or when you forget and treat them like everyone else, they feel wounded and hurt.

Take the previous example of the little boy who could not dress, who was hurt by the call to "hurry up." You may think that a bit much, but these little ones have not been able to build defenses. They have not developed the ability to sort out how much of the parent's urgency was aimed at them personally, and how much was for the rest of the family. You need to help them do that. You need to remember, as much as possible, to modulate your tone, or go to them with a warning or an explanation before you yell at them or anyone else. This will be one of the tasks of sorting out that I explain later. As you spend time with them, sorting these things out, eventually they will be able to do that for themselves.

Your time investment builds a strong foundation of love. They will learn who you are with them, and when you act in a different way, they will not be confused and think they caused the change. They will know within themselves who you the parent is, and not mistake the shout to the general family as a personal rebuke.

Exaggeration and over-reaction is a reflection of the force of the impact the environment has upon a child—whether that be their own inner environment or their outer environment. It also reveals the need for continued help in learning to control emotions, so life does not continue in chaos. Highly sensitive children more quickly reach the point of being overwhelmed, especially if he already has a backlog of emotional, spiritual, psychological baggage. Such children need lots of assurances and reassurances.

Providing Boundaries

A highly sensitive child may need more holding and reassurance than others when emotions overwhelm, so she can feel your boundaries creating banks for her own emotions. First, talk about the feelings, and associate the feelings with words, so she knows precisely what she is feeling. Then, establish what belongs to whom. Assure and reassure her that she is OK and loved. When a child has been the cause of the problem or is in the wrong, deal with the problem and the consequences, but clearly state that doing a wrong thing does not mean she is a bad person, and say it repeatedly. Your strength is like a levy.

By modeling boundaries, you teach a child not to fear feelings, but rather to let them pass through and inform. In time he will come to know that his emotions are neither bigger nor more powerful than he is. As you hold a child, as you talk through the feelings, bringing emotions under control, a child learns how to return to calm. The ability to find the way back to a calm state is key to good mental health.[3]

On his own, a child's emotions can become so big they crowd out logic. The brain literally shuts down the thinking portions of the brain and puts all energies into "fight-flight" responses. Such a child cannot reason. He is flooded, overwhelmed. Trying to talk and reason is a formula for futility! During these times, as much as you would like to use logic and reason with your children rather than be physical with them, the quickest way to diffuse the situation may be to physically remove them from their trouble spot and provide safe boundaries until reason can return. The sequence should be to comfort and calm, then teach.

Provide perspective, corral, harness, and give direction and purpose to the emotion. Give direction in what to do with emotions—bring emotions down below the panic mark, and then bring them to Jesus. After calming and prayer, you can help look with more logic and reason at whatever else may be appropriate. This takes the confusion and tyranny out of emotions. A key to learning is that emotions can inform, but need not be allowed to control. As you provide boundaries, banks, stopping places, and prayer, the child experiences relief and he learns that he can come to you. As you help him sort things out, he learns in time that he can come to the Lord in the same way. He will come to know that he can gain perspective, direction, and relief with the Lord. Praying releases the burdens so that the child does not carry weight unnecessarily, or be hurt by inappropriate burden bearing. Of course, answered prayers are always great faith builders!

Perceived Hurt

Highly sensitive children may be more vulnerable to perceived hurt—they may read a slight where none was intended, and withdraw in hurt, or react in anger. If you do not address the hurt and correct the misperception and the response it elicited, such children can come to erroneous, albeit bitter, conclusions.

Joey collapses in a heap in his room, weeping, but no one knows about what. Big brother Kevin hears the weeping and comes to help Joey. Joey does not know that Kevin is angry about an issue that has nothing to do with him. Preoccupied with his own trouble, Kevin *tries* to listen, but Joey notices the distraction, senses the anger, and assumes Kevin is angry that he has to listen to his story. His perception of the situation results in an inaccurate conclusion that hurts Joey further.

A highly sensitive child can be tempted to come to the conclusion that what he has to say is unimportant, which means he is unimportant, that he has less value than others in the family. You can see how self-talk can evolve. Most of us have experienced something similar.

Upon seeing his child in a precarious position in a tree, a parent may call out a child's name with urgency and command, "Come down immediately!" But the child senses anger and disgust, in spite of the parent's efforts to use a tone of voice that expresses fear and concern. He may feel crushed and humiliated in front of friends.

A child walks into a room just as a group of adults burst into laughter. She assumes they are laughing at her. A beloved uncle takes several boy cousins fishing, but leaves a girl behind. She concludes that boys are more valued than girls are. It is the perception of something and reacting to the interpretation of that perception that causes the hurt.

The parent whose child was in the tree feared his child would break a limb. But the child did not hear the fear, or the love behind it. He heard a harsh public reprimand. For healing, the father would need to acknowledge his child's perception, and ask forgiveness for humiliating him in front of his friends. Then, after calm had returned, the parent could share the fear he had that his child would fall. In the moment of fear, neither can entertain the other's perceptions, but when calm returns, they can.

Responding to Perceived Hurt

The adults in the example were laughing over a story one of them told. The timing of the child's entrance was coincidental, but she felt crushed by what the burst of laugher *meant to her*. For healing, the adults needed to apologize for hurting her, and then share the story so she could laugh as well (provided the story was appropriate for young ears!) To try to persuade her not to be hurt because that was not their intention will not heal. The apology acknowledges the hurt; the explanation opens the door to a different perception. It does not matter that the perception was erroneous. Hurts need at first to be treated as real. There is time enough, after hearts are healed, to answer mental questions of fact or fiction.

The uncle who left his niece behind did so out of love and concern for her health. He heard she was sleeping and assumed she was not well. It was not a matter of choosing others over her, but the hurt was still real and deep. The uncle could bring healing by asking forgiveness for not checking to see if she wanted to go, and then arrange another outing, making sure she was included. The second outing goes beyond healing to restoration of relationships.

Recall the example of the girl who felt she hurt her father's feelings. Her parents never did convince her that she did nothing wrong. If the father had simply forgiven her, that would have calmed her heart and spirit. As it was, she felt her parents tried to talk her out of her reality. Forgiveness would have acknowledged the hurt of her perception, then after loving reassurance, logic and reason could have brought assurance and understanding. When calm, a child is more able to hear and believe what a parent says.

To calm the storms caused by perceived hurt, acknowledge a child's perceptions, and act in a way that calms the turmoil and addresses the hurt. Step into his reality and gently bring him out. He has lost his way in the hurt and emotion. Learn to deal with your child's view of reality first, by treating those feelings as reality—for they are the reality the child is struggling with. Actual reality can safely be acknowledged only after the child's reality is settled. You do not need to say the child's reality is accurate because in some cases, it clearly is not, but the child is hurt nonetheless. After you address the hurt you can try to correct the perception, but often that is not even necessary.

Step into your child's reality, meet the perceived need there, provide reassurance, and let reason return before trying to bring the child into what you perceive as reality.

Performance Orientation

It may not be possible to prevent your children from developing some measure of performance orientation, but if there are things you can do and say that would mitigate the severity of the orientation, it behooves you to search them out, and implement them as much as possible. At times, you can see clearly how your words and actions contribute to the development of performance orientation; but at other times, it is difficult, especially when you struggle with it yourself.

Highly sensitive children are vulnerable to becoming performance oriented, because they can sense what is needed in the family, they know how and what to do to reduce stress and meet needs. Believing they must perform to earn love and acceptance, they quickly learn that they have value only when they produce. Appreciation of their performance confirms their belief.

As much as possible you need to take care to speak in ways that do not tie performance to value.

I was with a young couple and their toddler. When he would accomplish something—like successfully eating a spoonful of spaghetti without spilling half of it on the way to his mouth—they would say, "Good boy!" Then the time came when he acted up and his father removed him from the restaurant. In the car, he tearfully asked for reassurance. "I a good boy! I a good boy!" Both parents reassured him, but I saw that he was already making the connection between his performance and his worth and acceptability. I shared the understanding with the mother later, and she immediately started working on new habits of unconditional love and assurance.

Stepping Up

Some children are so sensitive they see needs within the family and are vulnerable to becoming parentally inverted[4]— stepping into a care-taking role just because they see a need, and believe they are responsible to do something about it. It may not be possible to prevent a child from taking on such a role, but you can watch, and take notice when you see a child stepping up to fill a gap. As much as possible encourage such children to also play and take time for themselves, so they do not surrender their childhood.

Sally was one who stepped into the gap. She was a very sensitive child, and as the eldest of several, she saw the family's emotional needs, sensed that neither parent was up to the task, and stepped forward. Father was emotionally absent due to the nature of his work, and when he was home, he was unavailable because of alcohol. Mother was emotionally absent because she had to work to make ends meet when the husband was gone. She also was emotionally unavailable when her husband was home because of the anger she held toward him about his alcohol consumption.

Sally felt her mother's hurt and anger and sensed that it filled her whole vision. Mother was so wrapped up in her own hurt that she could not see anyone else's needs. Sally felt her siblings' physical and emotional needs, and stepped into the gap. She became a second mother to her siblings, and a very responsible, dependable worker, working hard all her life. There was no room left for her to have needs or wants. She pushed away her own feelings, her own needs and wants, and cared for her family. She developed into a very angry adult. She was angry because of all she did not receive and because of all she did with no appreciation from Mom and Dad. She was angry because she felt forced to sacrifice her childhood. She was angry because no one saw what was happening, and no one helped.

She paid a horrific price for the lack of nurture and parenting. She spent years of her life carrying the burdens of her family in her own strength. When she moved into the workplace, she wore the burdens she sensed in the people she worked with. The load was becoming very heavy. She was angry and unfulfilled because she did not know who she was, or the way the Lord had designed her to be. She was especially angry with God because He never seemed to hear, or respond to her prayers. How could she help but stray from a path she did not know?

After years of work to heal the wounds from growing up in her family, she was able to move into her destiny as an intercessor and learned how to pass burdens on to Jesus. She wrapped so much of her identity in work, and what she could do for others, that when the Lord called her into the quiet life of an intercessor, it felt "wrong." It was difficult for her to justify this contemplative lifestyle with no paycheck to measure her worth. With patience, practice, and much grace, she "found her way" and the Kingdom of God is blessed by her intercessions, as are those individuals whom the Lord puts in her path.

Younger children may feel abandoned when an older sibling, actually a substitute parent figure, leaves home. Their presence cuts a wide swath; hence, their absence leaves a big hole. Some children take on a parental role so completely they become a substitute mate—having the role of parent in every way except the bed, which leads to difficulties for them later on in life.

I heard John Sandford tell the story about when many years after he and his younger sister and brother had all grown up and left the house, both the sister and the brother shocked him one day by saying identical words, "Did you know I was angry at you?"

"No, why?"

"You were my father, and you left me."

Stunned, John thought, *How did I get into that position?*

David and I have ministered to sons who felt their mother's pain when their father neglected his role as husband. We have ministered to daughters who became "the little woman," keeping house and caring for the family's needs after a mother's death. When a son or daughter begins to meet the parent's emotional needs, it robs the child of his or her childhood, and sets up problems in marriage later on.

Stepping Back

The child who steps up often has a strong and stabilizing influence or affect on the family; family members turn to that child often. Other highly sensitive children help stressful family circumstances by fading into the background. They see their parents as over busy, coping with family and finances, or other difficulties, so they volunteer not to add to the family load. They choose to have only minimum needs, but undertake the maximum to help meet family needs and draw off emotional overloads.

These children may appear very shy, timid because they choose to live in the shadows and contribute without fanfare. They quietly go about nurturing and caring for younger siblings, or find jobs to contribute to the family coffers. Actually, they may be neither shy nor timid, but one must persevere to find who this one really is. Parents must watch for this behavior, and do what they can to include such children, and make an effort to round out their tendency toward self-sacrifice— to make sure they do not sacrifice too much.

The Chameleon

As children grow older, during early childhood and school age, they will interact with other children. Sensitive children especially reflect the emotion(s) of those around them.

My husband and I could always sense which neighborhood child our youngest, Michelle, had played with. When she came home, she "was" that child. She talked and acted like that child, even to the voice tone and inflection. If we did nothing, she returned to her own nature within half an hour. She was a chameleon. She absorbed her friend's feelings and discharged them by acting them out at our house. She was not yet able to keep her own self separate from that of her friend. She did not know how to maintain the boundary between herself and her friend. She did not know where she stopped and where her friend began. She had not yet learned who she was, and what her own feelings felt like, as opposed to someone else's. She did not yet have the strength to maintain her sense of herself as separate in another child's presence.

Acting Out

When a child absorbs emotional, spiritual, and psychological trouble, turmoil, and confusion, but does not realize it and does not know how to discharge it, such a child can and will act in ways that appear inappropriate. The emotions may be more intense than warranted, exaggerated, more than the child's normal self.

For example, when a child comes home wearing the anger of a friend and strikes out at the parent or acts disrespectfully—if the parent is unaware of burden-bearing dynamics and responds only to the behavior, the child's confusion increases. You should not ignore the behavior, but address it within the context of sorting out.

Some hurtful reactions parents and siblings commonly have to such "excessive" behavioral displays are:

• **Name calling**—"Don't be a cry-baby," "That's a stupid thing to say/do," "You're acting weird," "Don't be a brat," etc.

• **Shutting down emotions and minimizing**—"Well, it's not that bad!" "Come on, dry up!" "Grow up!" "Don't bring that attitude into this house!" "I can't deal with that right now!"

• **Dismissing** the child without listening, rolling the eyes, sighing as if, "here we go again."

These reactions teach a child to ignore what she is feeling, to hide emotions, rather than process them, and as a result, she may arrive at conclusions about self, life, and God that actually prevent her from becoming the person the Lord designed her to be. She learns an incorrect or false picture of herself—that she has little or nothing to offer, that she and her feelings are stupid and a bother. Put downs are very damaging because they paint a negative word picture of the child and her future. If you do not bless, you curse, "You will never amount to anything. You are going to have to have thicker skin than that! You won't go anywhere in life being that sensitive." When the child hears these kinds of things, the child is prevented from becoming herself. How can she not stray from her way when she is older if she has never learned it is acceptable to be herself!

Laminated Behaviors

With a few simple but repeated words, parents can laminate onto their children the very behavior they find troublesome. "How many times do I have to tell you to...?" "You always...." "I should have known it would be Joe that...." When he hears the words, "Oh, that's just Joey!" he is confused, because innate knowing tells him that the laminated behavior is "not me," so he feels missed and misunderstood. Or, he may decide that the parent is right and he is wrong, that the troublesome behavior really is his own. He learns to distrust his perceptions of himself. This laminated behavior then becomes a barrier between parent and child, making it far more difficult to hear the child's heart and educate him in the way he should go.

Response to Correction

A tender, quiet, more introverted child senses what his or her parents want, learns quickly, and requires little correction. His tender little spirit responds to a look, a word, or a gesture. A less sensitive child needs more parameters and reminders, physical removal from temptation, needs a "time out," or a disputed toy removed.

Sometimes high sensitivity is more difficult to see when a child is extroverted. An extroverted child does not gravitate to the shadows, but chooses the center of activity. Rather than becoming the victim, he will choose to confront or manipulate problem people into calmness. Extroverted children do not hesitate to challenge a parent. They can zero in on what you value and accuse you of hypocrisy. You value honesty; they accuse you of not telling the truth. You value kindness, and they accuse you of not caring. You value honor and respect and they accuse you of not honoring or respecting them. They zero in on your sensitive spots with amazing accuracy.

As a teen, our eldest went nose to nose with her father, both of them extroverts, or so we thought. During these arguments, the youngest and I, both introverts, would retire to my bedroom, hold each other, and cry. One particular day, David won the battle, but later complained to God that Meilee had hurt him badly with her sarcasm. He clearly heard the Lord say, "And where do you think she learned it?" Meilee had an uncanny ability to sense what was important to him and accuse him of not being or doing that. In this case, David set a boundary because he loved and valued his daughter. He did not want her to be hurt. She turned it around and accused him of setting the boundary because he did not care about her, what she wanted or felt. The accusation hurt. Unerring accuracy in reading another can be a gift, but without grace, it wounds.

As an adult, Meilee saw an elderly lady sitting in the hotel lobby. She studied the lady for a moment, went to the break room and made tea. "Oh, how did you know?" Meilee didn't know how she knew; she just knew what was needed. The woman was distressed, alone in a strange city, waiting for family to arrive. Meilee was able to come alongside, to listen to her series of unfortunate events while praying silently within. The woman's stress level was lowered with prayer, kindness, and a cup of tea. She was no longer alone. This time, unerring accuracy in reading another had grace, and blessed a distressed woman.

High sensitivity overlays and modifies extroversion somewhat, so the child may simply appear to be strong willed. It is easy to miss that an extrovert child is highly sensitive and not treat that one as gently as you would a quieter child, thereby causing unintended hurt. A highly sensitive extroverted child also needs all the things introverted children need. He also needs recovery time, and the means to replenish energies, but how he goes about it may look and sound much different from the introvert. He will also be quick to see need, and solutions. He is very intuitive and creative, attuned to friends and family.

I did not realize our eldest was a burden bearer until after high school when she began to work. She related instances when she "knew things" about co-workers; experiences of "reading" someone's spirit, and responding in ways that were "perfect" and "how could you know!" The more I heard, the more I was sure she was a burden bearer, so I began to teach her so that burdens would not accumulate and weigh her down.

Then, I looked back over her childhood and could see the telltale signs, but because of her outgoing nature, I had never realized the significance. She taught herself to read somewhere around age three or four. She was always highly creative and enjoyed her quiet time. Her first grade teacher intended to retire at the end of the year and had already disconnected emotionally; she did not have the energy to reign in rowdy children, so the room was very noisy. Each day Meilee came home and went to her room without a word. After 45 minutes, she came out and joined the family. She needed quiet time to let all the other children's emotions dissipate so she could "be herself." She was, in fact, a highly social introvert. She renewed her energies in the quiet, arts, and books rather than activity. Parents, look for those telltale signs of needing time alone, high creativity, and uncanny accuracy in reading people.

Discipline and correction for a highly sensitive extrovert child is much more challenging and requires the wisdom of Solomon and the patience of Job! Parenting a highly sensitive child can reveal your own issues—and derail the parenting. Vocal expressions of emotion can hook or bump into your own unhealed areas, causing you to perceive expressions of emotion as issues of respect, or challenges to your authority. Such expressions of emotion usually reflect how the child felt at the moment—but stated passionately! This child, more than the quiet one, will put his little finger in your character flaws and describe them with unnerving accuracy. Is being late, your downfall? Don't be surprised when little extroverted burden bearer standing with hands on hips, says with a great sense of indignation, "Dad, you should tell the truth! If you say you are going to pick me up at school, you should be there!"

Sorting Me from Thee

Sharing a child's troubles, comforting him, and crying with him over tragedies—troubles with friends or the death of a hamster—models emotions appropriate to the occasion. Crying with a child helps draw the sadness below the overwhelmed mark. By synchronizing with children's feelings, you can know exactly what they are experiencing and more easily give them the vocabulary they need to define their emotions. The label and the feeling must be associated, and then they must learn the boundaries of that emotion, and determine if it is theirs or their friend's. They must learn to gain the information of an emotion, but not allow it to rule them. Then they must learn what their responsibilities are in relation to what they feel.

Is this something to take to Jesus, or is something else required—like an apology for angry words? Is an apology *and* prayer required? Did I also offend God when I offended my brother? Why did I yell, and hit my brother? Was the anger I expressed actually absorbed from the neighbor child I was just playing with and has nothing to do with my brother?

A parent must sort his child out—this is you, this is your friend. This is how you and I talk, but that is how your friend and her mother talk. Your friend's family uses that kind of language, but we do not. You were feeling happy when you went to play, but now you have come home sad. Was your friend sad? What was happening in that home? Is that a sad home? Do you think that might be why she likes to come to our house? Maybe your friend and her mommy are having a sad time. Let's talk to Jesus about it, shall we? Let's ask Him to help your friend and her mommy.

In a way, sorting me from thee helps children know where their responsibilities lie. Not everything a child feels originates from him, but he may not know that. Even before birth, a child experiences what the mother feels, unfiltered, so he comes into the world not realizing he is separate from others. A child must learn that he has his own feelings, others have theirs, and there is a difference.

Sorting what he sees, or senses in the spirit, from what is physical reality, and what is pretend is a second distinction you need to help make. It is important not to minimize a child's report that a neighborhood friend is going to fall out of a tree by telling him to stop making up stories. Visions look a lot like reality—children need to know that. The Lord reveals what was to happen so your burden bearer in the making could call upon Him to prevent the accident. It is especially important to listen respectfully when a child is upset about what he sees or senses. Again, provide boundaries for emotions, listen to stories with respect, and pray aloud with your child.

A common occurrence at our house was to have Michelle, our youngest, come home very upset about what happened on the playground. She could not understand why bullies went out of their way to make people miserable. She could sense the bully's feelings and fear of rejection, but at the same time feel the hurt of the taunted child. It was more than she could bear, so she came running home. We heard her out, empathized, and then prayed for the child who was hurt and for the bully who did the hurting. Then we prayed for ourselves, asking the Lord to heal the bruises to our spirits for having to witness meanness. By the time we finished praying, she was once again herself.

At four years of age, the son of one of my friends began reporting seeing people in the back yard. My friend looked out the window but no one was there. Little Matt pointed to them—no one his mother could see! She asked for descriptions, which he gave her. What were they doing? He told her. They prayed together asking Jesus to send the people away if He did not invite them. The people remained. They did not frighten Matt, and seemed to be there in a way that was supportive. After further prayer, she concluded that he must see angels. Matt's mother did what Mary did, and "pondered all these things in her heart."

She did not tell Matt to stop telling stories, or that he did not know what he was talking about. She believed he was seeing something, and supported him. She made her own discernment available to him, and with her coaching, he developed a strong prophetic gift without the wounding that could have come if she had not believed and supported him. He grew into himself easily; he did not have to overcome insecurity and self-doubt.

Kathy was 2½ years of age when she began screaming at nothing, and developed powerful fears of monkeys in the closet. Her father spent hours playing Dungeons and Dragons. This child was very highly sensitive. Maria, her mother, called asking for wisdom, for what to do. We finally concluded that the spirit behind the game began to frighten and oppress Kathy. I said, "Don't tell her there is nothing to be afraid of. She is seeing something that frightens her. So, teach her who she is in Christ, and thereby empower her. First, tell the monkeys that this is a Jesus house and they cannot stay here. Then teach her that she is a Jesus girl and Jesus will make the monkeys go away. Model it for her, and then help her understand that she has the authority; she can tell them to go away."

Within several weeks, they cleared the house of monkeys. The last one she flushed down the toilet! This mother was alert to call for help. There was too much terror in the child's fear to be just a childish fear, and far too much to ignore. Now the fear has gone, and this child does not doubt herself because her mother did not! I believe that she will develop into who she is just as Matt did.

Modeling How to Bear Burdens

It is quite easy to flow from sorting a child's feelings from a friend's feelings to praying for that friend. I would sit and hold our daughter, and pray for her little friend, and her family. When we prayed this way and the girls felt lighter and quickly returned to their usual sunny dispositions, we knew they had worn their friends' burdens home.

Both of our girls commonly came home with someone else's troubles, often bringing the source of the trouble herself! They brought hurting children, sometimes as foul in language as smell, and presented them to us! They were all smiles and I was dumbfounded. Where did they find these children? Why did they bring them home? They intuitively knew that they, as children, did not have the resources, but they knew someone who did! They were burden bearing in a way that was appropriate to their age and understanding. They brought the burdens home with them and dumped them in our laps, as they later learned to bring burdens to the Lord and dump them in His!

I know now that by listening to these children's stories, plying them with muffins and chocolate chip cookies, and praying with them, their burdens came to and through me to Jesus. Back then, later that night, David and I would pray together for the children, and for our daughters that their spirits would be cleansed, their sleep peaceful, and their dreams sweet. We instinctively did the right thing, though we had not yet come to the full understandings of burden bearing that we now have. Many other parents do as well, only it helps to know, which is why I write this book.

Children learn from parents. A highly sensitive, burden-bearing parent must be aware of the example set in regard to the use of that sensitivity. One woman I know referred to her mother as a witch with eyes in the back of her head. She always knew what my friend was doing, seemed to sense every move my friend tried to make, and cut her off at the pass every time. This ability to sense what others feel did not help my friend learn anything, other than either to resist or fit into her mother's mold. Her mother did not use empathy to discover "the way" for her daughter. Rather, she used it to control, and denied her daughter proper experiences of emotions for her own learning. My friend dared not make a mistake. Finally, as she is approaching middle age, and far from her mother, she is coming into her own identity as a burden bearer.

Unredeemed Burden Bearing

Having a highly sensitive personality does not automatically mean a child will bear burdens rightly. The child may have the necessary equipment but be untrained. She is simply sensitive until she learns how to attend to what she sees, hears, and senses, and how to respond appropriately with prayer. Teach him how to be himself—a burden bearer, one who carries the hurts, confusions, and troubles of others, as well as his own to Jesus, to the Cross. If you do not teach a child her design, she will bear others' burdens regardless, because that is how she is built. However, she will do it inappropriately, in an unredeemed fashion. Her spirit will function according to design, absorbing trouble and turmoil, but she will wear it as her own instead of discharging it to the Lord.

In time, burden bearing wrongly will result in the types of wounding related in Chapter 3. Everyone loses when we do not teach and train a child who has burden-bearing potential. The child loses, and God, society, the church, and the family lose.

Highly sensitive children end up in all walks of life. Some become pastors, carpenters, engineers, nurses, mothers, doctors, mechanics, clerks, businesspeople…regardless of profession or occupation, burden bearing is a spiritual aspect of their "way." It is their road to travel. It is their design, and if they learn early on to do it rightly, when they are old, they will not stray from this way of responding to empathetic information. It will become part of how they interact with life, and will go with them always.

This sensitivity is also the fountain of creativity out of which arts and literature flow. This is the source of inspiration, and the creative leaps in the sciences. One can be a burden bearer and an artist, a teacher, scientist, mathematician, or whatever. It is "both—and" not "either—or."

Just as children have to be walked to walk on their own, and talked to, to talk, so also they need to be walked through the burden-bearing process—set down, talked with about what they see and sense, and then prayed with. Parents need to model for them how to distinguish between their own troubles and those of friends. They need to see you take these things to the Lord.

Challenges for Highly Sensitive Parents

Parents can unwittingly make life harder for a highly sensitive child when they are wounded burden bearers themselves. Consumed with their own load, parents may miss the heart of their child. Burden bearing can muddle their own thinking and discernment, which compromises parenting. Burdens build up when they cannot discharge them as quickly as they come. Parents become short on patience, nurture, or whatever else their child may need, because of subconscious pressures and energy drains. Lack of energy may flatten or paralyze their emotions, which can be interpreted as withdrawal or lack of care and interest, thus making the parenting mechanical, and wounding the children.

Carrying burdens inappropriately is exhausting. I found that a normal child's request felt like a demand. When the dog cried to be let outside, I reacted like it was a conspiracy to wear me out. I knew I was overburdened and in trouble. I needed to find quiet with the Lord to give Him whatever was crushing me, and to understand how I came to be in that overwhelmed place. During these times, I dipped into anger to find the adrenaline to do regular household chores. I found some little detail to challenge and become angry about to generate that extra shot of energy. The overwhelming load compromised my parenting. When I understood this, I learned ways to discharge my load and find rest, spiritually and physically. I did not value taking stripes off the people I loved.

Parents can be misguided when they respond to a child through the lens of burdens within themselves they have not discharged. For example, a parent who has absorbed sadness from a friend, but forgot to bring that to the Lord, could respond with uncharacteristic sad negativity. The negativity was a result of the burden of sadness the parent was wearing, but a highly sensitive child could easily assume she caused the sadness. Then the reasoning becomes, "If I cause sadness, I must be bad. There must be something wrong with me." Subconscious absorbed anger acted out upon a child also has devastating results.

Parental burden bearing can cause difficulties when a parent is so full of a child's emotions that his spiritual vision is clouded or distorted. Parents may be unable to discern what the Lord reveals about their child when so filled with the child's emotion. They may not see clearly the way the Lord is showing them for the child.

As parents, when your child's behavior brings your own bitter roots to the surface your perceptions can become skewed. Your bitter roots rise up, and you revert to old ways that can prevent you from being a buffer between your child and the bumps and scrapes and falls of life. (See Chapter 4.)

As well as being a buffer, the parental role includes being a mentor through whom instruction and modeling teaches the child how to live life as a burden bearer. When you find yourself behaving in ways you do not value, extricate yourself from the situation, and ask the Lord to shine His light to reveal any hidden roots that may be entangled with your child. The revelation of your own unhealed areas is one of the benefits of parenting a highly sensitive child! It may not feel like a benefit or blessing in the moment, but you can see it in retrospect.

Parenting is interfered with when a parent is insensitive to a child. When a parent does not take the time to find the source of the tears, anger, or lashing out, a child cannot find an emotional stopping place. Rather than learning the banks and boundaries for emotions, rather than taking the information and using discernment, the child learns to push the emotions away and put a lid on. Then, as adults, emotions come up in a ball, all tangled up, and these adults do not know what they feel, or how to sort out the different emotions. Consequently, it becomes difficult for them to make decisions or find direction.

When you withdraw or disconnect, a child feels it, and assumes the worst about himself. Parental burden bearing can result in emotional inconsistency on the parent's part, which reflects in the child as insecurity. This underscores the importance of spiritual hygiene and keeping very short accounts with the Lord.

Other times, parenting misses the mark because a parent does not recognize high sensitivity for what it is, does not know how to address it, or provide training for the burden-bearing potential of a child. Lack of love did not cause these problems; the problems resulted from a lack of knowledge of the needs of such children and how to meet them.

High Sensitivity—a Parenting Benefit

Sensitivity enables parents to empathize with their children. Empathy helps children feel met and heard. That goes a long way in healing everyday hurts. In meeting a child's heart, you give him the ingredients to create security and healthy self-esteem. If you do not have the high sensitivity of a natural burden bearer, you can ask the Lord to give you what you need to raise your children. The ability to empathize helps you read hearts, and not yield to temptations to respond to words. Empathy also enables you to sense subtle changes in mood that signal when the child has absorbed some emotional freight he does not know what to do with. It alerts you to come alongside and help discharge the newly acquired load. It enables you to be consciously attuned to your children and thus able to be in prayer so you understand what you see and sense. The Lord can lead you to see the paths He designed for your children to walk.

High sensitivity will also enable you to carry your children in the heart during the hard times of growing up, when there are relationship difficulties. Our eldest experienced the death of a classmate who died in a skiing accident. Those kinds of events can prove to be difficult, and a parent can draw off overwhelming portions so that a child can continue to function. However, parents can only do so much about the great challenges of teasing and peer pressure, the agony of competitions, the winning and losing. Your being able to feel the exhilaration of winning, and at the same time feel the agony of the child who lost helps your children.

Burden bearing means that at the Lord's direction, you can draw off some of the hurts, troubles, or confusion your children experience, so they can continue to function. You can be continually bringing overwhelming portions to the Lord. At the same time, you can pray that the Lord strengthen their spirits so they can stand in the face of trials or temptations.

The Lord can also drop a burden for your child into your spirits to alert you when they are experiencing strong temptations, and thus call you to intercede on their behalf. You can pray that their spirits are strong so they can stand their ground. This is especially important in the teen years when they are actively individuating—experimenting with values to see which of the family values they choose to make their own.

Empathy, however, works both ways. A highly sensitive child will be able to sense when a parent is having difficulty and may ask pointed questions, "Mommy, are you and Daddy fighting?" When communications are open, a child may ask after a difficult phone call, "Is everything OK?" If it is not, you must admit it, pray together for wisdom and an appropriate response to the caller.

It is important to be honest when having a difficulty. To deny problems is actually lying to a child. It teaches him not to trust what he senses, or you! To admit having difficulties validates his sensing, and models that it is OK to not be perfect or know everything. However, you do not unnecessarily have to reveal details about the difficulty; only admit to having one. You can ask your children to pray for you so you have wisdom for what to do, for ability to understand, for the right words to say, etc. This validates your children and gives them a direction for what to do with what they sense, as well as modeling how to pray about problems.

Parenting Tips in Summary

Discern whether your child is a burden bearer. Begin to teach spiritual and emotional boundaries and responsibility immediately. This will give your child a foundation upon which to build later, during the developmental stage of initiative and beyond, when a child must define his own boundaries and develop discernment.

Help a child learn to listen to and identify his or her own feelings. Emotional vocabulary is very important. Vocabulary is critical to developing the ability to distinguish one's own spiritual, emotional, physical, and psychological load from that of others.

Do your best not to take personally what your child says or does. What is experienced and said may well have nothing to do with your relationship with your child. Do not make it a matter of authority or disrespect, unless that is really the issue. You are the adult. Do not make the child responsible for your feelings. Help children explore and identify issues.

Do not make an issue about things that are not an issue. If their eternal destiny is not at stake and they are in no physical or spiritual danger, allow them the enterprise of their own learning. Allow them the latitude to experiment and even make mistakes. You learn the most from your biggest mistakes. Better to make a mistake when parents are there to help pick up the pieces than to wait until adulthood when the cost of mistakes can be so much higher.

Be willing to accept inconvenience, whether from lack of sleep or by disruptions in schedules to accommodate crises, or to attend a child's event. These actions demonstrate the value you place on your child. They strengthen their trust in your word and strengthen their sense of identity and self-worth. Time taken to build the strong foundation of trust, strength of character, and to determine a child's way, pays dividends later in the form of less chaos in life, and wiser decision making.

Communicate, communicate, communicate. Listen for the heart, even when you do not like what you hear. Sort through the verbiage to find the message of the heart.

Parenting a highly sensitive child, a potential burden bearer, is challenging. It is a blessing because this child takes you to heights and depths you would not choose to explore given the choice. This child challenges just about every aspect of your personality.

Standing in the position of grandparent, I can say that it was worth it! Every challenge was worth it. Our children's sensitivity and creativity added richness and depth to our experience of their growing up years, and lots and lots of fun. Today I see two strong, creative women nurturing their families. I see them spreading love and laughter wherever they go. I see them growing in faith and living and working as healthy burden bearers. Their yoke is not heavy. I thank God and marvel at what He has done.

The next chapter examines situations that can be a problem for highly sensitive people. The purpose is not to raise fear, but to alert you of pitfalls you can avoid. Again, knowledge is a protection for those who have it!

Endnotes

1. Well into the writing of this book, a friend introduced me to the works of Elaine N. Aron. I recommend her books, *The Highly Sensitive Person, The Highly Sensitive Person's Workbook, The Highly Sensitive Child,* and *HSPs in Love.* A highly sensitive secular psychologist, she includes a checklist for the parents as well as the child drawn from her own practice and studies. She has a thorough treatment of how high sensitivity helps and hinders the parent-child relationship, and gives direction for navigating childhood—excellent resources.

2. Gary Smalley and John Trent, *The Blessing* (New York: Pocket Publishers, 1986).

3. James E. Wilder, *The Complete Guide to Living With Men* (Pasadena, CA: Shepherd's House, Inc., 2004), 42.

4. Full explanation of parental inversion and performance orientation in Chapter 4.

CHAPTER 9

Life Complications

Every good thing given and every perfect gift is from above, coming down from the Father of lights (James 1:17 NASB).

E mpathy was nearly lost in the Fall, along with the understanding of the good God intended for you to do with it. The enemy's tactic is to keep you ignorant of, and separated from, your identity and capabilities. Failing that, his aim is to cause you unwittingly to harm others and yourself with what God designed to be a blessing; thus causing grief to the Father. Because believers are woefully ignorant of their design and identity, the inherent vulnerabilities of high sensitivity complicate relationships and draw them toward danger. If you are a "fixer" you are particularly vulnerable.

Life's temptations and complications are rarely clear-cut or easily identifiable. For example, as a prayer minister, my husband might observe codependency as a married couple's issue, but untangling that condition can only happen as healing comes to the various wounds that made each partner needy in various ways.

Codependency[1]

Codependency happens when a relationship is based upon weaknesses rather than strengths. Both partners come to need and depend upon each other, but the relationship revolves around and feeds the very things that need healing. The role of one partner is to provide nurture and strength, which enables the sick partner to continue in sickness, addiction, or bad behavior. The weakness of the healthy partner is the need to be needed or fear of change. The weakness of the other is the illness. They strengthen each other's weakness rather than draw each other into wholeness and relationship with the Father. Both miss the path that leads to their inheritance and destiny. When the Holy Spirit comes, He enables them to drink from each other's strengths. Codependent people have not learned how to draw life from the Lord, so they fasten on to each other and make each other worse.

Burden bearers are vulnerable to codependent relationships *because* they are highly sensitive. You want to, and usually do, make hurting people feel better, but *some need to be needed*. High sensitivity does not give rise to the need to be needed; that need has its roots in early life experiences. High sensitivity informs you of ways to meet your need to give and help with uncanny accuracy. When high sensitivity is unredeemed, you may become a helper who enmeshes rather than sets free.

Entanglement has its reward; there is a pay back. It gives you a reason to narrowly focus and block out the rest of the world's turmoil. The reward is that you have to deal with only one trainload of problems at a time. As long as your friend or partner remains in need of you, you can isolate one slice of painful life and pay no attention to the rest. Needing that person to need you keeps your sense of self as a helper intact—a powerful incentive for remaining in a codependent relationship.

Codependant relationships provide a venue for the peace-maker. Peace is a good thing as long as it is not peace at any price. Don't let it become so important that you try to bring peace and calm into situations where none should rightly exist. That kind of peace covers over underlying problems, which will eventually work to the surface more hurtfully than had it not been delayed by a peacemaker. A wise old folk proverb says, "Do not cast water on a fire God is building."

Be Aware, Not Afraid

Do not hesitate to form relationships for fear of code-pendency. Recognize codependence and develop boundaries to strengthen your spirit and relationship with the Lord. The crux of the problem is, "Where do you draw life—primarily from other people, or from the Lord?"

People who have a strong relationship with the Lord and draw on His strength are able to develop mutually satisfying relation-ships based on the strength in others rather than the needs of oth-ers. The Lord helps you recognize what healthy needs are, such as the need for fellowship, worship, prayer, service. He helps you recognize when to ask for help when you truly have a need.

Movement toward strengthening your own spirit and relationship with the Lord precipitates a rocky time of change in codependent relationships. This is true even if the change is to make boundaries for the sake of physical, men-tal, emotional, or spiritual health. The equation is no longer balanced. Change on the part of one calls into question the role and sense of value and identity of the other. If you are the one embracing healthy change, it is wise to be in relationship with someone who is not codependent. Be accountable to that person—a small group leader, a trusted prayer friend, or a spiritual director, someone who can be helpful in keeping you on track. Such a friend will give feedback about your progress, be a sounding board, and help minimize the damage during turbulence.[2]

Emotional Infants in Adult Bodies

Some people do not have much life of their own. Rather than do the hard work needed to learn how to live life and find nurture for themselves, they attach an umbilical cord to someone they admire and live vicariously. The giving is one-way. Their emotional development froze at an immature stage, and their need sucks the life out of the host in the relationship.

Before I go further, I want to address any who may worry about being a life-drainer. Some of you honestly seek healing and desire all the Lord has for you, but recognize you are also broken and unequipped for life. You have found a friend, prayer minister, or counselor (a burden bearer) upon whom you can depend, and with their support you are learning to walk to wholeness. In reading this you may be saying, "Oh! That's me! I am an emotional infant! I am draining the life out of my friend! God forgive me!" People determined to have others feed them would not say those words. They might be momentarily jerked out of denial into a realization of their dependency but quickly return to the fog of denial. If you are afraid you are an emotional infant, you probably are not! Talk about it with a trusted friend and rest in their response.

Emotional infants do not become so in a vacuum, rather experiences caused, or tempted them not to develop the capacity to live their own life. These individuals lack key elements that could have built inner strength. Life was too hard, too painful, so they curled up in an emotional ball and stopped growing.

One of the main pitfalls in relationship with emotional infants is the great quantity of time and energy they consume if allowed to do so. They do not respect boundaries, spiritual, emotional, or physical. They will ask you to do their emotional and spiritual work for them. They will ask you to hear from God for them, give them advice and guidance in every aspect of life they can draw you into. The pitfall is their need of you; like a black hole, it can become all consuming—if you allow it.

You can know that you have encountered such a person. There are signs. Some days I go about feeling up and happy, and then *this person* comes along. She does have a name, but let me call her Janet. We spend time talking, give a hug goodbye, and suddenly I am so tired I want to go home and sleep. The hug did it! Embracing her was like hugging a vacuum cleaner—whoosh! I was completely depressed after a short visit. My visits with her soon became shorter and shorter. She clung and monopolized my time at church. Phone calls went on forever. She did not do anything offensive, but after a few such encounters, I tried to avoid her. That did "crazy making" things to my mind because I had no objective reason for not wanting to be around her. The sad part of the problem was that she did not seem interested in finding life for herself.

The key to remember is that emotional infants make an exchange. They exchange your life and energy for their lack of it. Proverbs 30:15 says, "The leech has two daughters. 'Give! Give!' They cry." Human leeches are people who have no life of their own so they take life by draining it from others.

Discerning an emotional infant can sometimes be difficult. At first meeting he may not look much different from a terribly wounded individual who for a period needs intensive care. A person can be so wounded, blocked, and tied in knots as to be unable to relate to God. This one needs to lean on someone else's faith. God calls us to bind up and heal the broken. Time will reveal underlying motivational differences between a broken person and an emotional infant.

A broken, wounded person can be very needy, requiring much attention, but becomes less dependent upon the relationship as healing happens. Following healing sessions, a wounded person learns to draw life from relationship with Jesus. Whereas perennial infants determined to be spoon-fed, do not want to do the hard work of learning how to draw life from the Lord and others in healthy ways. Some experiences in their background caused or tempted them to withdraw from life early on, and one of two things happened. Either they never built the resources of inner strength and character that push toward life, or they shut them down and disconnected. They accepted as truth the notion that there is no life inside them. Consequently, they are unable or do not know how to find nurture or benefit from it. Feeding off someone else is much easier. The result for the infant is that friends who are givers must withdraw for their own emotional and spiritual health. Learning happens when a boundary is drawn, enforced, and respected. If the person does not respect the boundary, you need to attach a cost to the transgression or break the relationship.

Let me illustrate the difficulty in discernment. After college, I shared an apartment with three other girls. Two had jobs, boyfriends, and interests. The other one, Karen, did not seem to have friends, things to do or places to go. David and I had recently met and were interested in pursuing our relationship, but Karen constantly intruded. I felt exposed. She did not read and comprehend my cryptic answers and nonverbal behavior, or willfully refused to take a hint. I avoided, she pursued. I felt a black hole of loneliness in her. She interrogated me until late at night and gave unsolicited counsel.

Finally my patience ran out and I drew my boundaries hard and fast. It was 2 o'clock in the morning and I had to go to work in a few hours. I told her that friendship was not practicing emotional nudity. My relationship with David was my relationship, and I would appreciate it if she developed her own friendships. From then on, she was not to consider herself included in any of our activities without specific invitation. I felt that I could never give her enough, so I would rather give her nothing than kill myself in an exercise of futility.

One part of my mind kept second-guessing. "Did I do the right thing?" Should I have been so harsh with her? Another part of my mind, knew to hold fast to the boundaries that I had drawn for my own health, while still being kind and polite. She did not know what to do with the mixture of immovable boundaries and acceptance. She had never experienced anything like it in her life. After that whenever she started to be inappropriate, all I did was raise one eyebrow—and she stopped.

Five years later, I heard from her. Not only did she have a solid relationship with the Lord, she was married! I was flabbergasted. From my initial experiences with her, I would have said she was an emotional infant, and probably would never be able to maintain a healthy relationship. Fortunately, Karen was one of the wounded ones who *can and do* develop when help and direction are given. God is in the miracle business. You can see how important it is not to refuse relationship on initial experiences, but to combine boundaries with loving acceptance. Wounded people learn and heal, whereas confirmed infants detach and find another source requiring less effort.

You can do several things when you discern that you are in relationship with people who refuse the Lord's call to learn how to live life for themselves.

1. *Pray.* Ask the Lord to detach them. Sometimes I pray, "Lord, I ask You to shake what needs to be shaken, remove what needs to be removed, and establish that which needs to be established." Another graphic prayer picture is, "Lord, I ask you to increase the salt of my spirit so that the life this one receives from me is well salted with You." In the natural, snails and slugs do not like salt, so they drop away. In the same way, an emotional infant will detach upon receiving a strong dose of the Lord of Life. This person prefers the Lord's life diluted, second hand, rather than direct. If a person is terribly wounded and trying valiantly to become whole, they will be able to tolerate the Lord's life. The person may sputter and object, but will not passively float away looking for another source of life to draw from.

2. *Speak tough truth.* Although it is difficult for a highly sensitive person, speak tough truth and take the risk of hurting feelings. Tell them something along the lines of, "Find your own life in Jesus. Do not get all your life from me. I am closing doors to you because I love you and know you need

to learn how to have a life of your own." This is what I did for Karen, and because she was wounded, not an emotional infant, she was able to find life.

3. *Teach.* Teach them that they need to choose life, they do have choices, and it is OK to choose. You may have to be in their face and insist they make their own choice. When you do this, they will either begin to make choices, or tire of the effort and detach. This may take a great deal of energy!

4. *Train.* Point them to spiritual disciplines for healing. Give them specific tasks such as reading Scriptures on a problem area of their life. Problems are something they talk about freely and have aplenty. Use a concordance to find appropriate Scriptures so you can hand them a list. "Read these Scriptures and meditate for a few minutes and write down what comes to you. Do this all week, and when you have done it, we can meet again." Give them set times and dates to prevent them from taking advantage of open-ended commitments. This sets boundaries for their access to you. You may need to set other boundaries, such as no phone calls, etc. Then, when you do meet, ask how the spiritual disciplines went; hold them accountable. Whether they learn or drop away; either way, they stop siphoning your life and energy.

5. *Listen to the Holy Spirit.* Do not be afraid of or flee from relationships, but learn to listen to the Holy Spirit. The Holy Spirit knows the intents and motivations of the heart and can warn you when to draw boundaries for your own well-being, or lovingly to break off a relationship to force a person to look at damaging life patterns. The Holy Spirit also indicates when you are to come alongside to walk a person through the pain of healing. You will not discern accurately

all the time—burden bearing, parenting, or helping someone mature—there is no exact science!

6. *Set boundaries.* Setting boundaries and limiting accessibility can become problematic because boundary setting must go both ways—you also need to set limits for yourself. How much do you give, how often do you give, and in what form? You sense the desperateness or the loneliness in others and want too much to make the distress go away. You may feel your own needs are not as great or important and give away too much of yourself. Although it may feel cruel, limiting access can salvage a relationship. Lack of boundaries is a formula for burnout; it can also lead to blaming and resenting God for not taking care of all these people. Setting boundaries challenges the deep core of those who are caretakers by nature or reflex.

Anorexia and Bulimia

The prayer ministry staff of Elijah House U.S. and Elijah House Canada[3] have observed a relationship between burden bearing and anorexia and bulimia. Burden bearing does not cause anorexia or bulimia, but intensifies and makes the condition worse. It may cause the problem to surface earlier than it would otherwise. Since I do not presume to diagnose, let me go directly to the connection with burden bearing wrongly.

The kind of person most susceptible to these devastating disorders seems to be those with a very compassionate, sensitive nature. They can sense and feel angers that are not expressed, trouble and confusion that is not discussed, fears that haunt. They feel responsible to take on the unrealistic goal of trying to fix everything and everyone, especially in the family. When they cannot fix the family, they fix themselves, by being pleasing—by being the perfect weight. At the same time, they cannot identify their burdens as coming from others. And, they don't want to blame anyone else for the problems they sense around them. So they blame themselves for being imperfect, and also for being different than others.

The love and care these sensitive, compassionate individuals possess for the pain in their families is what ensnares them into a very destructive thought pattern. Although anorexia and bulimia are two separate eating disorders, the prayer ministers I know who have worked with individuals battling these conditions have found that they are two different manifestations of an overloaded, crushed, and broken spirit.

An individual takes on the responsibility for fixing the family in the only way known, by subconsciously soaking up all the trouble. Being unable to identify the source of trouble as separate from himself, and not knowing how to take it to the Cross, his mind turns it around so that the trouble somehow becomes entirely his fault. This individual worries about everyone else and loses himself in the process. He absorbs the family's feelings of guilt, both valid and false. This is unredeemed burden bearing. When the family problems remain unsolved, he blames himself and feels even more worthless. He attempts to solve the problem by erasing himself through starvation. That opens a door and the enemy comes in to whisper words of death rather than life. The good gift of high sensitivity that God gave becomes a tool of self-destruction.

Consciously or subconsciously, he accurately assesses that by design he can do something, but is confused about *what* to do, or how to go about it—*because burden bearing is not a concept our society has grasped or taught.* Satan is happy to make the confusion worse with accusations and innuendoes, making him even more vulnerable to the stronghold of the mind-set of death.

In our prayer ministry, we encourage work on root causes to problems, but anorexia and bulimia presents a unique situation, especially in the case of severe anorexics. The prayer ministers I know who have had success with these conditions advise: *do no work on root causes* to the condition *until:* 1) the person is physically stabilized and a health professional verifies the physical stability, and 2) the individual makes significant inroads against historic strong habits of thinking. *Always* consult with doctors regarding physical stability of such people.

Anyone wanting to comprehend the thought process of anorexia and bulimia can read *The Secret Language of Eating Disorders: How You Can Understand and Work to Cure Anorexia and Bulimia* by Peggy Claude-Pierre.[4] She ably describes this life-devastating negative thinking and the kind of care that moves a person to safety. Severe anorexics and bulimics need physical stability, but in addition, they need the emotional stability from copious amounts of unconditional loving acceptance. *The habitual pattern of thinking must change if any physical progress is to be lasting.* Unconditional loving acceptance is thus the most powerful tool in this battle for the mind. Logic does not work. Working with anorexia and bulimia conditions is a delicate balance between listening to the Holy Spirit and doing what we know to be effective.

Before we leave this subject, it is important to note that not all anorexia and bulimia is family driven. Peer pressures set off many cases. Whatever triggers the problem; high sensitivity makes an individual vulnerable, heightens, and intensifies the torment of this potentially deadly condition.

The Occult

Humans do not have authorization to wander around in the spirit realm and are naïve to do so. Without the Lord's protection, it is a dangerous place. When you step into the spirit realm without the Lord's covering, you risk becoming the target of spiritual oppression, harassment, or outright attack. At the outset, let me say that occult practices are not merely satanism, black magic, and witchcraft, it also includes such things as clairvoyance, fortune telling, taro cards, Ouija boards, séances, consulting horoscopes, and those things mentioned in Chapter 1.

Some individual's empathy is so strong that it borders on mind reading. Mark Sandford refers to such a person as an "accidental psychic"—one who is not looking for psychic power, but to whom psychic experiences happen. With the advent of fiber optics, telephone calls are generally quite clear, but I remember the days when you could actually hear people talking in the background. It is something like that for the accidental psychic. This person is so sensitive as to truly "hear" and "see" things. In itself, this is no sin. It becomes sin if you deliberately seek to develop this natural ability from sources other than Jesus. Like all abilities, it needs to be brought to death on the Cross and only used when and if the Lord gives it back redeemed, in the form of the spiritual gifts, under direction of the Holy Spirit.

For a person who does not know the Lord, the lure of knowledge, power, and control that comes with the occult is very seductive. Knowledge gives a person the *illusion* of power. The acquisition of knowledge appears to be a way of gaining control over life, and therein lies the seduction. Control is power, and power can stop those who harass and torment you. Those already involved in occult practices give the novice acceptance, identity, and place. Invitation is also involved; the combination of control and acceptance becomes extremely attractive to a needy, wounded person, scapegoated by family, made fun of and called names, rejected, or hurt by the church.

One reason an accidental psychic may be tempted to become a deliberate one is they can seem to do good things with these activities. Sincere, caring individuals appear to be able to help people. Fortune telling, taro cards, horoscopes, Ouija boards, and séances may look harmless and helpful; but these are deliberate activities, not accidental ones. The enemy allows enough truth to make you dependent, and then deceives and leads you away from God, down endless trails that lead to captivity and destruction—emotional, physical, economic, and spiritual. You appear to thrive while damage is occurring on other levels. By the time damage is obvious, destruction is at hand.

In a generational occult family some in each generation embrace and engage in the occult practices. Those who do are often consciously aware that they deal with the demonic, but still choose to do it because of the illusion of power and control. Occultism can bring wealth—for a time. As with any loan, individuals have to pay it back, and when that time comes, the interest is horrendous.

When occultism rules in the family, relationships between members are distant and detached and/or cruel and destructive "for the curse upon those who involve themselves

in the occult is that they will be cut off from their people"
(Lev. 20:6). A typical scenario: no one has a real, intelligent, or
meaningful conversation with the father. Everyone must listen when he talks. The mother and father are divorced.
Mother speaks to certain family members only. Brothers and
sisters have off-again on-again relationships and rarely have
anything kind or helpful to say to each other. Being together
without sarcasm or an explosion is an unusual rarity. Several
have terminal diseases far before the age a person expects
such things. Addictions and physical problems run rampant
through the family—the ongoing toll is beyond words, but
they seem unable to make the connection between the occult
influences and their current difficulties. It is hard to walk
away from family, but it is also quite dangerous to remain in
a hurtful environment and have wounds chaffed open by
interaction with occult people.

Years ago, I saw how the lure of psychic power and psychic experience affected one woman. I was at a Christian conference; it was hot and the building was locked. I joined
several others under a shade tree and waited for the doors to
open. One of the women began to ask why I was there, was I
attending the conference on psychic abilities? I assured her I
was not. She welcomed me to join her conference, and told a
few awe inspiring experiences from the night before. Again,
she encouraged me to attend.

Then an odd thing happened. Something came over the
woman. There was an excitement in her and an eagerness for
me to have a psychic experience. Something made the hair on
the back of my neck stand up and my skin crawl. She asked if
I were a healer, corrected herself, and stated that I was indeed
a healer. When I denied it, she wanted to know if there were
healers in my family. I did not want her to know anything

about me, or my family! *It excited her* to be able to have psychic experiences, psychic power, and to be able to read people and bring others into her experience.

I felt as if I were fresh meat—as if she were smacking her lips at the thought of ensnaring me. Perhaps the spirit driving her was smacking its lips! I excused myself. I believe the Holy Spirit in me reacted to what was in her and directed me out of there. Had I not known the Lord, I could have fallen prey to the same seduction that controlled her. Without the Lord's guidance and protection, the very sensitivity He gave you for bearing burdens in the ministry of reconciliation can be diverted for purposes never intended.

For this woman, the bill had not yet come due. She was still using whatever satan loaned her to augment her natural sensitivity. The enemy never shows you the fine print, or practices informed consent—there are always hidden costs. How different from our Lord who is completely up front about the costs and benefits of salvation.

Demonic Attack

Demonic activity is not normally a topic of household conversation, so this section considers an aspect of your walk with the Lord that is just a little different. You have probably experienced a time when you met a stone wall at every turn, or so it seemed. Times when it felt you were finally going to achieve a goal, or come into your own, only to have success snatched away—again! Scripture says that the population of the spirit realm is not solely the good guys. Scripture says, that the enemy of your soul energizes and accelerates the down turns of life (Eph. 2:2). The Greek word for "works" is where we get our English word *energy*. Satanic forces literally energize disobedience. (See also Revelations 12:9.) Like any enemy, he does not want his strategies exposed. His assaults are usually subtle and play to your vulnerability or weaknesses. Your compassion and desire to help make life better becomes a weakness when uninformed, unredeemed, and therefore unprotected.

In the course of helping people come to wholeness, you follow the Lord into the spirit realm. Believers are hidden in Christ (Col. 3:3). However, there are times when the enemy can see, take note, and assign demons to stop you from burden bearing. If the enemy can see you, it is either because of sin or God's own discretion.

A word picture: How can you sin when you are following hard after Christ? Think of yourself as being under Jesus' robes of righteousness. If Jesus said to move out but you do not, and Jesus does, when He moves, you come out from under those robes. The same is true if you run ahead of Him. You are exposed by the sin of disobedience.

The story of Job illustrates God's discretion in allowing satan to see one of His own. "Have you considered my servant, Job?" (Job 1:8). Satan considers all prayer to be warfare against him, and prayer that focuses on God and his love for us is effective warfare. Such attacks are not always obvious frontal assaults—the subtler, the more effective. Discouragement, innuendo, half-truths, and allegations that pull on old wounds long healed are common means by which demons pull you increasingly off balance and make you ineffective. Attacks that derail you come in the form of your spouse or another person who is pushed off balance emotionally and is unable to be gracious at the moment. But, "Our struggle is not against flesh and blood, but against the rulers, against the authorities, against the powers of this dark world and against the spiritual forces of evil in the heavenly realms" (Eph. 6:12).

Like any worker doing a dirty job, you become coated with the stuff you bring to the Cross. This is outside spiritual dirt, not from your own sin, and can be easily washed off. Residue that goes untended may attract demonic forces. For this reason, it becomes essential that you tend to spiritual cleansing, asking the Lord to cleanse and hide you after times of ministry. If something wounds you in the process of ministry, or if you react wrongfully, you must quickly deal with the matter lest in the process of freeing another you give the enemy ground in your own life! "...and do not let the sun go down on your anger [hurt, fear, or any other burden you pick up], and do not give the devil opportunity" (Eph. 4:26-27 NASB). Your own sin left untended can also attract the demonic and lead to demonization—demons have access to harass, oppress, and make your life miserable.

Burden bearers are vulnerable to demonic attack because they are accustomed to carrying loads, and because they often reach out to carry them in their own strength. You can become involved in the routine of daily life and not be aware when a demon quietly attaches, counterfeiting his approach as a burden. You may become aware of a heaviness that comes upon you, but heaviness is nothing new, you brace and go on with life. The enemy knows that you are open to the Lord for any burden He may ask you to carry, so he takes advantage of your willingness to serve, or over-willingness based on fleshly motives, and your spiritual inattention. He sends a counterfeit burden, the kind of spirit that attaches, draws the life out, and uses up your physical and spiritual energies so you become ineffective.

You can suspect such an attack when you suddenly have no energy. You are fine; you have plenty of zest and suddenly *boom*, it is all gone as if someone pulled a plug. It will happen at odd times, generally with no specific pattern. According to Mark 5:10, Luke 8:29,31, and Luke 11:14-16, a demon is not dull-witted; it wants to stay, so it only drains energy off and on, so a person does not suspect. You may think your blood sugar is low, sit down for a snack and the energies come back. The best thing to do is have a snack *and* have prayer. If the problem is only blood sugar, the prayer will not hurt! It is also a possibility that the snack *appears* to help because the demonic stops draining as you sit down to eat so you will think you only need food—another ploy to not alert you to its presence.

I have been attacked in this way more than once. For me, it occurred during ministry trips when I was very busy and involved with many people. I allowed activity and ministry to encroach upon my private time with the Lord. Upon returning home, I did not recover as usual. The tiredness had an awful abnormal quality to it—a bottomless pit. I dragged myself to my prayer buddies for help reassessing how I was going about burden bearing. Sometimes accountability was all I needed, other times the Lord revealed a demonic spirit behind the exhaustion. After one ministry trip, He revealed that I looked like a pincushion from so many fiery darts hitting me.

The demon that drops you with abnormal tiredness has a name. It is a vampiric spirit—one that sucks your life's energy. Just as mythic vampires drained the blood from victims and so killed, these demons suck energy periodically and rob their victims of life—just enough to exhaust, always randomly so victims will not suspect. To free yourself or your friend, cast the thing away using Jesus' delegated authority and close all spiritual doors so that nothing can return. Pray for discernment—no one has to endure such a demon one moment longer than to see it and send it away. For further insight into demonic behavior, I highly recommend *The Screwtape Letters* written by C.S. Lewis.

Resist the temptation to spiritualize everything; some tiredness is just that—physical tiredness. If you have a physical condition that a doctor is treating, do not assume he is wrong, that you only have a spiritual condition, and toss your medication. A condition may be solely physical, solely demonic, or a combination of both. I believe that the Lord heals by miracles and by doctors. The Lord reveals the secrets of the human body to the scientists.

The sensitive, caring nature of the natural burden bearers makes them potential threats to the kingdom of darkness. You desire to bring life, not death; love, not condemnation; reconciliation, not rejection or retribution. These natural inclinations are the exact opposite of the goals of the enemy of your soul. Satan wants to take you out—or make you ineffective—simply because you are yourself. When you actively participate in the ministry of reconciliation—burden bearing rightly, he wants you gone, deactivated.

Confusion With the Prophetic

The empathy, or high sensitivity, which allows you to touch the heart of God and hear Him, can be so keen as to be able to read other people. Some are able to look at a person and read his or her mail, to hear the heart cries of fellow human beings. This ability has been the cause of a good deal of hurt and confusion within the Body of Christ.

In the restoration of the office of the prophet, some people have erringly been called prophets who have unknowingly read the desires of other people's hearts. People gave them the label prophet because of their accuracy and they readily accepted it when that is not their true calling. It is possible to read the desires of another's heart without being a prophet. *Exceptionally high capacity for empathy, and hence burden bearing, is necessary to be a prophet. However, not all highly sensitive people, or burden bearers, are prophets. They may speak prophetically, on occasion, but that does not make them a prophet.*

If empathetic people speak out the desires of the heart as if those were sure words from the Lord, the hearer may respond with great joy and wait in vain for the Lord to bring about the "prophecy." They can thus unwittingly set up a person for great disappointment in the Lord and do damage to their faith and trust in Him. Such a word given to a person who is resisting the Lord's call on his or her life may unwittingly be part of galvanizing him in his rebellion. Loren Sandford's book, *Purifying the Prophetic,* addresses this subject with incisive revelation in the first chapter.[5]

Another reaction to such words is to strive to bring the prophecy into reality, when it may or may not be the Lord's appointed time yet—or at all. You can entertain desires of the heart that are good but may not be the path the Lord wants you to follow. If the Lord allows you to see what is to happen in a person's life, assume it is for intercession rather than sharing. The Lord may want an intercessor to be calling on Him to prepare hearts, arrange circumstances, and protect the plans He has, so that what He wants to happen will happen easily and smoothly in the Lord's time. Speaking before it is time can derail what the Lord wants to happen and becomes an unnecessary temptation.

It behooves every burden bearer to consult with the Lord for direction on what to do with what you see, sense, and hear. Is it to inform so that you intercede specifically and intelligently, or are you to share it? It is wisdom to share with advisors what you see and sense first rather than to pronounce publicly. Allow room for the person to receive or refuse whatever you say. Share the possibility that you may be inaccurate, but to the best of your ability to hear, this is what "I *think* I heard the Lord say...." Your ministry is that of reconciliation, you do not want to be part of causing another to stumble!

Burnout

Burden bearers easily fall into burnout. Sensitive spirits, given their creativity and clear vision, easily see the needs that require attention, as well as how to meet them. Everyone is busy and over-worked, so the quiet ones simply take on more and more burdens. Sometimes it is the other way around— because burden bearers do such a good job, people notice and ask them to volunteer for every committee, fundraiser, Sunday school class, or small group and special event that comes along. Some of the tenderhearted become unable to do a good job when asked because the overwhelming pain around them disables them. When burden bearing is not under the direction of the Holy Spirit, boundaries are weak, or not there at all, and it is hard to say no. It can be difficult to guard private time with the Lord and down time to just "be," or family time, or rest for one's own health.

The needs around are real and the clamor of needs can drown out the Lord's voice so that you lose perspective and don't hear Him telling you to cut back, slow down, or stop. You can be so involved in the good that you miss the best. Everyone loses when one of the Lord's servants burns out. The Lord put Adam in charge—a delegated position—and has not changed His mind. God is still ultimately responsible for His creation and you are His servant—try not to lose sight of that. You need to hear from the Lord what your area of responsibility is, and is not, and take care not to overstep those limits so that you are well, and able to serve another day. As the family of God, we need to watch out for each other rather than take advantage and use each other up.

Do Not Be Afraid

All through the Old Testament, whenever God interacted with man, He always said, "Don't be afraid." As He gave Joshua his command, He repeatedly said, "Do not be afraid; do not be discouraged. Be strong and courageous" (Josh. 10:25) An angel touched Daniel and said, "Do not be afraid, O man highly esteemed. Peace! Be strong now; be strong" (Dan. 10:19). The Lord wants to touch you, strengthen you, and take the fear out of burden bearing.

The most common fear is of God Himself, what He will do to or ask of you. Yes, there are snares, pitfalls, and complications with a burden-bearing lifestyle. However, you do not need to be afraid of your heavenly Father. When these fears become conscious, you can talk about and address them. Many are unaware of their fears—I was. They can be very subtle; you may not come right out and say you distrust God, but have a habit of worrying or fretting. Worrying and fretting are symptoms of a fissure in trust rather than a full break. If you take a hard look at the things you worry about, and hear,

"But, Lord!" or "Yes, but...," you have identified an area where you cannot or do not trust, not fully. Why be fearful?

Doubt, Fret, Worry

Doubt feeds worry. Worry feeds fear and anxiety. By dwelling in these emotions, by allowing them to overwhelm, many believers plunge into discouragement and depression.

Several years after David and I moved to Canada, I was in a place where I was helpless to affect our situation. Our house had not sold; our furniture was in the States; we lived a temporary, unsettled lifestyle. Originally, we came for two years, on loan, and planned to return to Idaho. That did not happen and MS kept me from working. David was my sole support. What if something happened to him? Where would we be? What would become of me, of us? At the same time, our daughters were at a juncture in their lives where they needed to make decisions that would alter the direction and quality of their lives from then on. Again, I was helpless. I could only listen and help them sort through their thoughts and feelings, but the decisions had to be theirs. I could pray—and pray I did.

Time went on without resolution. My worries grew and loomed larger and larger. I began to question our decision to stay in Canada. We were paying rent and mortgage payments and the currency exchange hurt. What if...what if. When we made the decision, it seemed clear that God was behind it and He would provide. He has a very good record with us of keeping His word, but as I listened to our daughters, our situation seemed to become more and more precarious and I began to question David, God, and myself. As I doubted, worry grew.

My rational mind began to analyze my irrational feelings. I flipped through memories and saw how when God called, we followed, when we knew it was Him. End of discussion. Why was it different now? Finally the scales dropped and I saw that our daughters' burdens had become entangled in my emotions. Their burdens combined with and felt like my own. The combination distorted valid concerns into full-blown fears and tempted me to turn back from following Jesus.

Burden bearing can complicate your life when residue builds; molehills become mountains from the fear that God will ask you to do what you cannot. Valid concerns become niggling worries, which transform into full-blown anxiety. Fears about what God will ask are distorted and, as in a circus mirror, become huge, warped, and very scary. You may be tempted to act in a self-protective way, and pull yourself out of the Lord's will. When I realized I was unable to pass our daughters' burdens cleanly on to the Lord, I simply confessed that to Him, asked for grace sufficient to the task—and immediately felt the weight lift. Life fell back into perspective.

Fear of What He Will Ask

God asks what is appropriate developmentally. My husband had a dream of standing on a high plateau with the Lord. Jesus stretched out His arm and pointed as He told David what He wanted him to do. It was a glorious task. However, David came away from the dream feeling small and inept, a failure. He felt as though God had patted him on the back and said, "Go and make me proud," when he had no clue about what to do or how to do it. The dream was a picture of his fear born from early childhood experiences. God does not sit on a cloud with a cosmic fly swatter waiting for you to mess up. He does not wear your earthly father or mother's face. Yet many expect God to do to them the kinds of things they experienced with their earthly parents.

Negative experiences with an earthly parent can cloud your vision of your heavenly Father. You can project expectations and judgments onto Him that do not rightly belong there. The record in Scripture of God's dealings with His people reveals that harsh treatment always came as a last resort. God does not call you without instruction and He does not send you out without training and direction. He lived with the disciples and taught them before He sent them out. He will do the same with you.

After recovery from the MS attack, I still experienced burden bearing, but differently. Visions have increased, and I find insights coming together in my head without prior input in a way that is new to me. I experience fewer sensations. My body can no longer handle the stress induced by the physical and emotional sensations I experienced before. When I do feel sensations, it is as if they brush by me to inform, but do not course through my body as they once did. You do not need to be afraid of what He will ask of you. He will not require more than He designed you to bear—*I know this from personal experience.* However, we must overcome fear, worry, and anxiety.

Fear of Who God Is

The nature of God is an excellent devotional study. Keep Scriptures regarding His nature in your memory to have readily available when you doubt Him, when old tapes play and the Philistines begin to dance in your head. If you do not know His character, you do not know what He is like. See endnote 6 at the end of this chapter for Scriptures that reveal God's nature.

The Lord who designed you with a large capacity for empathy created you *in His own image*. God is capable of empathy on such a scale you cannot begin to imagine it. Empathy makes relationship with Him possible. He does not leave you alone; He is with you. He likes you; He enjoys your company. You can ask Him to reveal Himself to you personally so you can know that you know Him.

As I began this journey to learn how to live life as a burden bearer before it got the best of me, I would sit down to pray and some time later realize I had not voiced any prayers! I had come into His presence, enjoyed His company, and He mine—that was all! It surprised me. *God* enjoyed *my* company! He wants your company too; He enjoys being with His kids. No loving father I know wants his children to be terrified of him for any reason. Your heavenly Father is more loving than any earthly father. *Not* loving is not a part of His nature, so when you are afraid of Him, your fear grieves His heart.

Fear can permeate all of life and distort your perceptions as well as your reactions. To the degree that you are afraid of God, to that degree you will be unable to hear, see, or sense accurately; fear will skew your interpretations. It will make it more likely that you will bear burdens in your own strength. You may fear to leave burdens at the Cross, lest Jesus not act quickly enough, or not do it right. High sensitivity exaggerates and intensifies your fears and complicates life.

In the movies, a hero crossing a raging torrent continually tells himself, "Don't look down. Don't look down!" You may feel overwhelmed by the magnitude of the complications; the weight, the scope, and fear of the implications of burden bearing. It can sweep you away—if you allow it. First Corinthians 10:13 (NASB), "No temptation [or vulnerability] has overtaken you but such as is common to man; and God is faithful, who will not allow you to be tempted beyond what you are able, but with the temptation will provide the way of escape also, that you may be able to endure it."

The complications of life because of high sensitivity are part of the mix of experiences God uses to develop you into a Kingdom child—one who inherits. There are also profound blessings that come as you partner with the Lord in this ministry of reconciliation; these also help shape you into the likeness of Jesus.

Endnotes

1. For further discussion of codependency see Robert Hemfelt, Paul Meier, and Frank Minirth, *Love Is A Choice: Recovery for Codependent Relationships*, (Nelson Books, Nashville, TN, 1989) now replaced with *Love Is a Choice: Letting Go of Unhealthy Relationships*, 2003.

2. To find such an individual, ask your pastor or counselor or check with a social services person, or contact: Codependents Anonymous World Fellowship; Website: www.codependents.org; E-mail: outreach@coda.org.

3. See www.elijahhouse.org for more information.

4. Peggy Claude-Pierre, *The Secret Language of Eating Disorders* (New York: Vintage, 1998).

5. Loren Sandford, *Purifying the Prophetic* (Grand Rapids, MI: Chosen Books, 2005).

6. Biblical names of God that reveal His nature.
- **Advocate** - 1 John 2:1
- **Almighty** - Revelation 1:8
- **Alpha** - Revelation 1:8
- **Amen** - Revelation 3:14
- **Angel of the Lord** - Genesis 16:7
- **Anointed One** - Psalm 2:2
- **Apostle** - Hebrews 3:1
- **Author and Perfecter of our Faith** - Hebrews 12:2
- **Beginning** - Revelation 21:6
- **Bishop of Souls** - 1 Peter 2:25
- **Branch** - Zechariah 3:8
- **Bread of Life** - John 6:35,48
- **Bridegroom** - Matthew 9:15
- **Carpenter** - Mark 6:3
- **Chief Shepherd** - 1 Peter 5:4
- **The Christ** - Matthew 1:16
- **Comforter** - Jeremiah 8:18
- **Consolation of Israel** - Luke 2:25
- **Cornerstone** - Ephesians 2:20
- **Dayspring** - Luke 1:78
- **Day Star** - 2 Peter 1:19
- **Deliverer** - Romans 11:26
- **Desire of Nations** - Haggai 2:7
- **Emmanuel** - Matthew 1:23
- **End** - Revelation 21:6

- **Everlasting Father** - Isaiah 9:6
- **Faithful and True Witness** - Revelation 3:14
- **First Fruits** - 1 Corinthians 15:23
- **Foundation** - Isaiah 28:16
- **Fountain** - Zechariah 13:1
- **Friend of Sinners** - Matthew 11:19
- **Gate for the Sheep** - John 10:7
- **Gift of God** - 2 Corinthians 9:15
- **God** - John 1:1
- **Glory of God** - Isaiah 60:1
- **Good Shepherd** - John 10:11
- **Governor** - Matthew 2:6
- **Great Shepherd** - Hebrews 13:20
- **Guide** - Psalm 48:14
- **Head of the Church** - Colossians 1:18
- **High Priest** - Hebrews 3:1
- **Holy One of Israel** - Isaiah 41:14
- **Horn of Salvation** - Luke 1:69
- **I Am** - Exodus 3:14
- **Jehovah** - Psalm 83:18
- **Jesus** - Matthew 1:21
- **King of Israel** - Matthew 27:42
- **King of Kings** - 1 Timothy 6:15; Revelation 19:16
- **Lamb of God** - John 1:29
- **Last Adam** - 1 Corinthians 15:45
- **Life** - John 11:25

- **Light of the World** - John 8:12; John 9:5
- **Lion of the Tribe of Judah** - Revelation 5:5
- **Lord of Lords** - 1 Timothy 6:15; Revelation 19:16
- **Master** - Matthew 23:8
- **Mediator** - 1 Timothy 2:5
- **Messiah** - John 1:41
- **Mighty God** - Isaiah 9:6
- **Morning Star** - Revelation 22:16
- **Nazarene** - Matthew 2:23
- **Omega** - Revelation 1:8
- **Passover Lamb** - 1 Corinthians 5:7
- **Physician** - Matthew 9:12
- **Potentate** - 1 Timothy 6:15
- **Priest** - Hebrews 4:15
- **Prince of Peace** - Isaiah 9:6
- **Prophet** - Acts 3:22
- **Propitiation** - I John 2:2
- **Purifier** - Malachi 3:3
- **Rabbi** - John 1:49
- **Ransom** - 1 Timothy 2:6
- **Redeemer** - Isaiah 41:14
- **Refiner** - Malachi 3:2
- **Refuge** - Isaiah 25:4
- **Resurrection** - John 11:25
- **Righteousness** - Jeremiah 23:6
- **Rock** - Deuteronomy 32:4

- **Root of David** - Revelation 22:16
- **Rose of Sharon** - Song of Solomon 2:1
- **Ruler of God's Creation** - Revelation 3:14
- **Sacrifice** - Ephesians 5:2
- **Savior** - 2 Samuel 22:47; Luke 1:47
- **Second Adam** - 1 Corinthians 15:47
- **Seed of Abraham** - Galatians 3:16
- **Seed of David** - 2 Timothy 2:8
- **Seed of the Woman** - Genesis 3:15
- **Servant** - Isaiah 42:1
- **Shepherd** - 1 Peter 2:25
- **Shiloh** - Genesis 49:10
- **Son of David** - Matthew 15:22
- **Son of God** - Luke 1:35
- **Son of Man** - Matthew 18:11
- **Son of Mary** - Mark 6:3
- **Son of the Most High** - Luke 1:32
- **Stone** - Isaiah 28:16
- **Sun of Righteousness** - Malachi 4:2
- **Teacher** - Matthew 26:18
- **Truth** - John 14:6
- **Way** - John 14:6
- **Wonderful Counselor** - Isaiah 9:6
- **Word** - John 1:1
- **Vine** - John 15:1

CHAPTER 10

The Blessings of Burden Bearing

Be imitators of God, therefore, as dearly beloved chil-
dren, and live a life of love, just as Christ loved us, and
gave himself up for us as a fragrant offering and sacri-
fice to God (Ephesians 5:1-2).

B urden bearing is about relationship and intimacy, building up and restoring that which was stolen or broken.
The longer you bear burdens rightly, the more you return to
the relationship God intended for you at creation. The more
time you spend with Him, the more you think, walk, talk and
live like Him—and the more you become yourself. All other
blessings flow from this relationship. The blessings of burden
bearing create a beautiful tapestry of your life, woven into the
life of the Son, the Father, and the Holy Spirit.

Jesus' redemption of your life was and is a monumental
task, but the hardest part was not the dying—it was the suffering involved in bearing sin to the Cross while being completely separated from His Father for the first time. As you
join your Lord and Savior in this work of reconciliation and
restoration, you need to know that the blessings balance the
ways being highly sensitive complicates life.

The blessings of burden bearing flow from experiencing some-thing of the passion of Christ. Jesus' life was about His love for His people; this is what makes Him tick. His intense, passion-ate love put Him on the Cross. As you bear burdens, you encounter this love and find the blessings. Your restoration is the joy set before Jesus that gave Him the ability to endure the crucifixion. Similarly, bearing burdens may have its pain, discomfort, inconvenience, and confusion, but the blessings are worth it! What are they?

Blessed by Sharing in the Fellowship

You are blessed by sharing in the fellowship of His suf-fering. As you experience Christ's passion for His people, you come to know Him better. When you feel Jesus' suffering and grief for battered lives, you "comprehend the breadth and length and height and depth and come to know the love of Christ which passes all understanding" (Eph. 3:18-19 NASB). You limit your intimacy with Jesus by being unwill-ing to suffer with Him. Bonding happens between soldiers, law enforcement partners under fire, and victims of the same or similar kinds of traumas and tragedies—the fellowship of the foxhole. This kind of enduring bond of love develops when you enter into burden bearing, when you enter the fel-lowship of His suffering. Coming so close He can whisper His secrets to you, a direct path to knowing Him.

Scripture makes it clear that an element of suffering is involved in burden bearing intercession. Romans 8:17, "Now if we are children, then we are heirs, heirs of God and co-heirs with Christ, if indeed *we share in His sufferings* in order that we may also share in His glory" (emphasis added). Empa-thizing with others is not always comfortable. Jesus was not comfortable in Gethsemane, nor do I think is He always comfortable as He lives in you and me and continues to empathize and intercede for us. You have His Word that any suffering you may experience while connected with His children is well worth it (see Luke 18:29-30, Rom. 5:3-5, 8:18).

Philippians 3:10 says, "I want to know Christ and the power of His resurrection and *the fellowship of sharing in His sufferings,* becoming like Him in His death." Because of sitting in the Garden with Him (praying and bearing some of His burden), or carrying people in your heart, you enter into intimate relationship with Jesus and your Father. No one understands, as does someone who has also endured the same kind of experiences.

An incredibly deep bonding of spirits happens when you spend time with Jesus as He drinks the cup of another's trouble and touches other people's anguish. You don't bear the full load, just enough to know how to pray accurately and intelligently. Secular experiences demonstrate that working together on projects results in closeness, but when working together has life-giving or life-changing ramifications, there is a unique intensity. Relationships grow, and you come to have a deeper love and appreciation for Him and each other, which leads you to the next blessing.

Blessed To Know the Heart of God

Through burden bearing you come to know the heart of God better. You come to see people as He does when you experience God's love for them. You can then appreciate what He does or does not do, and because of that you trust His motives more even when you do not understand. You feel Jesus' burden and His love, which draws you closer to Him.

You see a glimpse of what He did, and continues to do for you.

> *I pray that out of His glorious riches He may strengthen you with power through His Spirit in your inner being, so that Christ may dwell in your hearts through faith. And I pray that you, being rooted and established in love, may have power, together with all the saints, to grasp how wide and long and high and deep is the love of Christ, and to know this love that surpasses knowledge— that you may be filled to the measure of all the fullness of God* (Ephesians 3:16-19).

You come into a wondrous experience of the dimensions of God's love by touching His heart each time you bring someone to the Lord in intercession. Going to Him for yourself is one thing, but going on behalf of someone else removes blinders and you see some of the vastness of His love. Gratitude wells up and you fall in love with Him deeper and deeper. His love surpasses knowledge; you cannot wrap your mind around it. You will never be able to comprehend God's love; it is not logical or rational according to any human standard.

When I pray for a wounded burden bearer, I sometimes ask the Lord to enlarge the capacity of his human spirit with as much voltage as Jesus used did when He changed the water into wine. We cannot contain all the measure of the fullness of God. When I pray for a wounded burden bearer, after bringing to death any hidden sins that compromise that capacity, I often ask the Lord to strengthen his spirit so it can contain all that he is now designed for.

Blessed To Understand the Cost of Sin

Everyone has reason to hate sin; however, when you deeply experience the love of God, you come to see and understand its cost, and hate it even more. Hating sin gives you new energy to break old patterns when you see how you participate in them. First Peter 2:24 says, "He himself bore our sin *in his body* on the tree, so that we might die to sin and live for righteousness; by His wounds you have been healed" (emphasis added). First Peter 4:1 says, "Therefore, since Christ suffered *in his body*, arm yourself also with the same attitude, because he who has suffered in his body is done with sin" (emphasis added). When you feel what sin does to His heart, you hate it in your life. He endured an incredible price to make it possible for you to receive His love and to love Him in return, you cannot bear to grieve His Spirit. The cost to Him becomes a hedge of protection for you. You do not yield to temptation so easily—this is indeed a blessing! (See also Ephesians 4:30 and First John 3:1,3.)

The crucifixion becomes very personal when you hurt with and for Jesus as He hurts for others. Hebrews 12:2-3 encourages you, "Let us fix our eyes on Jesus, the author and perfector of our faith, who for the joy set before Him endured the cross, scorning its shame, and sat down at the right hand of the throne of God. Consider Him who endured such opposition from sinful men, so that you will not grow weary and lose heart." *You* are the joy set before Him that motivated Him to endure the Cross. Realizing and experiencing His love not only for you, but for others becomes the motivation you need to change.

Blessed To Understand Scripture

Scripture becomes more alive as your love for Jesus grows. "...Christ Jesus, who died—more than that, who was raised to life—is at the right hand of God and is also interceding for us" (Rom. 8:34). Burden bearing drops the meaning of this Scripture from the head into the heart. You come to know experientially what it is Jesus does for you as He intercedes for you. You know because you do it for others.

"Therefore he is able to save completely those who come to God through him, because *he always lives to intercede for them*," (Heb. 7:25, emphasis added). Burden bearers who ask the Holy Spirit to manage their burden-bearing capacity live the truth of these Scriptures on a daily basis. You find yourself saying "Amen" a lot! A hunger builds as you live the Scriptures with Jesus and want them inside your heart to mull on at will. You come to love the law of God, as you understand more and more how it works.

Blessing of Being Safe

Suffering develops the sensitivity and courtesy to make you a safe person. It wears off your rough edges, making you slower to speak, more gracious, quicker to listen, and hold another's story with dignity and respect. People from many cultures and a variety of colors have at some point stopped mid-story, looked at me blinking and asked rhetorically, "Why am I telling you this?"—then continue with their story. People sense safety and share deep experiences they had locked away to fester for years.

One of the privileges members of His *fellowship of suffering* have is to pray *with* people. As you pray, you activate the laws of sowing and reaping that brought trouble to people's lives, but in reverse. When you help someone forgive and that person experiences restoration, the law of sowing and reaping works to bring blessing. As you sow forgiveness, you reap it. As you extend mercy, you reap mercy. As you give grace, you receive grace. Luke 6:38 (NASB) says that you will receive more than you give, "Give and it will be given unto you; good measure, pressed down and shaken together, running over they will pour into your lap. For by your standard of measure it will be measured to you in return." This is blessing upon blessing and joy upon joy.

Suffering with Jesus prepares you to live with His resurrection power. The Lord can give you more resurrection power for healing and restoring others because He knitted your heart together with His. You become more like Him and use His power as He would. This kind of knowing Christ through suffering with Him results in releases of power that bring new life to you personally, and to those for whom you intercede, or carry in your heart. Suffering with Him means you put aside your needs and wants for the benefit of others and in that, become like Him in His death. His death resulted in effective ministry that endures. The more you are like Him, the safer you become. Scripture says of Christ that, "He was full of grace and truth" John 1:14. The more you connect to the heart of God, the more His grace and truth will flow into you, and the more life will result from your interactions with others.

Blessed With a Stronger Faith

Hebrews 11:1 (NKJV) says, "Faith is the substance of things hoped for, the evidence of things not seen." The New International Version of the Bible renders it, "Being sure of what we hope for and certain of what we do not see." When God created humankind, He used clay, a substance. The things you hope for (Heaven, eternal life, and fellowship with Jesus and His people) are possible because of faith. You offer

God a grain of faith, and He blesses and multiplies it into the things for which you hope. Obedience and cooperating with God in burden bearing are parts of the substance God uses to grow faith and bring spiritual reality into your life. It strengthens your faith to see people come to life, captives go free, broken hearts mend, and oppression lifted. You see the differences burden-bearing intercession makes and your faith grows.

Blessings of Love

Burden bearing gives you a new love, understanding, and appreciation for the people He connects you with. Experiencing what another lives with has a singular effect. When you walk in others' shoes, you come to care about them. You stand in awe and admiration of how well they do, given the circumstances with which they cope.

As you touch the heart of God and can begin to feel how very, very much the Lord loves people—it changes you forever. As you bear troubles to the Cross, often you feel the Lord's love flowing back to the individual and taste His love for them. You can sense and feel the Father's love for His child and experience the comfort of His love for that person, which also comforts you. This is not a one-way street. You will never out-serve God. Your own capacity to love people will grow as you continue in the Father's business.

Blessed With Unity

Psalm 133, "How good and pleasant it is when brothers live together in unity! It is like precious oil poured on the head, running down on the beard, running down on Aaron's beard, down upon the collar of his robes. It is as if the dew of

Hermon were falling on Mount Zion. For there the Lord bestows his blessing, even life forevermore."

There is no "maybe" about blessing—God commands blessing when you dwell in unity. Burden bearing fosters the love that leads to unity. Unity, not disunity, is characteristic of the sons and daughters of God.

Sin is a fatal affliction. God did, and continues to do, some radical things to save His children. He brings you to death and raises you to life. He gives you a new spirit, a new heart. He adopts Gentiles into the family. He deals a death-blow to your sin nature, although it still struggles to control you much as a chronic disease struggles to come out of remission. Sin holds humankind hostage. It so thoroughly permeates humankind that, like any long-term hostage, your nature, your reflex, is to act like the one who took you captive.

When you are born again, it becomes your task to continually bring those habit patterns or patterns of thought, attitude, and behavior to death, all the ways that are contrary to God's nature, which is unity. To be divisive is fallen nature, and you can fall back into that behavior even though in Christ it received a deathblow. Burden-bearing intercession plunges you into an acid bath of love that eats away the dead sin nature. Burden-bearing intercession drops ropes of love over the walls of division and pulls you up into unity. You cannot help but come to love someone when you walk his or her walk, and experience something of the other's anguish. You cannot help but love when you experience the love of the Father flowing back through you as He meets needs. God is the One who created you. He knows the power of empathy and burden bearing for building unity. He knows that by empowering burden bearers, He strengthens His body, He repairs His people, and builds unity through love and gratitude.

As you touch the heart of God and experience His love for His people, your love, understanding and appreciation grows and unity builds. Burden bearing helps bring down the separateness that divides. It gives you God's heart for building up people rather than tearing down. Condemning, bitter criticism is your greatest service to the enemy! The understanding that comes from walking in another's shoes is essential to the building up of the saints. Indeed, without the blessings of burden bearing (unity, harmony, safety, grace, encouragement) the Church is little different from any other civic organization. Burden bearing builds harmony, unity, and common experiences, which creates common vocabulary and opens doors to common purposes and goals.

Blessed With Healing

You are blessed when burden bearing results in healing for yourself. As the Lord identifies with a person and their sin and connects him with you who voices the prayer He wants prayed, you will have difficulties if you have sin in that same area. It cannot pass on to the Lord cleanly in the area where you are not clean or transparent—some of it sticks! It reveals where you need healing yourself—that's a blessing! When this happens, you (and I) must go to the Lord and ask Him to reveal the problem, reveal the sin.

David realized he was in rage while listening to the husband of a client. The man's anger stuck and combined with David's own anger resulting in white-hot rage. The episode revealed that David needed more healing of his own anger. The time I listened for an hour to a woman's tale of woe and consequently ripped strips off David revealed that I needed to tend to my reactions to David's tendency toward tardiness.

Every time David and I take the sins revealed by burden bearing to Jesus for Him to draw through us to the Cross, we are glad to do so. Carrying someone else's sin in addition to our own is heavy. Confession and repentance bring relief. As you bring sin to death on the Cross, you can release the burden sitting on top of it so it can move on through you onto the Cross. You are lighter because the burden is gone but also because of the personal healing you receive in the process.

Blessed With Comfort

> *Praise be to the God and Father of our Lord Jesus Christ, the Father of compassion and the God of all comfort, who comforts us in all our troubles, so that we can comfort those in any trouble with the comfort we ourselves have received from God. For just as the sufferings of Christ flow over into our lives, so also through Christ our comfort overflows. If we are distressed, it is for your comfort and salvation; if we are comforted, it is for your comfort, which produces in you patient endurance of the same sufferings we suffer. And our hope for you is firm, because we know that just as you share in our sufferings, so also you share in our comfort* (2 Corinthians 1:3-7).

In the course of one weekend, Jesus took all the sin of all the people of all the ages into His body. This work began in Gethsemane and culminated at Calvary. His suffering involved sweating blood and weeping, therefore, know that there will be times when we too will sweat, and weep with those who weep, and for those who cannot weep, as we help people to the Cross through intercessory burden bearing prayers. Matthew 10:24 says that the servant is not above the master. In other words, when you follow Jesus, you should not expect to receive better treatment than He received. You can expect the world to respond to you the way it responded to Him. If He sweat, wept, and stumbled carrying the burden of sin on the way to the Cross, so will you and I. After He completed His work, He spent time in His Father's presence; so will you and I.

Many times after bearing others' troubles, confusion, and emotional pain to the Cross, we experience a sweet richness as we rest in the Lord's presence. It is the Lord's comfort, flowing over and through us back to them, that brings the richness to the experience. We are glad for the other person's healing and comfort, but we linger in the Lord's presence to soak up His love and compassion. His love is so wonderful that we want to come here repeatedly. We are blessed by being there, and then blessed again that someone else was helped.

It is also true that we will experience times when we feel separated from God as Jesus did on the Cross as you identify, connect with, or absorb part of another's burden. We can feel isolated in pain, longing for His comfort and unable find it. If we feel separated from God, it is not necessarily the confusion of wrongly burden bearing. We can experience this separation even when burden bearing rightly—there are three common reasons:

First, we may experience the exact feeling this person has—separation and isolation—so that we can intercede intelligently and specifically and with passion.

Second, the other person's emotional content can overwhelm us by pulling up matching unhealed issues in our lives.

Third, as we identify with another person's distress, the magnitude of what we sense can overwhelm. Our own ability to sense God's presence shuts down and we may need to call trusted friends for help, as well as God.

When overwhelmed, hold fast to what you know to be true of Jesus, regardless of what you feel. Feelings come and go, some are accurate and some inaccurate, but Jesus is changeless and eternal. He is our bedrock. He is what keeps us grounded. In times of feeling separated, speak the truth about Jesus aloud as King David did. It helps to comfort our mind and emotions: "Why are you so downcast, oh my soul?" (Ps. 42:5,11; 43:5). David continually talked to himself about the nature of God. When we speak the truth aloud, our spirit remembers; something clicks in and we come to ourselves. *Remember* that our distress is for their restoration, reconciliation, and salvation. It is important to *remember* that we also experience the Lord's comfort for the stress we feel as we carry others' burdens to the Cross in prayer what others carry—maybe not immediately, but the comfort will come. In the Lord's economy, comfort for the hurting also comforts our own distress. As we connect to His heart, we share Jesus' compassion for His people.

Blessed With the Nature of God

Burden bearing intercession furthers the Kingdom of God and accomplishes things for other people. It also builds the nature of God into your character. It is spiritual physiotherapy. You become like the One with whom you spend time. When you sense His heart and experience the value and caring He places on all His creation, those values change your values, your thinking, attitudes, and behaviors. Fear and darkness lose their hold as you become more aware of yourself as a son or daughter of God and begin to walk tall and confident in that awareness.

Blessed With Spiritual Protection

Rightly submitting to the Lord, and honoring His design is a spiritual protection. He will not abuse your capacity for empathy. He will not ask more of you than you can bear. When living in obedience, He will not allow you to know things you should not know, or see things you should not see. Redeemed burden bearing results in the easy yoke, the burden that is light (Matt. 11:30). Burden bearing will be light and easy, not in the sense of being pleasant, but easy in the sense of being appropriate to your stage of development and maturity. Asking Him to be in charge of the burden bearing means that the Lord will supply the resources to bear what He calls you to bear. And it will ensure that you will carry it in prayer only as long as Christ determines, and that you will then leave it at His Cross. It will not be grievous, or harmful. Unredeemed burden bearing can be heavy, grievous, and harmful for the burden bearer and for those nearby. Unredeemed burden bearing often results in violation and spiritual abuse.

The nature of the flesh (fallen human nature) is to peer because of curiosity, and finding something, to gossip, use or manipulate. When individuals are still in charge of their spirit's capacity rather than the Lord, they tend to abuse, knowingly and unknowingly. He protects you, not only from exterior spiritual forces, but also from yourself!

Blessed To Worship the Father

Redeemed burden bearing is an act of worship that pleases the Father, "Therefore, I urge you, brothers, in view of

God's mercy, to offer your bodies as living sacrifices, holy and pleasing to God: this is *your spiritual act of worship,*" (Rom. 12:1, emphasis added). To consciously say "yes" to Jesus' heart in you is to say "yes" to the burdens of others flowing through you on the way to the Cross. Scripture says your bodies are temples of the Holy Spirit, and it is fitting that spiritual acts of worship happen in the temple (1 Cor. 6:19).

Offering your body to the Lord to bear whatever He would have you experience in the course of burden bearing is also a sacrifice. Dedicating this capacity for burden bearing to the Lord for His uses, especially in light of His heart of mercy toward you, is certainly a spiritual sacrifice, an act of worship.

Be open to suffering for and with Him, to being inconvenienced for the Lord's sake. It may not feel spiritual, or like an act of worship, but He considers it such. Eternity is going to be full of surprises! You will understand the heart of God more each time you enter into His suffering and sacrifice. Like Paul, I urge you, in view of God's mercy, to offer your bodies as living sacrifices and dedicate yourselves and all spiritual capacities to Him (Rom. 12:1; 1 Pet. 2:5).

Blessed With a Personal Relationship With the Father

Intimacy with the Father does not come automatically after completing steps one, two, and three. It comes with maturity. The Father is present and active in your life from the moment of salvation, but you are more consciously aware of Jesus early in your spiritual walk rather than the Father. As you mature, you become more and more aware of the Father and relate to Him as well as Jesus and the Holy Spirit.

The Mystery of Spiritual Sensitivity

When Jesus rose from the grave, He spent time with His Father; that had to be a great comfort after the trial of the crucifixion. Jesus was very clear when He said that followers would experience what He experienced. Part of that experience includes the comfort of the Father's presence. "Whoever has My commands and obeys them, he is the one who loves Me. He who loves Me *will be loved by my Father,* and I too will love him and show Myself to him. ...If anyone loves Me, he will obey My teaching. My Father will love him, and *We will come to him and make Our home with him,*" (John 14:21,23).

What a privilege that Father God would show Himself to you! Jesus promises that knowing the Father is the result of loving obedience. In John 14:6 He says, "I am the way, the truth, and the life. No one comes to the Father except through Me. If you really knew Me, you would know My Father as well. From now on, you do know Him and have seen Him."

Your relationship with the Father builds with your increasing capacity to experience Jesus' heart. When you were born again, you received the Godhead—the full trinity—but at the outset were not capable of experiencing that fullness. It is a package deal, but you come into the full experience as you have the capacity to experience it. At the time of salvation, you can experience life with Jesus. Jesus is the focal point of relationship with God. As you mature and develop, you come to understand that you can also experience and feel comfortable with the Holy Spirit who widens your comfort zone.

Many are nervous relating to this member of the Godhead because some perceive Him as a bit wild—with time, you come to know that He is not. As you receive salvation for the asking, so you receive the release of the Holy Spirit for the asking. He has been there all along; you could not yet experience Him, or were unaware of experiencing Him, until your spiritual capacity grew. Jesus prepares you to experience the Holy Spirit, and the Holy Spirit prepares you to experience the Father.

Experiencing the Father does not necessarily come when you ask—there is something *you* must do. The Lord does many things for you, but when it comes to spiritual maturity, you have choices to make. You can and must choose the path of spiritual maturity—lay your life down for His people. Then He releases His life in you—He *comes* to you, reveals Himself, and abides with you. This is a mystery because He has been there all along, but actively choosing to lay down your life removes the last barriers. When the Father comes to abide in an individual, there is security and peace. You do not have to strive anymore—or work at ministry or loving God's people. The Father's love is just *there* and You can live in His blessing.

The call is to be willing to be imitators of Christ, to be living sacrifices as Jesus was, to be willing to accept burdens anytime, day or night, as Jesus did. The Lord is looking for those who will pray and prepare the way for His Kingdom, as Jesus did. One result and greatest reward is fullness of relationship with the Father. When the Father comes, nothing is the same.

CHAPTER 11

Bringing Healing

There is a time for everything, and a season for every activity under Heaven: a time to be born and a time to die, a time to plant and a time to uproot, a time to kill and a time to heal...a time to mend...(Ecclesiastes 3:1-8).

The healing process is a time of coming to life, of dying to some things, of planting and uprooting, of listening and speaking. Because burden bearers often resist asking for help, let me say this very clearly. *Healing will come faster and go to a deeper level if sorted out and prayed about with a trusted friend, a prayer minister, or a Christian counselor who focuses on inner healing*—one who listens as well as speaks, who knows how to plant as well as uproot, bring to life as well as bring to death. The added strength of a trusted friend can help you identify your own bitter root judgments and inner vows, to provide the loving presence that enables you to take responsibility for your part and do your own repentance. Doing your own repentance opens the door for the Lord's healing comfort.

Where To Begin

In one sense it does not matter where the healing begins, just that it begins. It is like taking hold of a stick protruding from a tangled mess and pulling, the tangle follows but as you pull the tangle begins to come undone. Some of you have pressing difficulties from current ongoing hurt that needs immediate attention. If current hurts are mended through repentance and forgiveness, then you can go back to remove accumulated burdens that you acquired because over the years you did not learn to do differently. You need also to tend to early wounds caused by the family, or lack of family, and their reactions to your responses to what you saw, felt, sensed, and experienced. Begin with what is obvious and be thorough. Repent of your responses—the conclusions you came to—that led to bitter roots and inner vows. Take responsibility for how you have and continue to participate in the patterns you discover. Present ongoing hurt intertwines with past hurts and reactions, so it may take some time to unravel the tangle. When bitter roots and inner vows have been identified, repented of and broken, forgiveness given and received, you can launch into a life of learning Kingdom language, ways, and values. The Lord will reveal other sinful reactions as you go about life, or additional aspects or angles to approach old ones.

The Healing Process

Tell someone you trust. Begin by telling your story. It is healing to express anguish in the presence of another human being who does not reject or go away. A loving countenance goes a long way in convincing your heart that God hears your prayers. "If this person still loves me, well, then, maybe God can too." When someone listens, empathizes, and prays with you, you no longer feel isolated and alone, there is a balm for the hurt of rejection and misunderstanding. Christ in the brother or sister meets you in the deep places of your being that you cannot access at will, but where you most need to be met. You feel the Lord giving you the same kind of emotional assurance He gave Job.

I understood this need to express hurt and the anguish over injustice at a new level when a nurse gave me a physical parallel. She explained that often a pocket of infection is "expressed," or lanced and the area pressed to push out accumulated infection in order to cleanse the wound in preparation for medication. Some wounds need further cleansing. She related how a bedridden patient developed a pressure wound. After expressing the infection, she had to reach into the wound with a Q-tip to see if other channels had developed. Sometimes a root system will develop in a wound, providing channels for infection to spread. These channels must be probed and cleansed if the wound is to heal.

The same is true of our spirits. The Lord may direct the one praying with us to ask probing questions, which take us to painful places in the moment but lead to ancillary pockets of toxic emotions that also need expression and to receive the Lord's healing touch.

Be forewarned that being listened to will seem awkward and unnatural at first, but do not flee away. Do not stop the process. The awkwardness will dissipate. Part of the healing is to have someone take you seriously, to listen to you, and affirm you. That happens as you tell your story to your friend and to God. God does want to hear your story, and He is a big God. He can operate the universe and listen to you as if you were the only one. Be assured that you are no inconvenience to Him.

Telling someone about the hurt and anger over God's *apparent* lack of interest and His non-intervention without being condemned helps your heart to heal further. The eyes can read the Scriptures, and the *mind* can believe that He cares, but the *heart* can still doubt. An added benefit from telling your story is that your friend becomes a witness to remind you when you doubt or forget what you asked the Lord to do. The friend can remind you when you minimize or forget what happened, when you forget what you know of His character and the standing He gives you. Then, confess.

Confess. At some point, the telling stops, and the confession begins. Confession lances your mental, emotional, and spiritual wounds so that you can "express" the infection that has accumulated in your spirit and emotions. The infection of an emotional wound is bitterness, anger, and resentment. It is necessary to clean out toxic emotion that has never found a place of release.

You need to discharge the collection of hurts from family members and the burdens you accumulated as you subconsciously drew off pain, troubles and torment, confusions. You begin by confessing to a friend, prayer minister, or counselor, that you accumulated this storehouse without knowing what you were doing, or how to do differently.

I found it worked well to inventory the hurts of each era and put words to any judgments or vows I made in response to those hurts. (Judgments and vows are explained in Chapter 4.) I also asked Him to lift out of my spirit the accumulated gunk I had unknowingly absorbed from others during that era and carried because I did not know I had picked it up, or what to do with it if I had known!

For example, my list included the pre-natal era, preschool era, elementary era, middle school, and high school, etc. I listed all the hurts I could remember in relation to teachers and schoolmates, and then on to the work place, church, extended family, and other authority figures—this took a while. I asked the Lord to take all the hurts, confusions, and burdens knowingly or *unknowingly* accumulated through the years. With His help, I off-loaded them at the Cross. As a safety check I asked the Lord to lift to consciousness anything I needed to know about any of these events, or even about the things I unknowingly accumulated, so that our enemy would have no place to claim legal access to my life. When I finished, I felt 40 pounds lighter!

A note of warning: You can do a very thorough inventory with the Lord and seem to have covered all aspects of your life. Yet at another phase in life and a different set of circumstances, He may take you back over territory you already covered. This is because at the time of the first inventory you covered all that you were prepared to face, and that took all the spiritual strength you had. The Lord was being the good surgeon who excised only what the patient could sustain in one surgery—though there remained others yet to come. It is the same spiritually; the Lord takes you to and through as much as you can bear at the time. If there is more to come, He will build you up, strengthen your spirits, and organize people and circumstances to cause the next level of what needs healing to come to the surface. Like the Disney character, Shrek, who declared, "Ogres have layers," so do people!

You must confess any hatred or resentment of the people with whom you grew up. Do a search, as thorough and ruthless as you are able, even looking for ways you may be angry with God. You may be angry with Him for not doing anything about your situation and angry with Him for "sending me here." If you feel that the word *hatred* is too harsh—then look for resentment. If you are aware of resentment, then you need to confess it because resentment feeds, or may grow into, hatred.

My specific anger issue with God was that He was holding me responsible, or accountable for judgments I made as a child, though I was completely ignorant of how God's laws worked. It seemed terribly unfair to me that God was holding me accountable for something I did as a toddler! (This was my feeling and understanding at the time.) As a toddler, I did not know that I judged God, my father, or life in general, or that judging activated the adverse side of laws of sowing and reaping. I was not pleased with this new revelation, but finally came to a place where I decided that His was the only game in town. I had better learn the rules—like them or not! For me, it came down to "No, life is not fair, but God is just and loving. He knows more than I do and if He says the universe runs this way, it probably does." If I wanted to steer my life in the right direction, He was kind enough to show me how to do that. I do not understand the logic and rational of a car engine, but I steer, I drive a car. I may not understand God's logic and rationale either. Much about God is mystery, but I still want a close relationship with Him. Having settled this issue, I could proceed successfully with confession, repentance, and forgiveness.

Now I have a fuller understanding. God does hold us accountable for *all* the judgments we made as a toddler, **but Jesus paid for them all** with His blood the moment we accepted Him into our lives. That is the good news of salvation. However, long years later some of you still hold onto a judgment like a favorite marble, and do not surrender it at the Cross. As a result, trouble from that unsurrendered judgment follows you. On the other hand, you may be able to remember resentments that you had as a child yet have no bad fruit in your life from those judgments. You, by expectation, do not draw out of others the hateful behavior, nor do you participate in it. Jesus covered that judgment with His blood when you were born again. Sometime, either before, during, or after the time of your conversion, you must have repented, for it is inactive. There is no bad fruit; you are no longer legally accountable for it.

The judgments that you made, usually sometime in childhood or teen years, will follow you if your heart, consciously or unconsciously, continues to hold on to them. *They are present, active judgments that had their beginnings* long ago, and continue to be currently active. Through the years there has been no resolution; you continue to respond to the *kind of hurt* you judged with anger, bitterness, or condemnation again and again. You know whether a judgment is active by the repeated pattern of present fruit in your life—addictions, bad job situations, difficulty relating to authority, relationships go sour.

You may think you have repented of a particular judgment, but if bad fruit remains, there is some aspect of that judgment that is still active, and needs to be repented of. You need to repent of the current practice, but you will also need to trace back to its roots and *apply the blood of Jesus* there to stop the reaping! If you do not, if you only confess the present behavior, God will forgive it, but it will again grow, flower, and produce bad fruit. The same happens to physical weeds. If you mow off dandelions, they will grow back until you kill the root. If you do apply Jesus blood to the root, but bad fruit continues, revisit the roots. Look at them from other angles; repent and bring undiscovered side roots to the Cross. Do this until the judgment no longer produces fruit. Many times ancillary roots, and subsequent judgments, grow from the original and produce their own bad fruit.

You are also held accountable for judgments made as born-again believers, adults, or teens. When you realize you just made a judgment, repent quickly before the reaping begins! When Mark Sandford moved back to Idaho from Florida, he had an accident on the snowy road. His father, who knows and teaches on judgments, judged his son. "Mark is spacey. That's how he always was. His spaciness caused the accident." John judged that the accident was Mark's fault without taking time to find out if that was true. He assumed it was based on an outdated picture of Mark. John's judgment put the law of sowing and reaping into gear. Later, he had an accident with his beloved car. He quickly realized it and repented all the way to the repair shop. He even went beyond asking the Lord for forgiveness, he apologized to Mark lest he have another accident!

At some point, you will probably confess that you unwittingly tried to do God's job, tried to be someone's savior. Be as specific in your confession as possible. However, specific does not mean you must rehash or relive every sordid detail. Ask the Lord to help by revealing strategic, repetitive events to pray through. When you can confess deepest hurts and the judgments or vows that came from them, you prepare the way for healing to come to many other similar hurts. Confession is not solely an admission after commission, it is also a much-needed expression of how badly particular incidents hurt—an expression of your sense of injustice or violation.

Talk with God about specific incidents that in a sense symbolized many such incidents. Tell Him how badly it hurt; admit to Him your responses, repent, and then forgive.

Forgive. You may not have ever expressed many of your emotional, psychological, and spiritual hurts and confusions. You also may not have ever expressed forgiveness toward those who misunderstood your responses of tears, anger, or withdrawal. You need to do this; and forgive those who called you names and damaged you with rejection or ridiculed you for your sensitivity. You need to forgive the people who did not hear your heart as a child or pursued you to find and know you. As a result, you felt invisible and because of that, you may now live with a keen sense of loneliness. You feel as if you live on the edge of life, and sometimes as if you are not even part of it. *Receive* forgiveness.

At some point, you will need to *ask* forgiveness for any less-than-gracious (sinful) responses on your part to what hurt you because negative, hateful, ungracious responses plant angry little seeds that give rise to other judgments, angers, condemnations, and bitterness. When you resent the people who hurt and misunderstood you, you hold their sins against them—as if you were God and had His wisdom and authority to determine how they should be punished. You define them according to a behavior. You hold something against your brother or sister.

Mark 11:25 says, "And when you stand praying, if you hold anything against anyone, forgive him, so that your Father in Heaven may forgive you your sins." (See also Matthew 5:23.) These judgments are how you throw people into a debtor's prison. They owe you—love, life, apologies, recognition. Release all of this to Jesus and let Jesus be responsible to fulfill you instead of holding people in your debt. In effect, Jesus said that God will do for you what you do for others. Matthew 6:14: "For if your forgive men when they sin against you, your heavenly Father will also forgive you." Matthew 6:15, "But if you do not forgive men their sins, your Father will not forgive your sins." Matthew 7:12, "So in everything, do unto others as you would have them do unto you, for this sums up the Law and the prophets." Luke 6:31 repeats the principle. You cannot hold something against someone if you do not want something held against you.

After you forgive those who hurt you, try to find words for judgments or vows you made in response to those hurts so that you can repent and ask the Lord's forgiveness for making them. When you come to see how judgments or vows affected your life by setting you up for continued reaping, you are motivated to repent. Then you are free to ask Him to break or nullify them and receive His forgiveness. Jesus said He came to destroy the works of darkness (1 John 3:8). Whatever separates you from the Lord is, in some way, a work of darkness. Separation from God is the enemy's aim and he will use anything and anyone to achieve it.

One final thing for which you need to receive forgiveness— for any way in which you participated, or continue to participate in the very behavior you hate. Scripture says that the one who judges is without excuse because that person does the very thing for which they have judged others (see discussion of Romans 2:1 in Chapter 4). You will either repeat the behavior or do something similar that has the same effect. Thus, the victim of emotional abuse often becomes the perpetrator of emotional abuse. The object of rage often becomes "rageful."

One caution—people do not always repeat the exact behavior they judged. For instance, many do not abuse others—but do abuse themselves. For example: a woman who judged her father for being harshly critical, may be gentle and patient with others, yet be harshly critical of herself. The child who grows up with an alcoholic father swears he will not be like his father...and he is not. He provides for his family. He is faithful to his wife, but she says, "You are just like your father!" How can this be? He is like his father in that he is emotionally unavailable and often physically absent from his family; it has nothing to do with alcohol or lack of provision. He is not addicted to alcohol; he is addicted to work.

A woman grew up with an obsessively tidy mother, in anger she determined she would not be like her mother, and she is not. She describes herself as a slob, just like her grandmother. Grandmother was obsessively tidy. Grandmother condemned that behavior but did not become like her mother; she went the other way. Grandmother was a messy housekeeper whose daughter became obsessively tidy. What is wrong with not wanting to be obsessively tidy? The judgment to be "different than mother" is based upon bitterness and therefore, cannot produce the desired righteous result. Consequently, the girl more than avoided obsessively tidy, she over corrected and became (in her words) a slob. Each participated in the family pattern in some way so that the pattern continued to pass down within the family—each generation judging the one before and becoming the opposite.

It is important to ask the Lord to reveal the ways in which you participate in hurtful patterns. It is common to lack awareness of your own participation. It often takes outside eyes to see and confront, but it will require revelation to your own heart to convict and come to repentance. When conviction comes, you may feel shame and dismay, for you know how hurtful the hateful behavior was to you. You surely do not want to perpetuate harm. I like the prayer Jabez prayed, "Oh that you would bless me and enlarge my territory! Let your hand be with me, and keep me from harm so that I will be free from pain" (1 Chron. 4:10). Some renderings indicate that it was his prayer not only not to *be* in pain, but also not to *cause* pain to others. This is surely your heart's cry, so you need the Lord to reveal any and all of the ways you subtly, or otherwise, participate in the patterns you condemned in others. God's revelation is meant to lead you to repentance and healing, not condemnation.

Prayers of forgiveness need to follow expressions of hurt, but you do not have to rush to forgive. Sometimes, like Job, you need to sit and ponder the enormity of what was done, to comprehend your losses, and then forgive. Confession makes room for cleansing and healing. Forgiveness removes the driving, grinding force, and the places where you stored all the hurtful experiences. Forgiveness is like removing the infection of bitterness that makes emotions toxic. You need to rid yourself of toxic emotions *and* the structures that hold them. Both need to go to the Cross. The structures are the ungodly judgments, vows, and habits of belief or thinking.[1]

In Summary

Ask a prayer partner to join you in talking with God about specific hurtful incidents. Ask God to show you what your sinful responses were to these hurts. Ask Him to forgive you for your judgments and choose to forgive the sinful actions, habits, or attitudes of those who hurt you. This frees you from those sins. Ask the Lord to forgive you of ways you participated in the very sin patterns that you condemned.

Repent of and renounce judgments and vows as the Lord reveals them and invite Jesus to take the place of your home-made armor. Ask the Lord to bring to death on the Cross any accumulation of bitter responses to this and any similar hurts—to cleanse you of wrong judgments and beliefs.

Ask the Lord to show you any area you missed that you need to address, and then rest in His timing. He will orchestrate people and circumstances to reveal what you are ready to face. He is faithful to prepare your heart and mind to recognize how you have been hurt and how you responded. You can count on God to help you talk it out, forgive, ask for forgiveness, and bring judgments and ungodly habits to death.

Remember the resurrection side of healing. Ask the Holy Spirit to fill your spirit, soul, and body where the toxicity was. You do not want to remove something without putting something in its place according to Luke 11:24-26. As you pray, remember the Lord is able to do even more than you know how to ask (Eph 3:20). After the healing, you need to learn a new way. Daily you will need to make Godly choices to develop new habits and learn to bear burdens rightly before they kill you! This will be the focus of another book.

Why We Must Forgive

In many cases, those who wounded us do not deserve forgiveness. Actually, no one does. Lack of forgiveness ties us to the hurt and keeps *us* captive in the role of the judge; whereas forgiveness cuts the tie. God becomes responsible for judging those who hurt and misunderstood us. When we forgive, we are free to heal. We would not hold a battery to our chests if it were leaking acid. Why hold tightly to unforgiveness when it leaks the acid of bitterness into our lives? We must stop sowing if we want to stop reaping.

Forgiveness—the "F" Word

For many, forgiveness is a dirty word. It may conger up memories of forced apologies or asking forgiveness because someone twisted our arm behind our back and asking forgiveness was the only way to stop the pain. There is usually a very good historical reason for feeling the way we do about forgiveness. However, God does not coerce. He is all about relationship. He wants us to understand the consequences of our choices, but does not twist our arm until we choose to live life His way.

Let us look at forgiveness. What does the word mean? Unfortunately, it has been vandalized. We must have a proper understanding of forgiveness if we hope to be free and whole.

Forgiveness is not saying what happened to you was right, that it did not hurt, or that it does not matter. Truth is, it was not right, it did hurt, and it does matter. Forgiveness is not making excuses or letting people off easy. Criticism, undercutting, minimizing are not all right, it does hurt and it does matter to God and to us. Forgiveness is recognizing that the hurt, trouble, anguish is bigger than we are and that we cannot cope with the accumulation of hurt and burdens on our own. To forgive is to release that accumulation to the Lord for Him to do with according to His own discretion. It is an invitation for the Lord to free and heal "me." It is giving Jesus the responsibility to determine justice for those who hurt us. Forgiveness does not let someone off the hook—it puts the offender on Jesus' hook.

You do not need to forgive and forget. Psalm 103:12 does say that God forgives and removes our sins from us as far as the east is from the west. It does say that God remembers our sins no more and does not hold them against us. I have not found any Scripture that says that we have to forgive and then forget about it and act as if nothing happened when we were hurt. God can afford to forget. When God forgets, He does not literally lose all conscious awareness of the offense, no! Forgetting is not amnesia; for if it was, there would be no record in Scripture of any specific sin that had been committed, then forgiven. God "forgets" in the sense of dismissing the case from court. A record of the offense remains, but it does not affect your life.

God can forget and still be appropriate because He has boundless wisdom. You and I do not. We need to learn from what happens to us. If you have no conscious recollection of everything you forgive, where would the learning be? You would go out and be hurt again! You are to forgive and remember. When you remember, you will not again walk into hurtful situations with your heart wide open. You forget only in the sense that God does, you dismiss it from court—in the court of your heart you hand the person over to God allowing Him to hold him accountable.

Forgiving someone does not mean you have to immediately trust the person. First Peter 2:17 says that we should "respect everyone." No exceptions. But, nowhere does the Scripture say you should "trust all men." Even Jesus did not entrust himself to men, for He knew what was in the hearts of men (John 2:24). And He said to not throw pearls before swine (Matt. 7:6). And when David snuck through camp and stole Saul's spear and water jug, Saul apologized and asked him to come back to Jerusalem, but David did not go back to Jerusalem, for he knew Saul's heart would not retain his momentary repentance (1 Sam. 24). Time proved David correct.

You can forgive a person who is not trustworthy because *you* want to be untangled; you need to be free to heal. If a parent (or other significant person) is a buzz saw that cuts you to pieces, forgive them for the hurt so you can go on with life, but you do not have to act as if nothing happened. No one knowingly walks back into the path of a buzz saw! It is possible to honor a parent or a person by respecting them, but at the same time give a wide enough berth to prevent new hurt from happening.

You respect your parents and others when you treat them the way you want to be treated. You can think for yourself; you can make your own choices, be responsible for your own thoughts and attitudes, responsibilities, and burdens as well as your own speech, deceptions, denials, blame, or tempers. You respect your parents and others when you ask or entreat them to be responsible for those same things. *Trust and respect (honor) are not the same.*

After confession and forgiveness, you have room in your heart and spirit for the Lord's love for the one you forgave. You will be more able to see the person through God's eyes of love rather than through the filter of hurt and resentment, but this does not necessarily come quickly.

A young man came to my husband for prayer ministry with such an active hatred for his father that he wanted him dead, and said as much. After he confessed and repented of the hatred, and asked forgiveness for it, in a vision he saw the Lord standing over his father with sword raised to strike the man down. In alarm he cried, "No, Lord." The Lord replied, "But you said you wanted him dead." The confession, repentance, and forgiveness cleaned the wound. Then the son could see his father more clearly, love flooded forward, and he interceded on his father's behalf.

This story indicated to me that God agreed with the son's assessment that his father's behavior was unacceptable. But the son went on to hate, whereas, God's heart was forgiveness, not vengeance. God knew the young man's heart, and to help him come to a place of repentance and forgiveness He showed him what the consequences of that hatred would look like. The son's error was not in the assessment, but in the hatred.

Healing Process Summary

- Recognize your hurts.
- Express the hurts without excuse for the ones who caused them, including yourself where you participated in the sin pattern.
- Confess and repent of (or renounce) our less-than-gracious responses.
- Give and receive forgiveness.
- Ask the Lord to cleanse, heal, and fill.
- Learn new responses—Kingdom language and Kingdom ways.

How Long?

How long will the process take? A lifetime. Complete healing is a lifetime process, but dealing with a specific root can be done very quickly. You may be often frustrated that your complete healing does not come as quickly as you would like, that it will go on forever. As you consistently track a bitter fruit in your life to the root, the process becomes much shorter, lighter, and easier.

I assure you, the Lord knows what you need to bring you to a place of wholeness and maturity. Think of your reactions to the hurts of your life as weeds on your inner landscape; it is much easier to pull a weed when the ground is moist than when it is bone dry and baked hard. If you put life on hold, and only pursue healing, lay hold of it and yank and pull, you may pull up what the Lord is not ready to reveal. You make the process more difficult, and you do it to yourself! Since God is all about relationship, He can reveal strategically what interferes with any given relationship. Pressing into Jesus is different than demanding that God act—now! You must not take by force what the Lord would give by grace. Trust. Trust His timing and His sequence of events. "God who has begun a good work in you will complete it" (Phil. 1:6).

Healing is an ongoing process that continues even as you are learning how to walk as sons and daughters of God, as you are learning to love your neighbor as yourself. Reflexive "natural" (sinful) responses are seeds that conceive and grow, (James 1:15), and are woven into the inner foundations of your being. Seed judgments and vows, attitudes and beliefs are integral to the logic you build and use to justify and rationalize your sinful behaviors and attitudes. This logic distorts your perceptions and does not reflect the truth about you, others, or God. It will take time and discipline, in the good sense of the word, to transform your logic, to replace the judgments and vows with truth, to adjust your attitudes and beliefs until they reflect His thoughts, ways, and values.

You may be impatient, but the Lord has all the time in the world. You become especially frustrated when you find yourself back at square one, forgiving the same people for the same offence again and again! I encourage you to be patient with yourself and with God. It is possible to pray through the prayers that follow in the next chapter and not find the release you desire. It is not because God did not listen or does not care. It is not that the prayers do not work. When nothing happens, the Lord usually wants to reveal some additional aspect that needs healing *before* He can give you what you asked for.

For example you may ask Him to take care of step number 4—and He will do that, but He will make sure that you address steps 1 through 3 first because they are the foundation for step 4. The Lord knows the best timing and the best sequence in which to bring healing so that it is lasting, not just a temporary fix. The Lord never withholds to be mean, but to protect. He sees the overall picture that you cannot see. You hurt and you want Him to fix it—*now*! He wants your lasting healing and a full and mature relationship with you, so He will organize people and circumstances in times and ways that not only heal but also develop the character of Christ in you.

Do not despair. Be patient with yourself and God, and get some help from a trusted friend or friends, a counselor, or prayer minister when you need it. Go through things again, and ask the Lord to shine His light to reveal the next step.

It is common to have to revisit an issue more than once. Having to do so does not mean the prayers did not work, or that you are defective in some way. Rather, it means the Lord knows what is ready to address, and what is properly prepared to heal. To revisit is to return from another angle. It is another layer.

Healing is about being restored to yourself, or being introduced to yourself in the first place, so that you can learn to act like yourself. You will need to confess hurt, receive healing, give and receive forgiveness many times as you learn to walk and talk like children of God. When the Lord starts something, He finishes it. You may not know what His schedule is, but you do know that it is His nature to love, comfort, encourage, and to build your faith. Be kind to yourself; healing comes a step at a time. If He asks you to take a step with Him and you can't or won't go with Him, He still loves you. Experiencing His patience with your "no" to what He wanted may be the piece of healing for today! Regardless of how it feels to you, He is right on schedule. Such a different attitude from those who wounded you!

During the healing process, several things happen that prepare the way for living a balanced life as a healthy burden bearer.

- You receive revelation from the Lord regarding His character.

- The Holy Spirit convicts you about your reactions to the Lord; you repent and ask Him to remove or redeem all that separates you.

- You bring the burden bearing capacity to the Cross and come to death to this ability.

- The Lord gives back redeemed in the form of spiritual gifts. When you go through the healing process and this list of things happen for you, you begin to walk in the power of the resurrection.

Back To Joy

God created humanity because of joy and for joy. Jesus' prayer for His disciples in John 16:24 was that "their joy might be full." Joy is the goal. God intends joy to be the natural state of a human being, your "baseline." To whatever degree you do not have joy you cannot be fully yourself. You have work to do—you must find your way back to joy! The most foundational joy you can have is being in right relationship to God, and then second, with people. Given the mystery of spiritual sensitivity, you are uniquely designed to help restore joy. Naturally, the enemy targets you to steal your joy, to damage the most, and eliminate first. Sin has turned the world upside down and backward so that your gift has become your curse. Sensitivity, the tool, and in some cases, the weapon, you were given to do the job designed for you from the beginning, becomes the very instrument of your wounding, a sword turned against you.

I have contended that God will do for you what you cannot do for yourself, but He will not do for you what you should do for yourself. He will not take away the responsibilities He gave. He will not force you to become a mature adult. He will not make you listen. He will not make you receive healing. He will not make you release burdens to Him. When you wrap your identity around the pain and trouble you carry, He will not forcibly insist that you "hand it over." He wants you to come to Him of your own accord. He wants to teach you to bear burdens rightly, to sense, feel, and hear His heart. If you come, He will lead and you will find your way back to joy.

I pray the Lord bless you and strengthen you in your inner being so that you have the strength to walk through hard places and that He may give you the courage to look where you would rather not. May you experience comfort, restoration, and the relief of healing from the hurts and wounds from growing up highly sensitive and by unredeemed burden bearing. I pray that He touch the very fabric of your spirit and soul so you can contain all that He would pour into you! May you know peace. May He show you how to find your way back to joy. Father You so love us! You know what we can bear; thank You for coming alongside to carry the overwhelming portion. Thank You for the host of people who join You in that work! Amen.

This is the beginning of a healing journey—a journey that takes a lifetime. We will have complete healing and understanding of the mystery of spiritual sensitivity only when we stand before our Father in Heaven.

Endnote

1. Loren Sandford, *Purifying the Prophetic* (Grand Rapids, MI: Chosen Books, 2005), 300-310.

CHAPTER 12

Prayer

P rayer is conversation you have with God. There is nothing magical at all about prayer, no special language, no
formulas, and no right way to say anything. You talk with
God, laugh, and pour out your heart as you would with any
friend; you share your needs, wants, and your hurts. As you
continue to relate to Him, you come to know Him—His character, attributes, and even His sense of humor, just as you
come to know another person.

Someone may point out that if God is all-knowing and
all-powerful He already knows what you think and feel, so
why pray. It is true that He does know it all, but He still wants
to hear it from you. Scripture frequently uses the metaphor
of the parent-child relationship to characterize your relationship with God. Every parent wants their children to talk to
them, to tell them about their day, how things went. Parents
want to know what their children think and feel. They want
dialogue—to hear actions, reactions, and some facts along
with all the color, texture, and intensity of their experience.
There are also those occasions when, as a parent, you
observed interactions, so you already know what happened,

but still want to hear it from them. All of this talking and relating creates trust, and builds a powerful bond.

God is not so different. He too wants you, His child, to share your thoughts, feelings, and experiences with Him in the same way, unedited. An open and honest relationship with God also builds trust and a strong bond. An additional benefit is that it helps you know what is in your own heart, which is essential for spiritual growth and maturity.

The remainder of this chapter is a series of sample prayers written for those who would like an idea of how to begin. Feel free to edit these prayers to fit your particular situation. They are offered to help you begin the healing process to understanding burden bearing and solving the mystery of spiritual sensitivity.

Prayer of Forgiveness

Father I come to you because You have said You want me to. I don't know how to make forgiveness happen. I can't cleanse my heart or change my feelings. I don't know how to trust, and I'm afraid to hold my heart open. But now I'm making a choice to forgive. I'm setting my heart and will to choose to forgive again and again until You make forgiveness real and complete in me—until it becomes a way of life.

Please God, give me the willingness and strength to persevere in forgiving until forgiveness is accomplished in me by Your power. You know the history between _____ (name) _____ and me. You know how ___ (name) _____ hurt me by _____ (what happened) _____. I release to You my right to hold this offence against him/her. I release to You my hurt, anger and/or resentment. Lord, I release _____ (name) _____ to you—You be the judge in this matter. I ask You to cleanse me of the effects of the negative emotions that I have carried all this time. I ask for Your healing touch, and I ask that You wash me and fill me with Your Holy Spirit.

Lord, after ____ (name) _____ did _____ (what happened) _____ to me I felt_____ (be specific about how you felt: worthless, helpless, etc.) I speak forgiveness to him/her and ask You to release me from to this person, emotionally and spiritually so that our relationship is no longer hindered by unforgiveness. I ask for the healing comfort of your Holy Spirit to be poured into the crushed and broken places.

Father, it is a hard thing to see and admit that I have also done hurtful things to others. I have repeated this hurtful behavior____(name the behavior) _____ and participated in this pattern. I hurt _____ (name) _____ by __ (action) _____. I ask Your forgiveness and ask that You strengthen me so that I may make matters right (where appropriate to do so). I ask You to be with me and give me courage and grace to ask for forgiveness, and give ____ (name) _____ grace to forgive me. I ask that You bless us with restored relationship.

I ask You to restore my spirit in all its crushed and broken places. Teach me who I am, teach me my worth, especially in relationship with You. Heal the wounded heart of the child within me. Let Your light shine into all the hidden places of my heart. Pour Your love in. Enlighten the eyes of my heart, Lord, so that I may see You and love You as You really are. Help me walk in Your ways. Help me pray this prayer until it is a reality in my life. Amen.

Prayer About Judgments

Lord, I recognize that I have judged. (State the judgement(s) as clearly as possible.) I was wrong about _____. My judgments do not reflect Your heart about _____,

about me or about You. I realize that in judging I locked myself into doing the same thing, having the same attitude(s). Forgive me, Lord. And where my assessment was accurate, but my response was sinful (bitterness, anger, condemnation), I ask Your forgiveness. I ask that You break the power of this judgment in my life so that the reaping of harm can stop. Break this judgment on Your Cross, make it into powder and blow it away with the breath of Your Holy Spirit. I ask that You stop this pattern of behavior and lift it out of my life or give me the wisdom, stamina, and perseverance to eradicate it. I ask that Your forgiveness and mercy would now flow rather than the destructive reaping of this judgment. Further, I ask that Your truth would wash through my spirit and mind and impact my thought patterns and belief systems so that I can know the truth as You see it. Amen.

Prayer About Inner Vows

Put words to the vow as specifically as possible.

Lord, I renounce this strong promise I made to myself. I ask You to break its power in my life, that my spirit and body no longer remember it. Set me free to be restored to Your original design for me. Please lift out of my life the requirement to feel, think, and act according to this vow.

Lord, this has been a defense, a hiding place to keep myself from being hurt; it has become my very own homemade armor. I know that this homemade protection blocks out the love, warmth, and nurture I long for. I come to You because I am powerless to change. Come into my life and dismantle this vow. I want You to be my defense. Lord, help me become vulnerable, able to risk love. Father, I forgive _____ (the people who wounded me and tempted me to make this vow and harden my heart).

As a set of my will and my heart, I choose this day to let You take down my walls of isolation and connect me to others within my family and Your Body, but in a way that honors and builds up rather than crushes and tears down. I declare this regardless of the storm of emotions or the absence of emotions. I give You the loaves and fishes of my trust—I trust Your timing and sequencing of events with as much trust as I have. Lord mend my trust in You. I know that people's love is not always trustworthy. But for those times when it was, forgive me, Jesus for not trusting the love offered me by _____ (my spouse, children, fellow Christians). I ask You to bring people into my life who know how to love unconditionally and still have the courage to hold me accountable. Amen.

Prayer of Release of Guilt and Shame

Lord, I release to You the guilt and shame that I have been wearing that was not mine to wear. I forgive those who called me names, labeled me, and scapegoated me; as a consequence I felt guilty and shameful. I ask your Holy Spirit to search out the recesses of my being to find it all. I give it to You. And, I ask You to heal the hurt and damage that happened as a result of wearing it. I repent of the ways I judged others and myself. Father, I didn't know what of the guilt and shame was not mine. I ask You to teach me and show me what truly is my own guilt and my own shame so I can confess and repent.

Lord, if I need to know more about the nature of any hurts I have incurred from burden bearing guilt and shame, please show me. Reveal to me any lie I came to believe about You, others, life, and myself. Help me give and receive forgiveness where it is needed so I can receive Your cleansing and restoration and move into the destiny You have for me. Amen.

Prayer to Break the Power of Names and Pronouncements
(words that picture our identity and future)

Father, in Your name I renounce the names spoken over me. (List as many names and words that pictured your self or your future as you remember.) _____

I renounce the destiny those names and pronouncements created for me. In Your name, I break the power of the names in my life. I no longer accept these names or pictures of my future and my destiny. I ask You to remove any spiritual imprint these names and pronouncements made in my life. They were not from You and they did not tell me the truth about who I am in You. I ask You to remove the confusion it caused me and heal the wounds caused by these names, words, and destinies that were declared over me. Lord I give You all the plans and purposes other people had for my life and all the identities others placed on me. I choose Your plans and Your destiny. I ask You to minister to my spirit and teach me who I am in You. Help me to see myself as You see me. I ask that You wash over me with wave after wave of Your cleansing love. Thank You, Father.

After the Healing

Prayer begins a process. You will go from revelation and conviction to confession, repentance, and forgiveness to a time of incorporating new ways of thinking, believing, and living. After the healing time, you need an unspecified time to regain equilibrium and adjust to these new ways of seeing and being and to allow them to strengthen. Some may need an extended recovery time after prayers of healing. Comparing the recovery time you need with that of others is not recommended. The Lord has a schedule and timeframe that suits each person. Your human spirit may need to be stronger before you take the next step, and only the Lord knows when that is.

Prayer of Dying

Lord Jesus Christ, I lay all my gifts on the altar—all my natural gifting, all ability to sense and feel things, all ability to know things. I place it all on the altar along with all other kinds of gifts: music, leadership, common sense, teaching, whatever abilities I have, I put on the altar. Put me to death in relation to them. I know You will give them back resurrected, refined, and directed by the Holy Spirit. Let it be so. Amen.

Prayer of Death to Self-Importance

Lord, I wish to be your servant. I give You my need to be important in the eyes of others. I set my heart and my will to seek importance in Your eyes only. For ways in which my heart holds onto and does not want to relinquish self-importance, then Lord I ask You to honor the set of my will to resist this tendency. Do for me what I cannot do for myself. Help me to die to my own importance, and grant me a sense of my importance to You. Amen.

Pray for Protection

It is a protection simply to know that you are a natural burden bearer. Knowledge can be a very real protection. "...The advantage of knowledge is this; that wisdom preserves the life of its possessor" (Eccl. 7:12). Stay in step with Jesus, walk in His shadow, don't lag behind, run out ahead, or try to hide from God's call to bear burdens for Him to the Cross, and become like Saul, hiding among the baggage (1 Sam. 10:22).

Prayer for Protection

Lord, God, I thank You for your faithfulness. I especially thank You for the faithful protection You give me because of burden bearing. I know that if the enemy happens to be around he can see when I do the work You call me to do, so I ask that You commission angels to guard me and those I intercede for and carry in my heart. I ask in particular that angels be commissioned to deal with the powers of darkness as they try to interfere with the work of Your Kingdom and as they try to overwhelm my life and discourage me from imitating You.

I ask that You wrap me up in Your robes of righteousness to hide my scent and sweep away any footprints so the powers of darkness cannot track me down to do harm. I ask that the brilliance of Your holiness radiate all around and blind the eyes of any that might follow. Hide me in Your cloud of glory, under Your wing. Keep me close to Your heart and wash me clean of any dusting of defilement so that I can rest deeply and peacefully in You. Amen.

Pray for Discernment

Ask for discernment as part of your protection, so that you know, as much as possible, the best way the Lord would have you pray. The more intelligently and specifically you pray, the more quickly and cleanly the burdens go through to the Cross. It pleases the Father when you ask Him how to pray. There may be times when the "who" or "what" is not important; what is important is that you pray and He will apply the prayer as needed.

Prayer for Discernment

Lord, teach me how a burden feels when You want to draw a burden from someone, through me for direct delivery to the Cross.

You are only asking me to join You in Your task, so help me learn what my own burdens feel like, then help me know what someone else's feel like. I don't always know the difference. As a result, I have carried them all. Teach me how it feels when You want me carry a portion of someone's load for a time so that it informs my intercession for them.

When guilt and shame are attached to the burden, help me know the difference between what I need to confess and what I need You to lift from me as You draw the burden to Yourself. Teach me to know when You want me to bear someone's burden, and when You want me to set out a spiritual "road flare" prayer to mark the spot and trust You to call someone else to do the burden bearing.

Jesus, You came to carry everyone's burdens and everyone's inner anguish and turmoil. I want to bear burdens to the Cross, as You designed me to, but I do not want to dishonor you by usurping your place in that work. Thank You Lord for Your patience and compassion as I learn what pleases You (Eph. 5:10).

Spirit, Mind, and Emotions

Pray for the unscrambling of the functions of spirit, mind, and emotions...and for the Lord to reintegrate them in harmony so that there is always some part of you at rest while you carry burdens. Scripture says, "The word of God is living and active. Sharper than any double edged sword, it penetrates even to dividing soul and spirit, joints and marrow; it judges the thoughts and attitudes of the heart" (Heb. 4:12). If the sword of the Lord can separate bone and marrow without harming either, the Lord is capable of untangling the body, mind, and spirit! Humankind was designed in such a way that the spirit of man is to set the direction of life. The mind's function is to make decisions, rationalize, and justify the direction made by the spirit, to convince the heart or the emotions that this is the best way to go. When so convinced, the heart and emotions come along happily, throwing in all your energy resources.

Unfortunately, sin has set your mind to working overtime. The blow of the Fall set up a division, a lack of unity between the body, mind, and spirit. Since the Fall, the spirit has been demoted, and the mind is too often in the driver's seat. Your ability to relate to God consciously, Spirit-to-spirit, is now impaired because your spirit has been sidelined. The mind cannot read the heart of God as the spirit can, so it sorts through information the best it can and then goes on to justify and rationalize and convince the emotions to be happy about the mind's decision.

The poor mind is overworked! Then, when burden bearing comes into play, empathetically acquired information can throw you into a tailspin. There is no identifiable source for the information, so your mind concludes that the feelings, sensings, or knowings originated from within, or that the information is to be ignored. It should be the spirit's function to decide when there is a question of whether feelings and sensations come from within or without.

Unfortunately, the mind has stepped into the spirit's role and because it was not designed to make that kind of distinction, it becomes confused and has a difficult time discerning. The confusion does not help your emotions since they are attuned to the other person's emotional state and interpret it as your own as well. Whew! You can begin to see why burden bearers do not want to be around other people!

When David asked me to join him in prayer ministry, I was good for one session but a mess for the rest of the day. It was exhausting. I paid a high price until I asked the Lord to separate these functions, which had become entangled and out of order. Now I can take on someone's inner turmoil but my spirit carries it. My mind can still function, either for my own needs or to put words to what someone else feels.

Many people have never learned to identify their own feelings, so they cannot tell their prayer partner what they feel. Separating the functions makes it less likely to confuse emotions absorbed from another with your own. The mind and emotions can be at rest; they are not doing the spirit's work. The result is far less exhausting. This side of Heaven you will never be able to be 100 percent correct in making this distinction as to what is your emotion and what is from another source, but it is wisdom to avail yourself of all the help you can find!

Make it an ongoing practice to ask God for the functions to be separate. The mind does not step aside easily nor give over control willingly. So from time to time it is wise to repeat the prayer, to make sure things are in order.

Prayer for the Unscrambling of Mind, Emotions and Spirit

Lord, You know the confusion that comes as a result of the mind, emotions, and spirit being out of order. I ask You to come and speak "Peace" in the confusion. I ask You to set me in order the way You designed me to be so that at all times some part of me can be at rest. Unscramble me and put me back together the way I'm supposed to be, with all my functions working in harmony. I want Your order and Your peace. Amen.

Prayer for Cleansing

(This is for cleansing after ministry, but you can modify it for cleansing from any situation.)

Lord, I thank you for granting me the privilege of ministering into _____'s life. I now want to release both _____ and the responsibility for his/her well being to you. Thank you Lord, for your love for _____, which is far greater than mine, could ever be.

Where I have become connected to _____ in any way that is outside your will, I ask you to forgive me and unbind the cords between us and cause us to be connected to you in those areas instead. Lord, only you can provide the life _____ needs. My energies will fail but Yours never do.

Father, please cut me free, by the sword of your Spirit, from any transference, spiritual or emotional, that took place during our time together, and nail it to the Cross of Christ. Wash me, Lord, and attach me to Yourself as well so that my energies may be renewed—restore me to your original design. Seal what was accomplished in _____'s life today, and protect it from the enemy. I give all of the honor, glory, and praise to You. Amen

Explore the Issue of Identity

The issue of identity has to do with knowing "who I am." I am not talking about your status, occupation, or title, but rather your sense of self apart from outside references. You may be swept along in the wake of strong personalities, or grievous needs and so caught up in the other's needs, thoughts, and desires that it is difficult to identify what you need, think, or want.

Prayer for Identity

Father, I ask You to remove from me all the residue of burdens I acquired during childhood that kept me from knowing myself—

burdens which were not mine to carry. I now know my spirit was open to family, friends and schoolmates, teachers and other authority figures from childhood years. I tried to help lighten their load by scooping up trouble, confusion, and turmoil, but I did not ask You to draw it on through me to the Cross. That accumulated burden was part of the squashing of my identity.

I ask You to remove what was not mine to carry and now teach me what is and is not mine to carry. Show me any way that I do not believe You do not care enough to meet the needs of family and/or friends. Show me any burden I continue to unknowingly hold on to in my spirit from family or friends, Lord I ask that You draw that through me and onto Your Cross.

(If you are consciously aware of who you may be identified with, and/or role(s) you were required to fill which you either willingly or reluctantly accepted, then spell that out to the Lord specifically.) I give You any identification I made with another which resulted in my living a destiny different from the one You planned for my life. I want to be free to be the person You designed me to be. I want to know You as You are, and relate to You unencumbered.

Lord, You know how I struggle with knowing what I want to be/do when I grow up. I have allowed myself to be pulled hither and yon by strong personalities and people's deep needs and have not found Your design, Your way for me. I ask You to help me set boundaries for myself. Teach me where I stop and others begin. Be my reference point. Lord, help me internalize what You show me. Lift confusion out of me and teach me who I am in You. Thank You Lord. Amen.

I believe the Lord does for you what you cannot do for yourself. He does the healing as you make yourself available to Him. However, He does not do for you what you can and should do for yourself. You do need to spend time at the

Cross. There are aspects of your life that need to die there—but, there is a life beyond the Cross, the resurrected life. As you live in Jesus His resurrection power motivates you to discipline yourself in ways that bring life into balance and to make lifestyle changes that will result in healthy, joy-filled lives. This is the part of your healing that you can do for yourself.

Here is another perspective. When you are in the trenches slugging it out, learning all there is to learn, you can feel small. Your contribution may feel like a drop in a bucket. But what might God see? How might He view your little drop?

CHAPTER 13

Another Perspective

As a group, burden-bearers struggle with how they view themselves. On one side, society tends to value aggression and production, making scapegoats, and calling names or labeling, while devaluing sensitivity. These experiences erode your sense of self and can bury you. On the other hand, the world may sometimes react negatively because burden bearers can be difficult people to live with. It can be especially difficult for others when your responses come from your own wounding, or when you operate in your own strength, without the grace and wisdom of the Holy Spirit. You do not understand them and they do not understand you—mutual misunderstanding!

Although the following story is not necessarily about burden bearers per se, it has some valuable lessons for burden bearers. It is primarily about King David and his learning how to be king, learning the power of his words, how to lead people, and yet, as with much of Scripture, you can find other lessons as well.

First Chronicles 12:18: "Then the Spirit of the Lord came upon Amasai, chief of the Thirty, and he said: 'We are yours, O David! We are with you, O son of Jesse! Success, success to you, and success to those who help you, for your God will help you.' So David received them and made them leaders of his raiding bands."

There were thirty men who were chiefs, which means each commanded a number of men, and Amasai was the chief of the chiefs.

First Chronicles 11:15-19 relates that "three of the thirty chiefs came down to David to the rock at the cave of Adullam, while a band of Philistines was encamped in the Valley of Rephaim. At this time, David was in the stronghold, as the Philistine garrison was at Bethlehem. David longed for water and said, 'Oh, that someone would get me a drink of water from the well near the gate of Bethlehem!' "So the Three broke through the Philistine lines, drew water from the well near the gate of Bethlehem and carried it back to David. He refused to drink it. Instead, he poured it out before the Lord. 'God forbid that I should do this!' he said. 'Should I drink the blood of these men who went at the risk of their lives?' Because they risked their lives to bring it back, David would not drink it. Such were the exploits of the three mighty men."

The phrase, "such were the exploits" makes me think these men were always brash and bold, that such behavior was characteristic of them.

Since Amasai was chief of the thirty, it stands to reason he was one of these three bold warriors. Amasai and the chiefs under him were so enthusiastic to serve their King's heart, that when they overheard David say, "Oh, that someone would get me a drink of water from the well near the gate of Bethlehem," they impulsively set out to make his wish come true. They did not stop to think of the strategic importance of a canteen of water in comparison to the overall mission, nor apparently, did they ask. They soon planned how to sneak out, go behind enemy lines and fetch the water, without consulting their king.

A couple of things leap out from this story. First of all, Amasai and his friends seem to be devoted to a fault. Second, they responded to a need without thinking about strategic repercussions. They risked the lives of three incredibly important, highly qualified and decorated men. If something had happened and they had been caught, the entire operation would have been put at risk. How could men who lived by raiding not think about the risks or potential negative outcomes? They did not ask the king if they could or should go. They did not inquire of the Lord if fetching water was an appropriate task for them. In taking on responsibility without consulting their earthly lord, they not only put themselves at risk, but everyone else.

In a similar way, when you bear burdens without the Lord's authorization, you do the same thing. When you go too far, or carry too much too long, you risk harm coming to many others, not just yourself.

But look at the king's response! He was grieved that they risked their lives. He may have been overcome with guilt as he realized the power of his words. King David considered the water to be the men's blood—how could he drink it! He poured it out before the Lord. Surely the men were willing to sacrifice their lives to meet the needs, desires even, of their king. The passage does not say what happened next. But based on what we know about David's character, I can imagine that having poured the water out to the Lord, he turned to Amasai with grief, guilt over his own part in the escapade, with worry and love on his face.

He probably grabbed Amasai by the shoulders and said something like, "You crazy man, you! I love you, brother! Thank God, you are safe!" Then the two might have embraced, and heartily thumped each other on the back, moved by awareness of their love and respect for each other. I also suspect that David held himself responsible, and went before the Lord to repent over his own propensity to blurt out His thoughts before he considered how they would sound to others. It would be his nature to do so, for elsewhere in Scripture David asked the Lord to help him, and put a watch over his lips, "O Lord, I call to You, come quickly to me. Hear my voice when I call to You. May my prayer be set before You like incense, may the lifting up of my hands be like the evening sacrifice. Set a guard over my mouth, O Lord, keep watch over the door of my lips" (Ps. 141:1-3). Whatever actually happened on that day outside of Bethlehem, King David would think twice before saying something so provocative again. He valued the lives and loyalties of his warriors.

In many of our families, all too often such a misguided act of love would be greeted with scorn and sarcasm, and no one would give us credit that we did a dumb thing out of love. No one would see how we are tempted to meet every need we see, and to turn wishes or desires into commands. Certainly no one would feel guilt over tempting us to act in a misguided manner. Definitely, no forgiveness is offered. Rather, our intelligence is called into question and our sensitive nature ridiculed.

There is no record that King David stripped Amasai of rank. He did not reject him; he did not condemn him. He seemed to have continued to value him as a person and a warrior. In the same way, I believe God values you as an individual—your relationship is important to Him, and not just for what you can do for Him. Read First Chronicles 12 in its entirety. Get a feel for the prowess of these men, and then remember that Amasai was the leader of these thirty commanders. In those days that meant that he was quicker, smarter, stronger. He was the best of the best. I believe this is how God sees burden bearers—as His "mighty warriors"!

Please read this account as many times as it takes to sink into the deep places of your heart. A burden bearer is a mighty warrior—not a rug mat. In the spiritual realm, burden bearers, you are a force to be reckoned with. Satan knows this, and that is part of why he wants to keep you feeling worthless, valueless. He wants you to remain ignorant of burden-bearing dynamics so that you assume that all the craziness you feel is your own. He wants the sensitivity of burden bearing to be the very thing that destroys your family, and you. He wants to keep you wounded!

The ability to bear burdens functions as a weapon against the kingdom of darkness, and satan wants you to fall on your sword instead of using it to free others. He wants you to sense the pain and troubles in your family, work place, and church, and be pierced by it. He wants leadership to be destructive, rejecting because of lack of compassion, knowledge, and understanding. He wants you to come to wrong conclusions about motivations. He knows that when you come to a realization of your identity in Christ, stand up, dust yourself off, and start walking as sons and daughters of

God that he and his kingdom will be as the Philistines were, vanquished!

Amasai was born with potential—a quick mind, a sound body, and excellent eye/hand coordination. But all of that would have been for nothing had no one taught and trained him. Burden bearers are born with a capacity for empathy. Like Amasai you need instruction and discipline to develop your potential. You will not become a mighty warrior in a day. You will need to learn which tasks to take on, and when to quit before you hurt others, or yourself. You will need to learn to hear the Lord's voice, and to discern between many different signals. You will need to be patient with yourself in the learning, until your responses become reflexes. You will need to learn what your weapons and armor are, and how to use them. One size does not fit all!

David could not wear Saul's armor or use his weapons. The Lord will issue to you what you need, and provide the circumstances in which to learn, before sending you to the front lines. The enemy's scheme is to press you into battle before you know what you are doing. Hearing the Lord's call is the first step. Coming into your identity as a child of the King, stepping up to be trained and equipped is next, and then, finally, you will take your place. For some it may be as a dancer who goes out before the soldiers, dancing before the Lord into battle, or into the Lord's presence to worship. Others will take their place in the ranks as warriors.

The Lord will hide some away in a lonely cave like Elijah's prophets in training. Some will be seers or visionaries, some watchers on the wall, some keepers of the gates, or quick response teams. Some will be Nehemiahs rebuilding, closing breaches in protective walls, and restoring glory. Some will be Ezras teaching what was lost and forgotten, or Annas praying in the temple, or Hannah praying at home. You can have a highly sensitive, burden-bearing personality whatever your natural field of expertise and the Lord can call you into service in that field. Whatever your position, you can be assured that you are not alone.

Heather, an intercessor and prayer minister, related the following story. She first heard of the attack on the news and later was called to pray, but it is best told in her own words:

A lady was killed by a cougar in Princeton, British Columbia, a few years back. She sacrificed her life for her young sons. That night I awoke with tears streaming down my face and quietly went to the living room with my Bible, and asked "Lord, what are the tears about?"

He showed me the mother, her heart to protect her boys, like a mother bear protecting her cubs. Then I saw the boys without this sacrificial mother's love, and the tears flowed again, freely. I began to pray and intercede for the boys, the husband and family and friends. This went on for a couple hours. Then the Lord said, "Stand, my daughter, put your right hand up into the air." Then the vision came of me standing with my arm up in the air (as the Statue of Liberty) and my prayers were helping to free the boys, especially from the burdens that were too heavy for them to carry alone. As I stood, with arm stretched out to the heavenlies, the Lord showed me legions of prayer warriors doing just what He called and anointed them to do—intercede. Then, I saw a baton in my hand, and another angel intercessor scooped it out of my hand and ran with the burden, passing it out to many others to help carry. Then the vision and the burden *were completely lifted and the Lord said, "You are released." He invited me to stay close to this vision for the next burden He would ask me to share in."*

The Lord wants you to learn what He showed Heather that night—you are not alone. No one has to carry the entire load all the way. Heather was called to lift it high. Then an angel came and passed it on to others who were also called to share in the task. Bearing the burdens of your family, your church, your nation, and the worldwide Church—this is too large a task for one individual. But you need not worry, the Lord has a host of intercessors, a host of burden bearers, and all you have to do is your part. To do more than your part is to put those you love, and yourself, at risk—or you prevent others from doing the part the Lord calls them to do.

Two parting thoughts—first of all, no one is alone. And second, like the warrior Amasai, you, oh warrior child of God, you are a spiritual force to be reckoned with—and well equipped at that!

As you take up your identity as a son or daughter of the Lord and commit to the task of learning what that means for you, I pray the Lord bless you and keep you; may He make His face shine upon you and be gracious to you. May the Lord turn His face toward you and give you peace. Amen.

When you lighten people's loads, when you bear burdens to the Lord, you are like Amasai and his men. In a very practical way you raid the Kingdom of darkness. You make off with satan's booty that he obtained through robbery, deceit, and murder.

After the Devastation

S ince the turn of the century there has been no end to disasters—natural and manmade. From 9-11 and Hurricane Katrina, to wars in the Middle East, earthquakes, tsunamis, and the killings in Africa, many feel, to some extent, downcast, coated, and vulnerable as if some kind of invisible blanket of gloom has dropped. As each disaster unfolds, fear, anxiety, grief, and anger is released around the world.

You may notice a tendency toward sadness or have trouble with depression in a way that you did not have before. Consider that we now live in a milieu of unfocused, non-specific tension, fear, and anxiety laced with grief and loss. You may be absorbing some of these emotions through daily interactions and especially the news. Anything you absorb can weigh on old wounds and make it seem like they are being resurrected, or make you wonder if you are developing problems in new areas.

Counteract these feelings by careful attention to spiritual hygiene, keep in touch with other burden bearers for prayer and reality checks, and don't neglect time with the Lord. Be proactive by praying for the people you encounter. Lift their fear and anxiety to the Lord, and allow His mercy and comfort to come back over and through you to them. Pray that God's people everywhere will be strengthened in their inner self and stand firm in their faith. Pray for the area in which you live, for the authorities in your state, province, nation. Pray for your leaders that they might turn to the Lord for wisdom for these times.

A Prayer

Lord God, I need You. Since the onset of the new century and considering all the natural and manmade disasters, I am more aware than ever of my need of you. I come to You as to a loving Father and ask for Your comfort for my fears and Your assurance that whatever happens I am Yours and You love me. I ask for the grace and the strength needed for these times. And Lord, You know how much that is. Give me each day what I need for the day.

Fill me with Your love, Your life, and Your light. I know that light consumes the darkness. As I go about my days I want to be Your light dispelling the darkness that has come with these events. Father, I pray for those who have lost loved ones and livelihood, for those whose families are separated. I pray for those with whom I live and work. For those who do not know You, I ask for their salvation so they may know Your comfort. May I be a source of love and peace for them that draws them to You.

For those who know You, I ask that they be strengthened in their inner self, that they may stand and be firm in their faith in the face of the unknown. May they choose You and Your ways. Lord I know that fear, anxiety, grief, and great emotional pain have become suspended in the air like so much fog. I lift to You this burden of fear and ask that You dispel it. Hold me close, wash me clean, emotionally and spiritually, of that which is not mine.

Remind me to come to You frequently lest I become overburdened, overwhelmed, and forget who I am or even that I may come to You for comfort, cleansing, and direction.

Lord, I pray for those in armed conflict, especially those who have lost their homes. I ask You to bring the fighting to a resolution as soon as possible with the least loss of life. The struggles that are going on now are only a surface manifestation of historical and multifaceted problems that only You can resolve. Lord have mercy on me for the part I play. Forgive me for ways that I participate in sin patterns that fuel conflict. Show me the way out.

I pray for my authorities and for those diplomats who negotiate. Give them wisdom to make decisions that are consistent with Your will so the world may live in peace. Lord, I thank You for those leaders who know You and do pray. Bless them Lord and keep them safe. As they hear from You and speak Your words, may their words have good effect. I ask these things for the local leaders, the provincial and state, as well as for national and international leaders. May Your Kingdom come and Your will be done on earth as it is in Heaven. Amen.

The Physical/Neurological Base of Empathy

To have a complete discussion of empathy, I must address those who are uncomfortable with assertions about humankind's abilities if not solidly grounded in science. There is a biological basis for the assertions made in this book. Empathy, the essence of high sensitivity, is a physical, as well as mental, emotional, *and* spiritual function.

People are biologically designed for relationships. Every human being is born with a portion of the brain specifically designated for the functions of empathy, which is essential for relationship—empathy has a home. Although the word *empathy* may not appear in Scripture, examples of both burden bearing and empathy are scattered throughout both the Old and New Testaments; and burden bearing could not happen if ability to empathize were absent. For example, Jesus at Lazarus' tomb, where we are admonished to "weep with those who weep" (John 11:33-36; Rom. 12:15b).

Biological, Neurological Basis of Empathy

Current brain research[1] has revealed specific areas of the brain that control, 1) your ability to *read* people and circumstances, 2) your ability to *feel* what another experiences, and 3) your *general take* on life—whether you tend to see life as happy, sad, threatening, etc. These areas are called the command center of the brain. Composed of such parts as the amygdala, the orbital frontal lobe, and the cingulate cortex, this command center is located in the right hemisphere of the brain and develops in the first two years of life. This portion of the brain is devoted to emotion.

Scientists have also found that emotions color and influence your logic and thinking, and reason, conversely, that thinking and logic influence your emotions. Both functions interrelate—neither portion of the brain, thinking or emotional, functions to the exclusion of the other.[2]

Development of the Cingulate

The cingulate is of importance in the discussion of burden bearing because its primary function is synchronization, "the ability to match another's state of mind or energy level."[3] This is the essence of what we know to be empathy. Synchronization allows you to match another's emotion or energy level so that you experience what they experience. You are born with this equipment—the cingulate—but have to learn early on to synchronize. "A child uses a parent to help organize his/her own mental processes"[4] between 2-9 months of age. With this organizational structure, a child then has the capacity to match emotional states of mind with someone else.

As a child interacts with a parent, he "exercises" or "stretches," and expands his own capacity to express, contain, or endure an emotion. For example, a parent may first look at a child, smile, then tickle and the child responds with delight. The parent leads the child through increasing intensity of emotions. The child quickly learns to identify the particular voice pattern that precedes the tickle. Repeated episodes result in anticipatory behavior at the first sound of that voice pattern rather than *after* the tickle. The child moves from a passive response to active.

This pattern of passive to active response applies to other emotions as well. His repertoire of emotions expands as he develops other responses to the voice and the tickle such as squealing, wriggling, rolling away, or shielding his "tickle spot." The length of time during which he is able to sustain a given emotion expands with frequent and sustained times of play. He is building emotional flexibility, the parent's brain being the blueprint for "how to do emotion."

What happens in this interchange is synchronization. Initially, the parent matches the emotions and energy of the child, for it is only after a parent takes the lead that a child will be able to follow. In fact, a child will not be able to match a parent until he is over nine months old; it takes that much practice! As a child tries to follow, the parent takes the child further into the emotion, or helps him hold it for a longer time, thus enlarging his capacity, or helps him transition into other emotions.

A parent's ability to sustain any given emotion, to contain, and move in and out of a wide range of emotions, with various intensities, is far greater than the child's. Therefore, it is the parent who matches the child, and provides the experience of being in sync, in attunement, in harmony. As a child makes the effort to match a parent, he builds emotional flexibility, agility, and vocabulary. Since a child's capacity is smaller, a parent or caregiver periodically breaks the interaction for periods of rest so the child does not become over stimulated or overwhelmed.

Parents do this intuitively following a game of peek-a-boo or tickling with cuddle time. To go from high intensity to quiet, back to high or even higher intensity, back to quiet and happy to be together, is what develops the child's capacity for emotion, emotional flexibility, and teaches him how to modulate his own emotions. This learned ability to quiet oneself is the greatest predictor of mental health across a child's lifetime.[5]

Being out of sync is perhaps the most frequent source of what most would call rejection, but an infant experiences it as a kind of "death."[6] A parent may not know how to be glad-quiet together and only wants to be together when the parent has an intense desire to be together. The parent then becomes upset when the child disconnects because of being overwhelmed by the parent's intensity. In other words, the parent does not realize the child is unable to maintain an emotional intensity equal to his or her own. The intensity is actually stressful, causing the child to cry or experience a disconnected state of being, a death-like state of collapse, which the parent may interpret as rejection, and pull away. The child comes out of the disconnected, death-like state of collapse and looks to reconnect to the parent who has pulled away. The child experiences this as rejection—as the parent "not glad to be with me." Of course, the opposite is also true. If a parent is not responsive to a child's signals to break off contact, the child does not learn how to modulate emotion, the direct precursor to not handling emotion well as adults.

With positive emotions, a child reaches to match the parent; but what about negative or overwhelming emotions.

Then the parent modulates and synchronizes with the child, calming the fear, dispelling the gloom or shame and walking the child out of the "lost" place. Once the child learns how to synchronize emotion from depending upon the adult brain (by 9 months of age), he begins the task of learning to regulate his own emotions. From the age of 9-12 months, he learns joy; he learns how to calm his own fears, how to find his own way out of the "lost places" of negative emotions, and how to break off stimulation before a "good" experience becomes painful.

As the cingulate develops, it is first able to relate to, and synchronize with, one other person, and only one. After age 9 months, the orbital prefrontal cortex begins its development and allows the properly synchronized brain to relate to it and two others. The cingulate, by itself, can only accommodate two. After 9 months, when the prefrontal cortex "comes on line," it adds awareness of the third while the cingulate continues to do for two.

The development of the cingulate is so important that to the degree that it is neglected or interfered with, an individual will have difficulties with relationships throughout life unless there is intervention.[7]

The experience of expressing one's emotional state and having others perceive and respond to these signals (be empathetic) appears to be of vital importance in the development of the brain. It "creates an attachment bond," "provides a source of security" and an inner expectation that needs are important and goals are achievable." It helps "organize the child's own mind," amplifies positive emotional states, and adjusts negative states to proper size.[8]

Such sharing of primary emotions does much more than allow a child to feel good. This empathy makes it possible for a child to develop normally, to be able to quiet oneself, and control one's emotions. These primary emotions are also called "vitality affects." They are expressed by "contours of activation of the body, facial expressions, non-verbal gestures and tone of voice and they form a foundational part, a precursor to what we think of as emotion such as sad, mad, glad, scared, surprise, disgust, and shame.[9] These primary emotions or "vitality affect" that you share empathetically are without words, like an awareness of a surge of energy or sense of deflation, impressions, sense of being alert or foggy, nervous or peaceful flows in the state of mind.[10] These early interchanges lay the foundation for how the brain is organized, and form the template for meanings and values that are assigned to emotions throughout your life. This makes the parent/child relationship of unimaginable importance.

Daniel Siegel, author of *The Developing Mind*, states, "Those parents who have the capacity to reflect on the importance of mental states are more likely to have secure attachments to their children. The ability to use 'mental state language' such as beliefs, feelings, attitudes, intentions, and thoughts, is associated with parents of children with secure attachments."[11]

Synchronization

The cingulate possesses cells dedicated to watching eye movement and others dedicated to observing body movement. As a child looks at a parent, a communication happens—right hemisphere of the brain to right hemisphere, from parent to child and back to parent—six complete cycles per second, too fast to be consciously controlled. It is also important to note that each cycle amplifies emotions, and within 30 seconds reaches full amplitude, or intensity![12]

These repeated alignments, when Mom first adjusts her brain to her child's mental state and the child responds by trying to adjust to Mom's mental state, six times every second of interaction are what allow Mom and infant to synchronize or join. As a child grows, these repeated times of matching of emotional states provide the joining that is essential for the developing brain to acquire the capacity to organize itself.[13] With communication going back and forth at that speed and synchronization being achieved this quickly, both parties feel the experience simultaneously. Is this not the essence of empathy?

All of the functions of the command center can and usually do occur without your direct awareness. When you say you have a "gut feeling" or a "sense" of something, what you experience is a flash into your consciousness of what is transpiring within the emotional brain, or command center.[14] The feeling is your physical responses to the messages of that command center.[15]

Cingulate Developmental Problems

Problems result from impaired ability to synchronize, but specific to our discussion are difficulties with discernment, knowing what is appropriate or inappropriate, misjudging others intent. Siegel calls this "emotional blindness."[16] A person can be emotionally blind, but still sense and absorb part of the burdens of others. However, the person will not understand "what has come over me." These kinds of difficulties lead to impaired social relationships, emotional insensitivity, emotional blind spots, and lack of awareness of your own feelings as well as those of others, while at the same time the drawing and absorbing quality of your spirit is at work.

The person becomes "heavy" but because he does not feel and understand his own emotions, he does not understand what is happening. Reading people is hit and miss, or becomes a mystery altogether. Being in someone else's shoes is difficult if not impossible, making burden bearing a difficult enterprise indeed! The misjudging of others has to do with the cognitive part of burden bearing and is why many natural burden bearers see high sensitivity as a curse rather than a blessing. Many are woefully deficient cognitively because of a lack of understanding of burden bearing and how it affects them. Consequently, far too many primarily wear the accumulated burdens, assuming they are their own.

The incredible importance of attuned parents in the full development of essential parts of the brain is unquestionable. This is obviously the Lord's design, the way He wants you to develop, and in that sense is the ideal. I must also acknowledge that forces of society mitigate against a parent's ability to provide the time and attention needed: the difficulties of divorce and single parenting, lack of modeling, knowledge, and skill in parenting, poverty, the need for two incomes. Providing an ideal environment requires planning and commitment.

About Neglect

Many have survived an infancy that afforded a less than optimal developmental environment, and many others have had what can only be described as "a bumpy start to life."

These children are not ruined; they are only different than they would have been. God loves and values them, nonetheless. If a child is neglected so that the cingulate does not fully develop, the child will have relational problems of one sort or another, more blind spots than would have been without the neglect. The child may have boundary difficulties, trouble modulating his own energy levels, or be empathetic to some people and situations, but not to others. Relational problems later in life will reflect his neglect. This does not mean that a neglected child cannot become a highly empathetic person.

A child can become empathetic even if parents were not available or were uninvolved during that critical developmental period. He will learn sensitivity the way any child learns, with the aide of a more mature brain, but he learns in spite of the neglect and from precious little loving care and attention. He may have an area in which he cannot be sensitive because there was no more mature brain to show the way *in that area,* but it was there in other areas. He may be sensitive to including others, of being a "team" but completely unaware of how it hurts to forget a birthday.

God has made people incredibly creative; some of us can obtain amazing mileage from only a shred of loving-kindness. Sometimes the Lord Himself intervenes, through visions, visitations, or by providing a person or persons to give the care and attention needed for cingulate development. Yes, neglected people do have difficulties, some of which are listed, but being able to absorb what is in another person, and so to experience what they experience and take it to Jesus— well, that is not necessarily among them! God is able today to take bits, loaves and fishes, and multiply them to accomplish what we need and He desires to accomplish.

How God touches people and makes a relationship when the deck is stacked against them is a miracle, at least to me. Why it happens for some whereas others struggle with intractable deficiencies is something to grieve over, share with the Lord what you see, and release to Him. We cannot comprehend the evil of neglect. Trying to understand it tears up the hearts of the tender-hearted, and takes our focus away from Jesus. For our spiritual and physical health, we need to lift neglected ones to Jesus and release the "whys" to Him. Our job is to seek His face and reflect His character in all we do and say.

Remediation

The good news—not all is lost. Although many brain functions are hard wired, other areas of the brain remain flexible throughout life, allowing for remediation along the way. Remediation requires help. You may need many people in your life, professionals and non-professionals, people who know how to share life, love, and joy. Indeed, the development and organization of your brain may be a community project! For your part, when you become aware of a need for remediation, one of the most important things you can do for yourself is to hold still. You can make yourself stay in a place where you can learn emotional language (experience the feelings and learn the words associated with them) and not flee from the exercise.

My nonprofessional's speculation is that as you learn emotional language, you begin to activate, to soften, or make flexible that neglected portion of the brain so that it can make the associations that should have been made at age 3-9 months. For example, if you as an adult know you do not have secure attachment with your parents, you can organize times and activities that have the potential to build relationships and rectify the problem.[17] If parents do not want to partici-pate in such activities, find people who are willing to fill those relational positions. If you avoid talking about states of being (feelings) because you are not adept with the language or because feelings make you uncomfortable, commit to keep working at it until you are comfortable. You can ask someone you trust to make you aware when you are being insensitive.

Remediation of Neglect

The prerequisites for remediation are: 1) awareness that you are somehow different; 2) awareness that you miss a great deal of what goes on; 3) awareness that you respond differ-ently than others, or do not respond at all, and have a desire to change. Remediation requires a passionate desire for wholeness and a deep determination to walk through what-ever is necessary. It takes someone who knows how to reme-diate and someone willing to love, nurture, and mentor a neglected one. This is not a task to take lightly, but at the Lord's direction. The process of nurturing someone into sen-sitivity will undoubtedly reveal your own character flaws, which will throw you upon the Lord's mercy and accelerate the development of Christ's character in your own life.

Theorize With Me

Could this portion of the brain house something of your original design? What if God designed people primarily for relationship with Him? What if heart-to-heart communica-tion is your first language, quite literally? What if God built you to sense each other's state of being long before you use verbal language, the language of the mind; but humankind lost the ability to use this soul language effectively? Obviously humanity's design is for relationship—your brains do not develop properly without it!

What if you were able to synchronize your state of being with God at all times? Do you suppose that was what Jesus did when He went off by Himself to be with his Father? Was Jesus able to come into sync with God and stay in sync? If so, He was could download the Father's thoughts and match His state of being. If that is so, then He could do what the Father did, and say what the Father said. When He said to Philip, "anyone who has seen Me has seen the Father," He did not speak metaphorically (see John 14:9).

Wonderment

I committed myself to the Lord and gave Him access to my brain as well as my spirit. I wonder if the Holy Spirit who is present in me, but also equally present worldwide, accomplishes burden bearing by simple stimulation of the cingulate. I speculate that it would work like this: the Holy Spirit acts almost like a satellite, picking up distress in one person and communicating it across time and space to a burden bearer. The Holy Spirit would communicate in a fashion similar to right hemisphere to right hemisphere communication that research has documented occurs between two people. Since the Creator wants you to communicate with Him, He has included in your physical equipment the cingulate to communicate not only with Him but also each other heart-to-heart. He gave you legs so you could walk and ears to hear, and a cingulate to communicate empathetically. We are "fearfully and wonderfully made!" (See Psalm 139:14.)

Endnotes

1. Daniel Siegel, *The Developing Mind*, (New York: The Guilford Press, 1999). This work is a synthesis of current knowledge from independent, usually isolated areas of research. This work presents an integrative framework for understanding the interface of the brain and the social environment.

2. A good source for this discussion is *Descartes Error* by neurologist Antonio Damasio.

3. James E. Wilder, *The Complete Guide to Living With Men* (Pasadena, CA: Shepherd's House, Inc.), 35.

4. Siegel, 121.

5. Wilder, 42.

6. Wilder, quote from lecture notes, Thrive Conference, 2003.

7. Wilder, 42.

8. Siegel, 149.

9. Siegel, 158.

10. Siegel, 128-129.

11. Siegel, 155.

12. Wilder, 41,42.

13. Siegel, 278. quoting A.N. Schore, (1994).

14. Here Siegel uses the words "emotional brain" to refer to the command center because this part of the brain, the amygdala, the cingulate, and the prefrontal lobe are the major parts of the brain that control and process emotion.

15. Ibid.

16. Siegel, 136.

17. Daniel G. Amen MD, *Change Your Brain, Change Your Life* (New York: Three Rivers Press, 1998). This book gives examples of various kinds of cingulate problems and presents ways of dealing with them.

Author Contact Information

To contact the author, visit her Website:
www.fromgodsheart.com.

Additional copies of this book and other
book titles from DESTINY IMAGE are
available at your local bookstore.

Call toll-free: 1-800-722-6774.

Send a request for a catalog to:

®

P.O. Box 310
Shippensburg, PA 17257-0310